RUSSIA'S WORLD ORDER

A volume in the

NIU Series in Slavic, East European, and Eurasian Studies
Edited by Christine D. Worobec

For a list of books in the series, visit our website at cornellpress.cornell.edu.

RUSSIA'S WORLD ORDER

HOW CIVILIZATIONISM EXPLAINS THE CONFLICT WITH THE WEST

PAUL ROBINSON

NORTHERN ILLINOIS UNIVERSITY PRESS
AN IMPRINT OF
CORNELL UNIVERSITY PRESS
Ithaca and London

Copyright © 2025 by Cornell University

All rights reserved. Except for brief quotations in a review, this book, or parts thereof, must not be reproduced in any form without permission in writing from the publisher. For information, address Cornell University Press, Sage House, 512 East State Street, Ithaca, New York 14850. Visit our website at cornellpress.cornell.edu.

First published 2025 by Cornell University Press

Printed in the United States of America

Librarians: A CIP catalog record for this book is available from the Library of Congress.

ISBN 9781501780011 (hardcover)
ISBN 9781501780028 (epub)
ISBN 9781501780035 (pdf)

Contents

Notes on Transliteration vi

    Introduction   1

1. Two Concepts of History   10
2. Russian Historical Determinism   33
3. The Origins of Russian Civilizationism   48
4. The Emergence of Russian Civilizationism   63
5. The Eurasianist Strand of Russian Civilizationism   75
6. The Isolationist Strand of Russian Civilizationism   91
7. The Rise of Russian Civilizationism   105
8. The Triumph of Russian Civilizationism   118

    Conclusion   132

Notes 135
Index 157

Notes on Transliteration

In the notes, I have strictly followed the Library of Congress system for transliterating Russian words and names. In cases where I have used translations from Russian, the transliteration of names may vary, so that one author's name may appear in several versions. In the main text, however, I have altered the Library of Congress system to reflect general English usage. For this reason, I have translated the Russian *ë* as *yo*, not *e*. Because Russian names ending in *uŭ* are popularly rendered as ending in *y*, not *ii*, I have used the former—Danilevsky, not Danilevskii. I have also generally used a *y* for the Russian soft sign—thus Leontyev, not Leont'ev. Where there is a generally accepted transliteration for a Russian name, I have used that—for example, Yeltsin, not El'tsin. Also, to reflect common practice, the names of tsars are given in English—Alexander I, Nicholas I, and so on.

RUSSIA'S WORLD ORDER

Introduction

In 2004, somebody in Moscow had a bright idea. The Russian government should assemble people of influence from around the world—high-profile journalists, prominent scholars, and the like—and give them an opportunity to talk with their Russian counterparts about the state of the world. At the end of it all, they would go home with a better understanding of the Russian point of view and, with luck, would then use their influence to persuade their fellow countrymen that they ought to take that point of view into consideration. It would be a cheap and relatively easy way of swaying international public opinion in Russia's favor. And so was born the Valdai Discussion Club.

Since its inaugural meeting in 2004 in the lakeside resort of Valdai, some four hundred kilometers northwest of Moscow, the Discussion Club has expanded into a global network that issues regular reports on various aspects of international affairs. The key event of its calendar remains its annual meeting, at which Russian president Vladimir Putin invariably gives a keynote speech. For club members, it is an opportunity to see Putin in person and ask him questions. For Putin, it is a chance to address the world on the topic of international relations. His annual Valdai speech is a highly anticipated occasion for everyone wanting to know what is going on in the Russian president's mind.

Putin's address to the Valdai Club in October 2022 was perhaps one of the most important to date. Any good general seeks to fight on ground he himself has chosen. Delivered in the aftermath of Russia's 2022 invasion of Ukraine, Putin's speech laid out the ideological ground on which he is choosing to fight his geopolitical conflict with the West. It is terrain that Putin clearly believes favors the Russian side.

At the heart of the speech was the word "civilization" (*tsivilizatsiia*). Putin used variations of this (civilization, civilizations, and civilizational) no fewer than fifteen times and then repeated these words several times again in the question-and-answer session that followed. He also used the phrase "flowering complexity," originally coined by the Russian philosopher Konstantin Leontyev (1831–91) in an 1876 study of the rise and fall of civilizations. And finally, he cited Leontyev's contemporary Nikolai Danilevsky (1822–85) to argue that the world consists not of one civilization that all nations are destined eventually to join but rather of multiple distinctive civilizations each developing in their own way. International peace required recognition of this reality, Putin said: "Respect for the ways and customs of peoples and civilizations is in everyone's interest." The problem, he claimed, was that the part of the world known as the "West" refused to recognize this. Instead, the West regarded itself as the only valid civilization and was attempting to force everybody else to adopt its ways. According to Putin, "the smoothing out and erasure of all and any differences is essentially what the modern West is all about. What stands behind this? First of all, it is the decaying creative potential of the West and a desire to restrain and block the free development of other civilizations." This policy was a mistake, he claimed, arguing that "the world is diverse by nature and Western attempts to squeeze everyone into the same pattern are clearly doomed. Nothing will come out of them." The Western-dominated, unipolar world would in due course be replaced by a diverse and multipolar one, said Putin. "The significance of today's historical moment lies in the opportunities for everyone's democratic and distinct development path, which is opening up before all civilizations," he concluded.[1]

A year later, Putin did it again. In his speech to the Valdai Club in October 2023, he used the word "civilization" even more than in the previous year—twenty-three times. "There are many civilizations, and none is better or worse than any other. They are all equal, being expressions of the aspirations of their own cultures, traditions, and peoples," he said. Putin continued, "Civilization is not a universal construct, one for all—there is no such thing. Each is different, each is culturally self-sufficient and draws its ideological principles and values from its own history and traditions. Respecting oneself undoubtedly derives from respecting others, but it also implies respect from others. Consequently, a civilization does not impose anything on others, but also does not allow anything to be imposed on itself. If everyone abides by this rule, it will guarantee harmonious coexistence and creative interaction among everyone participating in international affairs."[2]

Speeches like this are not normally delivered off the cuff. They are carefully scripted affairs, generated through a long bureaucratic process involving the input of a large team of drafters and advisers. The repeated use of the word "civilization" was not a random stylistic device. It was a deliberate choice of language, designed to send a specific message to a specific audience for a specific political purpose. The tone of Putin's speeches makes it clear that his intended audience was not the West. Rather, he was appealing to people from other parts of the world, and his purpose was to win their political support against the West. The focus on civilizations was the chosen tool.

The modern Russian state, unlike its Soviet predecessor, has no official ideology. Indeed, the Constitution of the Russian Federation specifically states that "no ideology shall be proclaimed as state ideology or as obligatory."[3] That said, over the past decade, a particular worldview has become increasingly prevalent in state discourse; it permeates presidential speeches, policy documents, and even educational curricula. This is the philosophy of civilizationism. In Russian political discourse, talk of civilizations has very definite connotations rooted in over two centuries of political philosophy. To decode Putin's message, this book endeavors to explain what civilizational theory is, where it came from, and how and why Putin has chosen to embrace it.

Civilizationism differs from other ideologies such as communism or liberalism in that it does not propose a model for how nations should develop. In fact, it rejects the entire concept of a single model. Its focus is not on how individual countries should organize themselves but on how the world as a whole should be organized. At its heart is a concept of cultural and civilizational diversity, of a world not of dull uniformity but of "flowering complexity." As this book will explain, this vision of the world stands at odds with the one promoted by the West. It also contradicts the Western understanding of the flow of history.

Civilizationism is more than a philosophy. It is also a powerful political tool. Russia's leaders are using it to resist what they see as the West's efforts to export its values and institutions to the rest of the world and to smother worldwide civilizational diversity under a bland homogeneity of universal Westernism. They are throwing down an ideological challenge to the West and its claims to represent universal values. It is a challenge that the West needs to understand if it is to have any chance of responding effectively. To this end, this book examines the history of Russian civilizationism, its numerous variants, and its impact both on Russia and on the world at large.

Russian civilizational theory has many strands. Some are very hostile to the West. An example is the thinking of Aleksandr Dugin (b. 1962), which is examined in chapter 5 of this book. Other strands of civilizational theory, however, do not necessarily view Russia and the West as enemies. Philosopher Vadim Mezhuev (1933–2019), for instance, regarded Russia as still being in the process of making its civilizational choice. He envisioned a civilizational dialogue between Russia and the West, which he imagined producing a universal civilization that combined the best elements of Western material and technical progress and Russian spirituality.[4] Talk of a "dialogue of civilizations" is common among Russian civilizational theorists, while many such theorists recognize the existence of common, universal values that transcend civilizations. It is not, however, these strands of thought that have come to dominate Russian political discourse. Rather, it is a version of civilizationism that places more emphasis on the differences between Russia and the West. This version will be the focus of this book.

Civilizational theory of this type originated as a reaction to the universalist pretensions of Western liberal internationalism. The "West" is a fluid and ill-defined term. Nowadays, it tends to be used in a way that includes the countries of Europe and North America, the former British colonies of Australia and New Zealand, and possibly also Japan and South Korea. What demarcates the West is not geography so much as a set of political, economic, and social institutions and values, notably liberal democracy and free-market capitalism. Western liberal internationalists like to portray these institutions and values as universal. That is to say, they argue that they are valid for everybody everywhere. All societies will benefit from becoming Western. More than that, all societies *ought* to become Western and in due course are bound to do so, such are the advantages of the Western way of life.

Western liberals are not alone in considering their values to be universally valid and to believe that the entire world order will in due course end up being based on them. Communists hold a similar perspective, although their view of the final end point differs. Whereas to liberals, the end of history is a world consisting of free-market democracies, for communists it is a world in which the workers control the means of production and social inequality has been abolished. But the basic idea that history follows scientifically determinable laws of progress that lead all societies to converge on a single social model is common to both modes of thought.

Civilizational theory rejects this conception of history. In its place, it puts forward two simple propositions: first, that no single society can claim to embody universal civilization; and second, that history moves not in a single direction but along numerous different lines of development. Consequently, civilizational theorists generally stand in opposition to concepts of Western hegemony and a unipolar global order and in their place advocate for a multipolar, "polycultural" world.

Civilizational theory has long roots in Russian history. Despite this, since at least the time of Peter the Great (reigned 1682–1725), it has largely lingered on the intellectual margins of Russian society. It has certainly not been the lens through which the Russian state has viewed the world. Indeed, during the Soviet era, Russia's rulers very much considered that history marched in a single direction, toward communism. In the past thirty years, however, Russia has undergone a profound ideological shift, and civilizational thinking has become almost de rigueur. The belief that Russia is a separate civilization from the West and that it must struggle against Westernization in the name of a multicivilizational world order has become pervasive. More importantly, it has now been adopted by the Russian state as the ideological framework that it is using to justify its political battle with the West.

This represents a significant change. When Putin first became president, in 2000, he expressed the belief that Russia was a European country. At that time, Putin and other Russian officials claimed that their ideal was the construction of a "common European home." Bit by bit, however, their language changed. References to Russia as an integral part of European civilization were gradually replaced by talk of Russia as a "unique" or "self-contained" civilization of its own. And instead of talking about common, even universal, values, the Kremlin began more and more to talk of a world made up of multiple civilizations each with values of their own that others should learn to respect.

It was no coincidence that this change in rhetoric took place alongside a serious worsening of Russian-Western relations. It is perhaps an exaggeration to say that at the time of writing, in 2024, those relations have never been worse, but if so the exaggeration is a slight one. Political, economic, and cultural ties have been severed, and the West has sent hundreds of billions of dollars of military supplies to Ukraine for the specific purpose of fighting Russia. As yet, Russia and the West are not directly at war with one another. Nevertheless, they are engaged in an intense political battle. With this, many commentators have concluded that Russia and the West are now embroiled in a "New Cold War."

It is debatable whether the situation today is indeed comparable to the original Cold War, which lasted from about 1947 to 1991. There are some significant differences between the two periods. First, during the Cold War, there was a relatively even balance of power between the Soviet Union on the one hand and the Western bloc on the other. Today, the imbalance of power between the two sides is enormous, in favor of the West. Second, the Cold War was a global power struggle, whereas the current tensions between Russia and the West are more localized, and the two are not competing to control the countries of the developing world in the way they did from the 1950s to the 1980s. And third, the Cold War was as much an ideological as a geopolitical struggle, involving a clash between two fundamentally opposed visions of human society—capitalism and communism. In the eyes of many, this important element of the Cold War is absent today.[5]

This last point needs some qualification. It is true that current Russian-Western tensions do not originate in ideological differences. That said, both sides in the current political conflict need to justify their actions to domestic and international audiences. They therefore seek to frame their conflict in ideological terms. US president Joe Biden (b. 1942), for instance, regularly speaks of a struggle between autocracy and democracy, a framing that has been described as "the organizing principle of his foreign policy."[6] On one side of this struggle, in his view, lie the United States and its allies. On the other lie Russia and the People's Republic of China. The Russian state is said to fear the success of democracy in other countries, lest its example encourage the Russian people to overthrow Putin. Consequently, Russia is described as doing all it can to "destabilize democracies" such as Ukraine while propping up dictatorships such as that of Bashar al-Assad in Syria.[7] "We stand at an inflection point in our history in my view," Biden has said: "The choices we make . . . in this moment are going to fundamentally determine the direction our world is going to take in the coming decades. Will we allow the backward slide of rights and democracy to continue unchecked? Or will we together, together, have a vision . . . and courage to once more lead the march of human progress and freedom forward?"[8]

Biden's statement indicates a belief in a type of progress that marches forward in a single direction toward a clear end state. He is far from alone in holding this position. For instance, his predecessor but one as US president, Barack Obama, regularly talked of countries being on "the right side of history" or "the wrong side of history" and also spoke often of "the arc of history," indicating a firm belief that history has a specific direction, identified with progress toward Western liberal values and institutions.[9] This conception of progress stands in clear opposition to civilizational theory, which envisions history as following multiple paths toward no particular end. In addition, Russians do not appear to view the world in the way that Biden describes it. Rather than waging war against democracy, Russia has shown itself to be consistently indifferent to other states' political systems, being far more concerned with whether those states are friendly than with what sort of regime they have. It enjoys friendly relations with many authoritarian states, but it also has friendly relations with many democratic ones and shows no preference for one over the other. Russian leaders have never expressed a dislike of democracy per se, merely a dislike of the foreign policy pursued by the democratic states of the West.

As Putin's 2022 and 2023 Valdai speeches made clear, the Russian government frames its conflict with the West not as a struggle against democracy but rather as a battle against attempts by the West to preserve a unipolar world order in which it has hegemonic power. Civilizationism provides a philosophical grounding for this framing. With its aid, the Russian state is telling the rest of the world that the root of the problem is that the West believes that it alone represents civilization and that the only way to create peace is to spread Western values and institutions around the world. Rather than peace, the Russians argue, this strategy creates conflict. Instead, the aim should be the creation of a multipolar, multicivilizational world, in which each civilizational center respects the rights of others to develop in accordance with their own logic.

The ideological campaigns conducted by Russia and the West are to some extent at cross-purposes to one another. In speaking of democracy versus autocracy, the West is presenting the ideological dispute as one whose primary concern is how states organize their own internal affairs. The Russians, by contrast, are painting the conflict as one about the shape of the international order. How states organize their internal affairs is not relevant to this, and indeed civilizational theory is by its very nature indifferent to such matters, as what it stresses is the need for diversity, and therefore it does not inherently prefer one internal system to another.

So far, the West has sought to defeat Russia by economically and politically isolating it. In response, the Russian government is appealing to countries of the developing world for support. Moscow is telling them that the West is repeating the colonial practices of its past, seeking to impose its ways on others and denying them the right to develop in their own way, according to their own values and their own civilizational logic. It is attempting to homogenize the world along the Western model. Russia, by contrast, claims to be fighting to defend the right of different civilizations to determine their own future and to create a world that celebrates the diversity of civilizational reality.

It is a logic that potentially has considerable appeal, especially in countries with experience of Western colonialism. Civilizational theory thus provides Russia with a means to win the support, or at least the neutrality, of what is often called the "Global South," thereby undermining the West's efforts to isolate Russia and force it to submit. So far, it appears that this strategy is having some success. According to a March 2023 study by the Economist Intelligence Unit, governments representing 36 percent of the world's population were, at that time, actively opposed to Russia or leaned toward the West, while governments representing 32 percent of the world's population actively supported Russia or leaned toward it, with about a third of the world being neutral. This represented a slight shift in Russia's favor from the position twelve months previously, suggesting that the world was evenly divided but that the fight for the world's hearts and minds was moving marginally in Russia's favor.[10]

Given that Russia is using civilizational discourse to achieve this, it is important that this discourse be studied and understood. Russians have their own political and philosophical language. They use words and phrases such as *"sobornost'," "passionarity," "katechon,"* the "common task," and "flowering complexity," terms that have no meaning to the average Westerner and require explanation. In addition, Russian civilizational theory is quite diverse and complex. There is a tendency in Western commentary to take a single aspect of it and then treat it as the entirety of the theory. There is also a tendency to mix up civilizational thought with related but somewhat different strands of thinking, such as Slavophilism. The result is a habit of ascribing to Russian leaders ideas that they have never expressed and probably do not believe. This leads to considerable misunderstanding of what Russians are saying.

A single speech using the word "civilization" hardly proves anything. However, a whole series of speeches and documents doing so definitely means something. Similarly, a single quotation from a single source hardly proves that the Kremlin has adopted a given ideology. But a mass of quotations from sources with similar inclinations could suggest that it has. Putin cites a wide variety of people, many of whom disagreed with each other on important issues. No single one of them can be considered an ideological guru. But overall, when one looks at who gets quoted and who does not, a pattern emerges. People who have argued that societies everywhere follow the same path of development and that Russia's destiny is to become a part of the West do not get mentioned. Nor does Putin ever quote anybody saying that Russia's future is to be communist. The names that pop up in chapter 2 are notably absent from Russian official rhetoric. But people who have argued that Russia is different and has the right to develop in its own distinct way do

INTRODUCTION   9

appear again and again. Thus, Putin mentions the likes of Danilevsky and Leontyev, along with others such as the Russian novelist Fyodor Dostoevsky (1821–81), the Soviet dissident Aleksandr Solzhenitsyn (1918–2008), and the Soviet ethnologist Lev Gumilyov (1912–92).[11]

In this he is not alone. A 2014 survey of Russian international relations scholars asked them which Russian thinkers they considered most important. By far the most popular choice was Danilevsky, followed by Leontyev, Aleksandr Panarin (1940–2003), Vladimir Vernadsky (1863–1945), Gumilyov, Nikolai Berdiaev (1874–1948), Vladimir Solovyov (1853–1900), Nikolai Trubetskoi (1890–1938), Aleksandr Herzen (1812–70), Pyotr Savitsky (1895–1968), and Pitirim Sorokin (1889–1968).[12] All of these are associated to a greater or lesser extent with ideas of Russian exceptionalism and through that with civilizational theory. This provides firm evidence of the powerful influence that civilizational ideas now exert on Russian thought.

The list above also suggests that understanding the current intellectual trends in Russia requires one to move beyond a single thinker and to look at civilizational theory as a whole, in its many varied manifestations. This book aims to do just that, in the process providing readers with a detailed analysis of the origins and nature of the ideological discourse being used by the Kremlin in its political struggle against the West. To this end, this book begins by summarizing the two main trends of thought opposing one another in this ideological struggle: first, the idea of history marching toward a single end, mainly associated with the West; and second, the idea of history moving in multiple civilizational directions. Next, the book examines how Russian thinkers until recently mostly adhered to the first conception. It then analyzes different variations of Russian civilizational theory, discussing many of the men mentioned in the previous paragraph (it should be noted that Russian civilizational theory is a very male-dominated school of thought). Finally, the book turns to the current day and the manner in which Putin and his government have adopted civilizational theory and adapted it for their own political purposes.

Some readers may sympathize with the ideas expressed in this book. Others may find them bizarre or even downright dangerous. Whether these ideas are valid is, however, beside the point. Right or wrong, they have proved to be extraordinarily influential and need to be understood. Consequently, this book does not seek to judge; it seeks merely to describe and provide context. In this way, it is hoped that readers may come to a fuller comprehension of what Russians are saying and how they are framing their struggle with the West.

Chapter 1

Two Concepts of History

The intellectual conflict described in this book is a competition between two metahistories—that is to say, two different philosophies of history. The first philosophy views history as unilinear, as marching in a single direction toward a single goal, usually defined as something resembling the Western world. History involves everybody becoming Western. The second, by contrast, views history as heading in no particular direction. Instead, it involves different groups of people each marching along their own path toward their own distinct goals.

Another way of putting this is to view it as a conflict between the concept of civilization, singular, and that of civilizations, plural. The first metahistory is a story of humanity's advance away from barbarism toward civilization. The second is a story of distinct civilizations, each with their own character and destiny. Civilization is universal; civilizations are not.

In its original usage, the word "civilization" was entirely singular. The first recorded use of the term was in France in the mid-eighteenth century, and the first recorded use in English was in 1772.[1] Being civilized then meant having institutions and manners similar to those of Western Europe and was regarded as undoubtedly a good thing. Civilization was thus both a description and a value judgment.[2] Giovanni Borgognone and Patricia Chiantera-Stutte note that civilization in this sense "was used to order and classify peoples and countries as superior and inferior. . . . The idea of civilized people, juxtaposed with barbarians—or, in other words, the colonial communities—was the basis for the development of the Eurocentric contemporary domination."³ Progress was a "movement from *barbarism*, the rude, uncultivated, uncivilized state of mankind, to the higher condition of refinement in thought and manners—in a word, to *civilization*."⁴

Over time, however, an alternative conception came into being. By the second half of the nineteenth century, "civilization" began to be used also in the plural.⁵ This accompanied the idea that there was more than one standard of civilization and that the division of the world into civilized and barbarian was invalid. Both these viewpoints have had a strong impact on Russian thinking about the nature of the world.

Russian thought has drawn heavily from that of the West. Indeed, it is one of the ironies of Russian intellectual history that what one might term anti-Western thinkers have often been highly Westernized people, well versed in Western philosophy, who have drawn on that philosophy to criticize the West. Before we turn to Russia, we therefore first have to make a detour into Western philosophy concerning the nature and purpose of history.

The West as the End of History

British philosopher John Gray remarks that "if a simple definition of western civilization could be formulated it would have to be framed in terms of the central role of millenarian thinking."⁶ By this, Gray means that the core idea of the Western world is that history is moving toward a utopian end, "the arrival of some kind of holy kingdom."⁷ This end was once understood in religious terms, and many scholars have associated the belief in an "end of history" with the Christian religion and specifically with the idea that history will end with the second coming of Christ. Russian philosopher Nikolai Berdiaev, for instance, claimed that the pagan world was "dominated by the idea of the frequency and recurrence of events, and this had made all conception of history impossible. The Christian consciousness, on the other hand, held that events were immediate, non-recurrent and unique, and it imposed this conception on historical reality."⁸ Similarly, Gray argued that the idea that history has a purpose and will one day come to an end "is a Christian inheritance. Most religions lack any conception of history as a story with a beginning and an end . . . [but] Christians believed that it had . . . a predetermined purpose, and when that was achieved it would come to a close. . . . This idea entered western thought only with Christianity, and has shaped it ever since."⁹ Seen this way, modern political philosophies such as socialism and liberalism derive from Christianity, with God removed and the promise of a spiritual heaven replaced by the prospect of a very material heaven here on Earth.[10]

The idea that only Christianity (along perhaps with Judaism) contains a notion of history reaching an end point is, of course, highly disputable. Nevertheless, within the context of the Western world, there may be something to the thesis that Christianity helped generate a belief that human affairs have a higher purpose. On its own, though, this idea is not sufficient to explain modern forms of historical determinism. There is no particular requirement that humanity should progress, either materially or spiritually, prior to the end times. The apocalypse can just as easily arrive after centuries of stagnation, or even regression, as after centuries of progress. The ending can come at any point. The concept that the end is something toward which one advances gradually over time is something very different and requires an explanation that goes beyond religion.

Arguably, it is also a relatively modern idea. While conceptions of progress may have existed far back in time, to gain serious traction they needed people to be aware of change of considerable rapidity and scale and for people to consider that change to be positive. Only in that way would it be progress rather than something else. Unsurprisingly, therefore, the growing belief in progress among Europeans coincided with the economic advances made in Europe from the Renaissance period onward, along with what were also considered advances in the arts, sciences, education, and the like.

The scientific revolution in Europe in the seventeenth and eighteenth centuries added a new element to this. Newton's laws of physics showed that matter was governed by rules that humans could understand. It did not take long for people to pursue the theory that human societies were also governed by knowable rules. At the same time, religious faith declined in many circles, being replaced by a belief in the power of reason. The idea emerged that progress consisted precisely in this—in the replacement of faith with reason.

Charles Darwin's theory of evolution added yet another factor to the mix—namely, the concept of the survival of the fittest. Applied to human societies, this meant that strong, advanced societies were destined to force out weaker, backward ones that failed to evolve. In the eyes of so-called social Darwinists such as British philosopher Herbert Spencer (1820–1903), the lesson was clear—either the weak would become like the West, or they would perish. Either way, the Western model would eventually triumph everywhere. As Spencer put it, the "forcible supplantations of the weak by the strong . . . [aided] civilization by clearing the Earth of its least advanced inhabitants, and by forcibly compelling the rest to acquire industrial habits."[11] It is a logic that still underlines a lot of thinking about the inevitable march of Western civilization.

Spencer's reference to the "supplantation of the weak by the strong" indicates another key element of this worldview. It compares two blocks—the West and the rest—almost always in a manner favorable to the former. The belief in the superiority of the Western way could not arise without there being some "other" to whom the West could feel superior. For much of Europe's history, however, the only major other with whom it had contact was the Muslim world, which was not in any sense—technologically, intellectually, or militarily—inferior to Western Europe. Belief that European models constituted the end point of history did not develop until Europeans came into contact with peoples at a different technological level.

This came to pass with the colonization of North America from the early seventeenth century onward. Europeans looked condescendingly down on the native peoples of North America as examples of humanity in a state of nature. This perception influenced the new science of anthropology, giving rise to concepts of social evolution that saw history as progressing in a linear way through certain distinct stages.[12] At the end of the eighteenth century, French nobleman Marie Jean Antoine Nicolas de Caritat, Marquis de Condorcet (1743–94), wrote that "the first state of civilization in which the human race has been observed is that of a sparsely populated society of men making their livelihood from hunting and fishing . . . next is added a crude sort of agriculture." In the next stage of development, wrote Condorcet, some people develop a surplus, exchange part of their surplus for labor, and devote themselves to other tasks. With this, new classes come into being, industry and arts begin, and human relations become more complex.[13] Civilization arrives. Likewise, in his 1877 book *Ancient Society*, the American anthropologist Lewis Henry Morgan (1818–81) laid out an influential three-stage model of social evolution, consisting of savagery, barbarism, and civilization. He wrote, "It can now be asserted upon convincing evidence that savagery preceded barbarism in all tribes of mankind, as barbarism is known to have preceded civilization . . . this sequence has been historically true for the entire human family."[14] In most renderings of this model, civilization has been defined in terms of Western values and institutions. Social evolution is thus portrayed as a process of moving through a series of steps at the end of which one adopts the ways of the West.

Perhaps the first person to put this idea into print was the German philosopher Immanuel Kant (1724–1824) in a 1784 essay titled "Idea for a Universal History with a Cosmopolitan Aim." In this, Kant wrote,

> Whatever concept one may form of the *freedom of the will* with a metaphysical aim, its *appearances*, the human actions, are determined just as

much as every other natural occurrence in accordance with universal laws of nature. History . . . allows us to hope from it that . . . it can discover within it a regular course; and that in this way what meets the eye in individual subjects as confused and irregular yet in the whole species can be recognized as a steadily progressing through slow development of its original predispositions. . . . Individual human beings and even whole nations think little about the fact, since while each pursues its own aim in its own way and one often contrary to the other, they are proceeding unnoticed, as by a guiding thread, according to an aim of nature.[15]

For Kant, the aim of history was the "achievement of a civil society universally administering right."[16] Efforts to limit freedom, he wrote, suppressed enterprise and so weakened society. Consequently, restrictions on freedom by necessity gradually disappeared. "Finally," he added, "war . . . will become so dubious an undertaking, and the influence of every shake-up in a state in our part of the world on all other states, all of whose trades are so very much chained together, will be so noticeable, that these states will . . . prepare the way for a future large state body . . . in the end that which nature has as its aim will finally come about—a universal *cosmopolitan condition*."[17] But for all the talk about a "cosmopolitan condition," it is clear that Kant viewed this as an extension of European ways of life rather than anything else. "Our part of the world," he wrote, would "probably someday give laws to all the others."[18]

Kant further expounded on the theme of historical progress in a famous 1795 work titled "Perpetual Peace." In this he argued that republican governments (by which he meant those featuring freedom, equality, and the rule of law) were less likely to go to war than others, for the reason that if the decision to go to war rested with the people, not with autocratic rulers, they "would think long before beginning such a terrible game, since they would have to call down on themselves all the horrors of war."[19] The advantages bestowed by republics would be such that they would inspire other states to join them, creating a federation of peaceful states that "gradually extends further and further," until eventually it secures "perpetual peace."[20]

Kant's vision has been extraordinarily influential, and to this day it lies at the root of what is possibly the predominant strand of Western thinking on international affairs—liberal internationalism. By promoting human rights and free trade—in other words, by promoting Western institutions—liberal internationalists believe that they can achieve Kant's perpetual peace or at least bring the world closer to it. Democratic peace theory, meanwhile, somewhat follows Kant in claiming that well-established democracies do not fight each other (the idea that they are less warlike per se is hard to maintain) and that the spread of democracy will therefore bring peace in its wake.

Another late eighteenth-century optimist was the aforementioned Marquis de Condorcet, although the circumstances of his own life did not perhaps bear his optimism out. A mathematician, he shared Kant's faith in the power of reason and promoted liberal causes such as female suffrage and the abolition of slavery. In due course, he gave his support to the French Revolution. A member of the Girondist faction, he was deemed a traitor by the rival Montagnard group when the latter took control of the revolutionary government in late 1793. After a warrant was issued for his arrest, he went into hiding, at which point he wrote what was probably his most famous work, titled *Sketch for a Historical Picture of the Progress of the Human Spirit*. Captured in 1794 while trying to flee Paris, he was imprisoned and died two days later in mysterious circumstances, possibly having committed suicide by poison.

With its idealistic faith in human perfectibility, Condorcet's *Sketch* encapsulated the mood of the era in which it was written. "No limit has been set to the perfection of human faculties; the perfectibility of man is really indefinite. . . . No doubt this progress could proceed more rapidly or less, but never will it be retrograde," wrote Condorcet.[21] He added, "The sole foundation of the belief in the natural sciences is the idea that the general laws, known or unknown, which govern the phenomena of the Universe, are necessary and constant; and why should this principle be less true for the development of the intellectual and moral faculties of man than for the other operations of nature? . . . Our hopes as to the future state of the human race can be reduced to these three important points: the destruction of inequality among the nations; the progress of equality within nations; finally, the actual perfecting of man."[22]

For Condorcet, this meant the spread of European ways to the rest of the world. He wrote, "Are all the nations one day to approach the civilized state already reached by the peoples most enlightened, most free, most emancipated from prejudices, such as the French and the Anglo-Americans? Is not this immense distance which separates these peoples from the servitude of nations subject to kings, from the barbarism of the African tribes, from the ignorance of savages, destined little by little to vanish? . . . In answering these questions, we shall find . . . the strongest motives for believing that nature has set no limit to our hopes."[23]

Similarly optimistic was another Frenchman, Auguste Comte (1798–1857), who is viewed as the founder of the philosophy of positivism. Comte considered it to be a law that every branch of knowledge passed through three successive stages: the theological, the metaphysical, and the scientific, or positive.²⁴ As he put it, "In the theological state, the human mind . . . supposes all phenomena to be produced by the immediate action of supernatural beings. In the metaphysical state . . . the mind supposes, instead of supernatural beings, abstract forces . . . inherent in all beings. . . . In the final, positive, state, the mind has given over the vain search after absolute notions, the origin and destination of the universe, and the causes of phenomena, and applies itself to the study of their laws. . . . Reasoning and observation, duly combined, are the means of this knowledge."²⁵

According to Comte, "the first characteristic of the positive philosophy is that it regards all phenomena as subject to invariable natural *laws*."²⁶ Having established the laws of natural science, it remained only to determine the laws that direct human society. "This once done," he wrote, "the positive state will be fully established. It can never again change its character. . . . Having acquired the state of universality which has hitherto been the only advantage resting with the two preceding systems [theological and metaphysical], it will supersede them by its natural superiority, and leave to them only a historical existence."²⁷ Human society, in other words, would pass through the same three stages as scientific knowledge, and once positivism had triumphed, history would finally have reached its end.

The German philosopher George Wilhelm Friedrich Hegel (1770–1831) provided yet another three-stage model of human progress, one that would prove to be enormously influential thereafter. Hegel believed that universal history involved the gradual manifestation of God's spirit (*Geist*), which he defined in terms of freedom. History, therefore, was an advance toward freedom, although in Hegel's eyes, human beings were social creatures, and thus true freedom was not individual but communal and was possible only within the context of a rationally ordered state. The state, according to Hegel, was "the reality within which the individual has and enjoys his freedom, but only in so far as he knows, believes in and wills the universal."²⁸

In accordance with his famous dialectic method, Hegel described history as proceeding through several stages, each of which had a different organizing principle: first, the family; second, civil society; and third and finally, the state.²⁹ It was in the last of these, he believed, that freedom found its culmination—"the state presents the first realization of freedom," he wrote.³⁰

An important development in the decades following Hegel was an increasing tendency to view economics as bound by universal laws. In the late eighteenth century, Adam Smith (1723–90) had partially endorsed this idea, but only partially. Smith described human society as "a great, an immense machine" and the universe more generally as "a complete machine, a coherent system governed by general laws."³¹ At the same time, though, Smith recognized that humans were subjective actors whose behavior was uncertain. He therefore considered economic laws to be context dependent, a fact that was lost on some later admirers such as the Russian reformers of the 1990s (see chapter 2).[32] The latter perhaps owed less to Smith than they did to economists of the second half of the nineteenth century. These came under the sway of mathematics and helped turn what was previously known as "political economy" into what we now call "economics." With that, they established the concept that economics was a science based on universally valid laws.[33]

Among the believers in universally valid economic laws was Karl Marx (1818–83). Marx supposedly "turned Hegel on his head." In his philosophy of dialectical materialism, he maintained Hegel's dialectical conception of progress as a matter of action, reaction, and synthesis but stressed the supremacy of material factors as the driving force in history in contrast to the emphasis that Hegel had put on spirit and consciousness. He wrote, "I was led by my studies to the conclusion that legal relations as well as forms of state could be neither understood by themselves nor explained by the so-called general progress of the human mind, but that they are rooted in the material conditions of life. . . . The mode of production in material life determines the general character of the social, political, and spiritual processes of life. It is not the consciousness of men that determines their existence, but, on the contrary, their social existence determines their consciousness."[34]

According to Marx, "At a certain level of development the material forces of production in society come into conflict . . . with the property relations within which they had been working before. . . . Then comes the period of social revolution."[35] One "social formation" then replaces another, until eventually a formation (communism) comes into existence in which the antagonism between the material forces of production and property relations is resolved and humanity reaches its final form. Marx believed that "in broad outlines we can designate the Asiatic, the ancient, the feudal, and the modern bourgeois methods of production as so many epochs in the progress of the economic formation of society. The bourgeois relations of production are the last antagonistic form of the social process of production . . . the productive forces developing in the womb of bourgeois society create the material conditions for the solution of that antagonism. This social formation constitutes, therefore, the closing chapter of the prehistoric stage of human society."[36]

Few people in the West would nowadays claim to be Marxists, but in reality most probably are to some degree. For they tend to share, at least partially, Marx's belief that the economic substructure determines the political and cultural superstructure. The idea that economic development will automatically bring with it beneficial changes in other areas of life is widely accepted and paradoxically underlay a Western theory of historical development that challenged Soviet communism during the Cold War, thus building on Marx to fight Marxism.

The context for this was the emergence of a large number of new states that gained their independence from colonial powers after the Second World War. Soviet communism proved attractive to many of these states' leaders, as it seemed to provide an economic model that they could copy to rapidly industrialize without becoming dependent on Western capital. To prevent these countries from coming under Soviet influence, American economists therefore created an alternative theory of development known as "modernization theory."

Modernization theory had its origins in Franklin D. Roosevelt's New Deal in the United States. The Tennessee Valley Authority project, begun in 1933, constituted a model of how to develop economically deprived areas through the combined efforts of the state, private enterprise, and nongovernmental organizations. The American economist Eugene Staley (1906–89) proposed the export of this model to poorer parts of the world as a means of preventing them from falling under communist or fascist influence.[37] For Staley, modernization was "irresistible and universal" and followed a predictable pattern. Increased production generated "progress in democratic self governance," which in turn provided "opportunities for self-development and respect for individual personality," which then reduced a country's vulnerability to communism.[38]

In 1960, another American economist, Walt Rostow (1916–2003), built on these ideas in a book titled *The Stages of Economic Growth: A Non-Communist Manifesto*. Rostow argued that all societies passed through five stages of economic growth, the third of which he named "take off" and the last of which was the "age of high mass consumption."[39] Writing of the United States, Rostow claimed that it was possible to see "the whole pattern of the nation's domestic evolution—in many ways unique—as a version of the universal modern experience . . . the economic evolution of the United States from the 1780s to the present can be seen as a special version of a general experience."[40] In other words, the end of history would be a worldwide American-style consumer society.

Modernization theory dropped out of academic favor in the 1970s due to the American defeat in Vietnam and the dismal failure of American efforts to promote development in the Third World. However, it left a lasting legacy in the form of the aid and development programs that Western states continue to support throughout the world. In addition, it underwent a major revival in a slightly different form following the terrorist attacks on the United States in September 2001 and the launching of the so-called Global War on Terror. At this point, counterinsurgency experts dusted off modernization theory and promoted the concept that development assistance in places such as Afghanistan would enable those societies to "take off" onto the path to economic prosperity and liberal democracy and thereby turn into allies of the United States. The enemy was now terrorism, not communism, but the logic was much the same.

This, however, is to jump ahead somewhat, for before then another event occurred that reignited belief that history had proved the correctness of Western ways. This was the collapse of communism in Eastern Europe and the Soviet Union, and with that the end of the Cold War.

It was this occurrence that provided the backdrop for Francis Fukuyama's 1989 essay "The End of History?" which Fukuyama (b. 1952) followed up in 1992 with a book, *The End of History and the Last Man*. By the "end of history," Fukuyama meant not the end of historical events but rather the final triumph of a given idea of human development—liberal democracy. "The triumph of the West, or of the Western *idea*, is evident first of all in the total exhaustion of viable systemic alternatives to Western liberalism," wrote Fukuyama in his original article.[41] He claimed that "what we may be witnessing is not just the end of the Cold War . . . but the end of history as such; the end point of mankind's ideological evolution and the universalization of Western liberal democracy as the final form of human government."[42]

Fukuyama drew on the thinking of the Russian émigré Alexandre Kojève (1902–68), who argued that Hegel had been "essentially correct" in foreseeing "the imminent universalization of the state incorporating the principles of liberty and equality."[43] According to Fukuyama, it would take some time for every part of the world to put these principles into action, but beyond these principles there was nothing new to be established. Humanity's intellectual journey was at an end.[44] Fukuyama wrote, in a manner that was extraordinarily dismissive of non-Western ideas, "Our task is not to answer exhaustively the challenges to liberalism promoted by every crackpot messiah around the world, but only those that are embodied in important social or political forces and movements, and which are therefore part of world history. For our purposes, it matters very little what strange thoughts occur to people in Albania or Burkina Faso, for we are interested in what one could in some sense call the common ideological heritage of mankind."[45]

If in his 1989 article Fukuyama was talking primarily about the triumph of Western ideology, in his 1992 book he went further and boldly predicted the triumph of Western institutions too. He wrote, "The unfolding of modern natural science has had a uniform effect on all societies that have experienced it . . . and guarantees an increasing homogenization of all human societies, regardless of their historical origins or cultural inheritances. All countries undergoing modernization must increasingly resemble one another . . . the logic of modern natural science would seem to dictate a universal evolution in the direction of capitalism."[46] "There is a fundamental process at work that dictates a common evolutionary pattern for *all* human societies—in short, something like a Universal History of mankind in the direction of liberal democracy," he concluded.[47]

The start of the Global War on Terror in 2002 led many Western leaders to double down on the universalist rhetoric. The struggle against terrorism was fought in the name of supposedly universal values—human rights, democracy, and so on—all of which were seen as emanating from the West and spreading out from there. Liberal imperialism acquired a new impetus.

Among those leading the intellectual charge was the British academic Niall Ferguson (b. 1964), whose 2011 book *Civilization: The West and the Rest* contained a heady brew of liberal idealism, Marxist historical materialism, modernization theory, social Darwinism, Eurocentrism, and civilizational condescension. An unashamed believer in the supremacy of Western civilization, Ferguson commented that "there are those who . . . [claim] that all civilizations are in some sense equal, and the West cannot claim superiority over, say, the East of Eurasia. But such relativism is demonstrably false."[48] What made the West superior, he claimed, was its mastery of six "killer apps"—competition, science, property rights, medicine, the consumer society, and the work ethic.[49] Ferguson worried, however, that the West was entering a period of decline. A self-confessed "fully paid-up member of the neo-imperialist gang," he urged Westerners to once again take up what Rudyard Kipling (1865–1936) had called "the White man's burden" and to guide Afghans and others to the benefits of civilization by means of a new form of colonial rule.[50] "The things that once set the West apart from the Rest are no longer monopolized by us," he wrote; "a growing number of 'Resterners' are sleeping, showering, dressing, working, eating, drinking and travelling like Westerners."[51] If the West was declining in relative terms, it was precisely because its ideas had triumphed.

Despite the many differences in the theories outlined above, they share an intellectual core. Whether through changes in consciousness (Hegel, Comte) or economics (Marx, modernization theory), all societies, it is believed, are bound to follow the laws of social evolution and to pass through the same stages of development, until they eventually reach the end of history. Such are the advantages of this end-state model that any peoples that fail to adopt it are doomed to extinction. Progress flows from the West to the rest. Any who resist are standing against the judgment of history.

Civilizational Theory

It is perhaps inevitable that when an idea becomes popular, some contrarian will come along looking to poke holes in it. So it was that in the late eighteenth century, the growing belief in reason and in the existence of natural laws guiding human societies generated a reaction from those who thought that there was more to life than mere reason and more to human development than a single linear track that all must tread.

Among the first contrarians was the German philosopher Johann Gottfried Herder (1744–1803). Poor and largely self-educated, Herder enrolled at the University of Konigsberg in 1762, aged just seventeen. There, he so impressed Kant that the great philosopher agreed to teach him free of charge. Before long, however, Herder turned his back on his teacher and denounced what he called "the excessive homage paid to reason."[52] Herder is regarded as one of the founders of the philosophy of "historicism," which rejects the idea that one can judge other peoples by the standards of one's own present time and place. Rather, they must be considered in the context in which they themselves lived. Given this, it is meaningless to consider any one set of values or institutions to be inherently better than any other or to regard history as a progression from worse to better systems. As Herder wrote in his 1774 work *Another Philosophy of History*, "One does not develop anything but that *for which time, climate, need, world, fortune* gives occasion."[53] He noted, "We have construed for ourselves an *Oriental Despotism* by singling out the most extreme and violent occurrences from what are usually decaying empires. . . . And as, in our European terms (and perhaps emotions), one cannot speak of anything more terrible than despotism, so we console ourselves by alienating it from itself and *putting it in a context* where it could *not* have been *the terrible thing* that we dream up *on account of our own condition*."[54]

Herder believed in progress but viewed it as consisting of the flowering of multiple cultures, each revealing part of the universal truth, rather than of all cultures converging on a single model. As he wrote, the future would be built on the basis "of the common reason of [the] whole fraternal race." Herder asked, "Should the *general, philanthropic tone of our century* so generously and readily bestow 'our own ideal' of *virtue* and *happiness* on every remote nation, every ancient age of the world? Is it the only judge, to be *assessing, condemning,* or *prettifying* their mores all by itself? Is not the good *dispersed* throughout the earth?"⁵⁵ Brimming with sarcasm, he then answered his question by mocking French philosophers such as Voltaire (1694–1778) for their belief in the inherent superiority of Western ways, using language that despite being 250 years old remarkably resembles that of modern antiglobalists:

> When has the world been as universally *enlightened* as it is now? . . . The *whole world* is well-nigh glowing with *Voltaire's lucidity*! How this seems to go on without end! *Where are* there no European colonies, and where *will* there not *be* any? The fonder savages grow everywhere of our liquor and luxury, the more *ready* they all become for our *conversion*! Everywhere they are brought closer to *our culture*, by liquor and luxury especially, and before long—God willing!—all human beings will be *as we* are: *good, strong, happy men!* . . . In Europe slavery has been abolished because it has been calculated how much more these slaves cost, and how much less they yield, than free men. There is only one thing we continue to permit ourselves: to *use* and *trade three continents as slaves*, to *banish* them to silver mines and sugar mills. But these are not Europeans, not Christians, and in return we receive silver and gems, spice, sugar . . . All this for the sake of trade and for the *mutual fraternal assistance* and *community* among nations. . . . The system of trade!! The greatness and uniqueness of the project is obvious! *Three continents devastated* and *regimented* by us . . . what a rich and happy deal! . . . Who could praise everything in *such* an age as ours? Enough: we are *"the crown of the tree*, swaying in *heavenly air*! The *golden age* is nigh!"⁵⁶

"Every people," wrote Herder, "had its period of growth, flowering, and decline."⁵⁷ The same applied to the West—rather than being the end of history, it too would eventually give way to others. As Herder wrote, "The more *means* and *tools* we Europeans invent to enslave, cheat, and plunder you other continents, the more it may be left to you to *triumph* in the end! We forge the chains by which *you* will pull *us* [one day] and the *inverted pyramids* of our constitutions will be *righted* on your soil."⁵⁸

In Herder we see many of the themes that became common in civilizational theory: the idea that values and institutions that arise in one context do not necessarily suit another; the denunciations of Western arrogance and colonialism; the view of societies as organic beings that are born, live, and die, meaning that none can be the final form of human development; and a belief in the value of diverse forms of social evolution. In the century that followed Herder, however, rapid technological progress, along with imperial expansion and the spread of science and education, meant that many Westerners were more inclined to the optimistic message of the likes of Condorcet and Comte. A serious shock was required to dent the belief in continual progress and the superiority of Western ways. That shock came with the First World War, followed by the Russian Revolution and the rise of communism and fascism. Suddenly, reason and liberalism seemed less like the end of history than they had before. With this, the path lay open to a revival of alternative models of human development.

Oswald Spengler's book *The Decline of the West* thus arrived at exactly the right time. A former schoolteacher who had taken up writing after receiving an inheritance from his mother, Spengler (1880–1936) avoided military service in the First World War due to a heart ailment and devoted the war years to writing *The Decline of the West*. The first volume hit the bookstores in 1918. The second volume followed in 1922.[59] Perfectly fitting the zeitgeist of the moment, it was a huge hit and had a great impact on civilizational thinking thereafter.

Like Herder, Spengler denounced the idea of history as a linear process leading toward the Western mode of life. He wrote,

> The Cultures that are to come will find it difficult to believe that the validity of such a scheme with its simple rectilinear progression . . . was, in spite of all, never whole-heartedly attacked. . . . It is not only that the scheme circumscribes the area of history. What is worse, it rigs the stage. The ground of Western Europe is treated as a steady pole, a unique patch chosen on the surface of the sphere for no better reason, it seems, than because we live on it—and great histories of millennial duration and mighty far-away Cultures are made to revolve around this pole.[60]

Spengler proposed an alternative:

> I see in the place of that empty figment of *one* linear history which can only be kept up by shutting one's eyes to the overwhelming multitude of the facts, the drama of a *number* of mighty Cultures, each springing with primitive strength from the soil of a mother-region to which it remains firmly bound throughout its whole life-cycle; each stamping its material, its mankind, in *its own* image; each having *its own* idea, *its own* passions, *its own* life, will and feeling, *its own* death. . . . Each Culture has its own new possibilities of self-expression, which arise, ripen, decay, and never return. There is not *one* sculpture, *one* painting, *one* mathematics, *one* physics, but many, each in its deepest essence different from the others, each limited in duration and self-contained, just as

each species of plant has its peculiar blossom or fruits, its special type of growth and decline.[61]

Western values, wrote Spengler, "are local and temporary values—most of them indeed limited to the 'momentary' intelligentsia of Western-European type. World-historical or 'eternal' values they emphatically are not.... The future of the West is not a limitless tending upwards and onwards for all time towards our present beliefs, but a single phenomenon of history, strictly limited and defined as to form and duration."[62] "Cultures are organisms," he added: "Every Culture passes through the age-phases of the individual man. Each has its childhood, youth, manhood, and old age."[63] Every given culture possesses a unique soul, and "it dies when this soul has actualized the full sum of its potentialities."[64] This was as true of the West as of any other culture. Consequently, he concluded, "In a few centuries from now there will no more be Western Culture."[65]

The First World War was a profound shock to many of those who had previously believed in the myth of steady progress toward a utopian future. Among the disillusioned was the British historian Arnold Toynbee (1889–1975), who, like Spengler, was medically excused from military service during the war and worked instead in the Political Intelligence Department of the Foreign Office. Afterward, he moved to the Royal Institute of International Affairs (Chatham House), whose annual *Survey on International Affairs* he edited from 1925 to 1954. Author of numerous books on world history, Toynbee acquired great popularity, especially in the United States, appearing regularly on TV and radio after the Second World War.[66]

Toynbee began his intellectual life as a typical liberal internationalist.[67] He noted that before 1914 he had "expected that life throughout the World would become more rational, more humane, and more democratic ... we thought that mankind's course was set for an earthly paradise, and that our approach towards this goal was predestined for us by historical necessity."[68] The experience of the First World War shattered this belief and encouraged Toynbee to look for a new explanation of the grand scheme of human history.[69] At first he sought inspiration from Spengler but soon rejected Spengler's idea that civilizations were all doomed to extinction, viewing this as allowing no room for human agency.[70] "Spengler was, it seemed to me, unilluminatingly dogmatic and deterministic," Toynbee said, added to which, Spengler offered "no explanation" for the rise and fall of civilizations: "It was just a law of nature which Spengler had detected, and you must take it on trust from the master."[71] "We are not doomed to make history repeat itself," Toynbee added; "it is open to us, through our own efforts to give history in our case, some new and unprecedented choice. As human beings, we are endowed with this freedom of choice."[72]

Toynbee was looking for a scheme that would allow Western civilization to survive. The key to that, he thought, was recognizing that it was just one of many civilizations. "I am a Westerner," he said, "I value Western civilization, and I don't want to see it go under. . . . It is very important—and in the West's interests—that we should come down to a footing of equality in good time, rather than be overthrown, clinging to power, and then have the roles reversed. But this is not anti-Western, it is pro-Western; a wish for preservation of Western civilization as one among a number of different civilizations."[73]

Whereas Spengler had written of "cultures," Toynbee wrote of "civilizations," which he defined as "the smallest unit of historical study at which one arrives when one tries to understand the history of one's own country."[74] As an example, he argued that you could not understand the history of the United States "unless you looked beyond the bounds of the United States—out beyond her frontiers to Western Europe. . . . But, to make American history and institutions intelligible . . . you need not look beyond Western Europe into Eastern Europe or the Islamic world."[75] In this way, one could define the boundaries of something one might call Western civilization.

Toynbee commented that "the West's ascendancy over the rest of the world during the last three centuries has been reflected in the recent Western way of looking at mankind's history as all leading up to the modern West. I think this West-centered way of looking at history is a palpable case of subjectivism; it seems to me to misrepresent the reality and, in so far as it distorts it, to make it unintelligible."[76] He argued that ideas such as human rights could not be exported to other civilizations without considering the differences between them. International peace depended on a dialogue of civilizations rather than on a process of foisting Western models upon non-Western societies.[77]

While Toynbee considered every civilization to be different, he nevertheless perceived common patterns in their birth, growth, and decay. Through a study of various civilizations over time, he concluded that a civilization arises when a "creative minority" responds to a physical challenge by creating a new set of values and institutions that it persuades the passive majority to accept.[78] "It is only the thrust of genius that has ever forced the inertia of Humanity to yield," he argued.[79]

According to Toynbee, over time the creative minority begins to rest on its laurels and loses its creativity, becoming what he called a "dominant minority." In the process it loses the support of the masses, who become what Toynbee called an "internal proletariat." The bonds holding society together begin to disintegrate, causing conflict. As a last resort, the dominant minority unites all the parts of the civilization into "a universal state," but this cannot save it. Citing Rome and the rise of Christianity, Toynbee argued that within the universal state, the internal proletariat develops its own new civilization in the form of a "universal religion."[80] As he put it, "In the last rally but one, the dominant majority succeeds in temporarily arresting the society's lethal self-laceration by imposing on it the peace of a universal state. Within the framework of the dominant majority's universal state the proletariat creates a universal church, and after the next rout, in which the disintegrating civilization finally dissolves, the universal church may live on to become the chrysalis from which a new civilization eventually emerges."[81] With this, the original civilization comes to an end, and a new one is born. It would be incorrect, though, to speak of the death of the original, as large parts of it survive in the new civilization.

Toynbee hoped that Western civilization could avoid this fate but argued that in order to do so, it would have to accept that it was just one of many civilizations. He commented,

> It will be harder for us to accept the not less plain fact that the past histories of our vociferous, and sometimes vituperative, living contemporaries—the Chinese and the Japanese, the Hindus and the Muslims, and our elder brothers the Orthodox Christians—are going to become a part of our Western past history in a future world which will be neither Western nor non-Western but will inherit all the cultures which we Westerners have now brewed together in a single crucible. Yet this is the manifest truth, when we face it. Our own descendants are not going to be just Western, like ourselves. They are going to be heirs of Confucius and Lao-Tse as well as Socrates, Plato, and Plotinus; heirs of Gautama Buddha as well as Deutero-Isaiah and Jesus Christ; heirs of Zarathustra and Muhammad as well as Elijah and Elisha and Peter and Paul; heirs of Shankara and Ramanuja as well as Clement and Origen; heirs of the Cappadocian Fathers of the Orthodox Church as well as our African Augustine and our Umbrian Benedict; heirs of Ibn Khaldun as well as Bossuet; and heirs (if still wallowing in the Serbonian Bog of politics) of Lenin and Gandhi and Sun Yat-sen as well as Cromwell and George Washington and Mazzini.[82]

Another influential thinker whose original worldview was shattered by the First World War and subsequent events was the Russian American sociologist Pitirim Sorokin (1889–1968). Born in the Komi region of northern Russia, Sorokin fled his native country following the revolution of 1917, after which he settled in the United States and became a professor of sociology at Harvard University. Like Toynbee, Sorokin was a onetime believer in universal linear progress who changed his mind in light of the turmoil of the early twentieth century. He explained, "The World War and most of what took place after it were bewildering to one who, in conformity with the dominant currents of social thought of the earlier twentieth century, had believed in progress, revolution, socialism, democracy, scientific positivism, and many other 'isms' of the same sort. For good or ill, I fought for these values and paid the penalty. . . . If anybody had seriously predicted in 1913 a small fraction of what has actually taken place since, he would have been branded then as mad. And yet what then appeared to be absolutely impossible has indeed happened."[83]

Sorokin's contribution to civilizational theory lay in the production of what one might call a metahistory of metahistories—that is to say, he compared and contrasted various theories that asserted a nonuniversal, nonlinear model of human development and thereby created a theory of theories of history. In this way, he helped establish civilizational thinking as a legitimate area of academic study.

In his original work on the subject, Sorokin avoided the word "civilization," preferring instead the term "cultural supersystem." Subsequently, he put the word "civilization" in quotation marks, as if to denigrate it as unscientific. Finally, he removed the quotation marks altogether.[84] In this way, he gradually came to accept the civilizational discourse.

In his comparisons of civilizational theories, Sorokin criticized the models developed by Danilevsky, Spengler, and Toynbee. The groupings they described often lacked sufficient internal unity to be true cultural supersystems. Moreover, they mixed together groups of different types. Some of their civilizations were language groups, others state groups, others single nation-states, and so on. There was no consistency in what they described.[85] In addition, wrote Sorokin, their view of civilizations as organisms with a life cycle of birth, growth, and death was "neither logically nor factually tenable."[86]

Sorokin therefore rejected both the linear model of historical development and the Danilevsky-Spengler-Toynbee model of civilizational life cycles. "What may resemble a limitless linear trend is likely to be merely a limited trend of considerable duration," he wrote: "This generalization applies also to the laws of the 'universal stages' through which mankind as a whole or a given society or cultural system is supposed to pass. . . . The dominant form of the direction of sociocultural processes is neither permanently cyclical nor permanently linear, but varyingly recurrent, with incessant modifications of the old themes."[87]

Sorokin thought that cultural supersystems fluctuate between three different value sets. They do not die; they merely move onto something else. The three value systems he described as ideational, sensate, and idealistic. According to Sorokin, ideational cultures believe that "the true value and the true reality is the super-sensory, super-rational God." Sensate cultures believe that "the true value and true reality is sensory" and tend to be materialistic. And idealistic cultures believe that "the true reality and value is partly sensory, partly rational, partly supersensory and superrational infinite manifold."[88] One can see a certain similarity between this and Comte's three-stage model of development (for some reason, patterns of three are extremely common in these theories). The difference is that whereas Comte saw the third stage as something from which there was no going back, Sorokin envisaged a process in which after completing stage three, cultural supersystems went back to stage one. Eventually, each culture system would become too one-sided, lose its creativity, and give way to a different system after a period of internal crisis and war.[89] Ideational cultures became sensate cultures, which then became idealistic cultures, which then became ideational ones, and so on ad infinitum.

Sorokin associated linear theories of progress "from 'the caveman to superman,' from barbarism to civilization'" with sensate cultures. By contrast, he believed that ideational cultures favored "divinely guided, cyclical or eschatological" theories.[90] In Sorokin's view, the West was a sensate culture and was therefore dominated by linear theories such as those of Condorcet, Comte, and Hegel. But that was changing, he believed. The political crises that rocked Europe in the early twentieth century showed that the West was moving from a sensate to an idealistic culture. With that, civilizational theories were gaining more support, as witnessed by the popularity of authors such as Spengler and Toynbee.[91]

Sorokin identified six commonalities among these civilizational theories, a number he later increased to thirteen. Among other things, he considered that there was general agreement that there were higher-level cultural unities, or civilizations; that they were few in number; that each was different from the other; and that each embodied a distinct "ultimate value."[92] The fact that so many different authors with different ideological perspectives agreed on these points suggested that they were correct, he argued.[93]

Sorokin identified civilization with culture. Writing in the 1950s and 1960s, another American, Carroll Quigley (1910–77), a professor at Georgetown University, provided a more material definition. His civilizational model was strongly influenced by Toynbee's, but Quigley rejected the Englishman's religiosity in favor of an economic approach.

According to Quigley, there were five levels of "social aggregate." These were "collections of persons, whose only significant relationship is that they are in the same place at the same time"; "groups of persons, whose relationships are sufficiently patterned for members to be able to identify who is, and who is not, a member of the group"; "societies, which are groups whose patterns serve to satisfy most of the members' basic needs"; "producing societies, which are societies whose economic patterns serve to increase the amount of food in the system"; and finally, "civilizations," a civilization being "a producing society whose patterns include an organization of expansion."[94]

What Quigley called an "organization of expansion" consisted of three parts: the existence of incentives to innovate, "an inequitable distribution of the social product so that there accumulates within the society a surplus of wealth," and a form of social organization that ensures that the accumulated surplus "is used to mobilize resources to exploit the innovations being made."[95] The three elements of a civilization are therefore "incentive to invent, accumulation of surplus, and application of this surplus to the new inventions."[96] Expansion can be in the form of population, territory, wealth, or knowledge. According to Quigley, the rate of expansion is at first rapid but then slows. This is because civilizations become "institutionalized"—in other words, they are taken over by "vested interests more concerned with defending their own interests . . . than they are with the organization's macro-goals."[97] If the civilization fails to reform itself, it descends into an "Age of Conflict" until eventually the entirety of the civilization is absorbed into a "Universal Empire." In the meantime, members of the civilization begin to reject it and opt out of the system, seeking satisfaction in sex, drugs, religion, "or other irrationalities." The society becomes one of "atomized and alienated individuals," and it collapses.[98]

Civilizational theory attracted few converts in Western academia during the Cold War. It did, however, prove popular among certain elements of the European far right, including the French *Nouvelle droite* (New Right). The most notable member of the latter was, and is, the French journalist Alain de Benoist (b. 1943), who is considered responsible for popularizing the concept of "ethnopluralism."

A founder of the French think tank Groupement de Recherche et d'Études pour la Civilisation Européene (Group for Research and Studies for European Civilization), de Benoist believes in the centrality of identity in human life and criticizes Western liberalism for eradicating identities and turning everybody into a homogeneous mass of mere consumers.[99] He denounces liberalism as an "ideology of sameness," a "universalist ideology, which . . . aims at reducing the diversity of the world . . . to one uniform model."[100] In its place, de Benoist offers the ideology of ethnopluralism, according to which each ethnic grouping will be able to develop in its own way, according to its own principles, free of outside interference.

Ethnopluralism is meant to protect a world of diverse cultures. As such, it provides a tool for condemning Western imperialism and colonialism and for asserting the right of non-Western states to develop in their own way. At the same time, it justifies isolating Europe from non-European cultural influences. Critics complain that it is racist, as it rejects cultural mixing and in effect proposes a "separate but equal" doctrine that "professes extreme tolerance towards different cultures but only as long as they remain far away."[101]

De Benoist supports the creation of a multipolar world and believes that in such a world "the future belongs to large civilizational and continental groups."[102] He wrote in 1986 that, "Globally, the major contradiction is no longer between right and left, liberalism and socialism, fascism and communism, 'totalitarianism' and 'democracy,' it is between those who want a one-dimensional world and those who support a plural world founded on a diversity of cultures."[103] It is an opinion that remarkably foreshadows the rhetoric of the Russian government almost forty years later.

As the Cold War wore on, various scholars began to turn to culture for explanations of social development. This so-called culturalist revival provided the context for Samuel Huntington's 1993 essay and subsequent book on "The Clash of Civilizations."[104]

In his article, Huntington (1927–2008) declared that "in the politics of civilizations, the peoples and governments of non-Western civilizations no longer remain the objects of history as targets of Western colonialism but join the West as movers and shapers of history."[105] "A civilization is a cultural entity," he wrote.[106] More specifically, a civilization is "the highest cultural grouping of people and the broadest level of cultural identity people have short of that which distinguishes humans from other species. It is defined both by common objective elements, such as language, history, religion, customs, institutions, and by the subjective self-identification of people."[107]

Huntington's central thesis was that "the fault lines between civilizations are replacing the political and ideological boundaries of the Cold War as the flash points for crisis and bloodshed."[108] "The fundamental source of conflict in this new world will not be primarily ideological or primarily economic," he wrote: "The great divisions among humankind and the dominating source of conflict will be cultural. . . . The principal conflicts of global politics will occur between nations and groups of different civilizations. . . . The fault lines between civilizations will be the battle lines of the future."[109]

In his 1996 book *The Clash of Civilizations and the Remaking of World Order*, Huntington explained that national identities were breaking down, to be replaced by civilizational identities. Consequently, "a civilization-based world order is emerging," in which "global politics is the politics of civilizations."[110] Huntington argued that "in the twentieth century the relations among civilizations have thus moved from a phase dominated by the unidirectional impact of one civilization on all others to one of intense, sustained, and multidirectional interactions among all civilizations."[111] In this context, he claimed, "the West's universalist pretensions increasingly bring it into conflict with other civilizations. . . . The survival of the West depends on Americans reaffirming their Western identity and Westerners accepting civilization as unique not universal."[112] "Western belief in the universality of Western culture suffers three problems," Huntington concluded: "It is false; it is immoral; and it is dangerous."[113]

Any theory that seeks to fit the entirety of human history into a neat framework is bound to come in for criticism. Unsurprisingly, both of the trends of thought described in this chapter have multiple detractors. For some, the view that history is marching inexorably in a single direction is a fig leaf justifying Western imperialism. For others, it is simplistic or just plain wrong. For instance, in a 2022 book examining the early history of humanity, anthropologist David Graeber and archaeologist David Wengrow poured scorn on theories of social evolution that paint a linear model of development, arguing that ideas and institutions that are said to be products of modern, and in particular Western, society are nothing of the sort and in many cases have existed for almost as long as humanity itself.[114] The fact that the authors felt it necessary to spend seven hundred pages making this argument is testimony to the dominant place that linear ideas of social evolution hold in the Western popular consciousness.

Civilizational theory is equally subject to criticism, being denounced as a means by which oppressive regimes can justify "dodging inconvenient questions regarding the poor application of human rights and democratic norms in their home countries."[115] Because they study global history, civilizational theorists tend to be jacks of all trades and masters of none, making errors that those who specialize in the history of a specific country or region can easily exploit to undermine their credibility. Beyond that, they are often charged with cherry-picking evidence and twisting facts to fit theory. Toynbee, for instance, was said to be "guilty of . . . ignoring facts that do not fit neatly into the system and bending others so that they do."[116] Sorokin, meanwhile, has been accused of being "unscientific, metaphysical, and often authoritarian in his analysis; guilty of reification; theoretically simplistic in the development of concepts and use of ideal types; statistically naïve and empirically unsatisfying; historically inaccurate . . . and dominated by his values and scornful of science."[117]

For our purposes, however, the rights and wrongs of the various theories are neither here nor there. What matters is that they exist and have exerted a powerful influence on both the Western and the Russian imaginations. As we shall see, Russian proponents of unilinear historical development have drawn heavily on the likes of Comte, Hegel, and Marx, while their opponents have drawn on Herder, Spengler, and Toynbee. Niall Ferguson comments that "hardly anyone reads Spengler, Toynbee or Sorokin today."[118] That may perhaps be true in the Western world, but Ferguson's comment reveals the limits of his own Western-centrism. For Spengler, Toynbee, and Sorokin are all popular in post-Soviet Russia. Senior Russian politicians have cited Toynbee, while Russia has a Sorokin Research Center at Syktyvkar State University in the sociologist's native Komi region, and Foreign Minister Sergei Lavrov has quoted Sorokin in an article for the journal *Russia in Global Affairs*.[119]

Russians first adopted and then rejected the unilinear concept of history, and now civilizational theory appears to hold sway. In the rest of the book, we shall examine how this happened.

Chapter 2

Russian Historical Determinism

Russian civilizational theory is a reactive philosophy. In other words, it came into being (and continues to exist) as a reaction to something else. That something is Russian historical determinism, the belief that Russia is destined to follow the same rules of historical development as those that guided the progress of Western Europe. This chapter therefore examines the various understandings of those rules in Russia since historical determinism first began to exert a powerful influence there in the early nineteenth century.

Roughly speaking, one can identify two main strands of Russian historical determinism: conservative and radical. The first agrees that history is marching in a single direction but urges caution in how one reacts to this knowledge. Conservatives believe that change needs to be gradual and organic, happening in accordance with existing values and institutions. They regard the premature transplanting of institutions from a society further along the single path of development as highly disruptive. Different peoples may all be going in the same direction, but they need to do so at their own pace and in their own way. In Russia, this mode of thought has largely found expression in what one might call "conservative liberalism," a philosophy that seeks the liberalization of Russian society, but in an orderly manner guided by the paternal hand of the state.

Radicals, by contrast, tend to derive an *ought* from an *is*. Because society is progressing along a given path, they conclude that anything that obstructs that path ought to be removed, ideally as rapidly as possible. The end of history is something to be accelerated, not patiently awaited. One can identify two currents within this stream of thought: radical liberal and revolutionary communist. Both have sought rapid and decisive change, but with different objectives: a Western-style liberal democratic order in the first instance and a communist society in the second.

The nineteenth and early twentieth centuries witnessed a slow movement away from the moderate position toward the radical one, culminating in the Bolshevik revolution of 1917. Radicalism then ruled the roost for several decades, until in the late Soviet period communist theorists began to become more conservative and to consider the possibility that different societies might benefit from advancing toward communism in different ways. This proved to a be a short-lived trend, as faith in communism disintegrated and was replaced by a radical liberalism that sought post-Soviet Russia's rapid transformation into a Western-style society. Negative perceptions of the consequences of radical liberalism then led Russians to decisively reject it in turn. Civilizational theory's moment arrived, and historical determinism's two-hundred-year grip on the Russian imagination finally came to an end, at least for now.

"If one were to ask in which direction the Russian people is destined to march, I would say that the question has already been answered: it must march towards European civilization."[1] Writing in the early nineteenth century, economist Nikolai Turgenev (1789–1871) aptly summarized the basic worldview of Russian Westernizers both in his time and thereafter. Noted for his 1818 *Essay on the Theory of Taxation*, Turgenev was a close associate of members of the conspiratorial Northern Society, set up in the Russian capital St. Petersburg in 1822 with the aim of turning Russia from an absolute to a constitutional monarchy. The model for this clearly came from Western Europe. In his *Ideas on the Organization of a Society*, Turgenev noted that "the Russians, too, want to participate in the destinies of enlightened Europe."[2] Though he later denied being a member of the Northern Society, he at the very least inspired many of those who were. "I acquired the nefarious liberal ideas which led me into such horrible errors from reading books and from the company of Nikolai Turgenev, who more than anyone was instrumental in imparting such views," said one such member, Mikhail Mitkov (1791–1849).[3]

Fortunately for Turgenev, he was out of the country in December 1825, when members of the Northern Society launched an abortive coup d'état in

St. Petersburg following the death of Emperor Alexander I (reigned 1801–25) and the accession to the throne of his brother Nicholas I (reigned 1825–55). Some participants in what became known as the Decembrist Revolt were executed. Others endured years in internal exile. Sentenced in absentia to death (a punishment commuted by Nicholas I to life imprisonment), Turgenev spent thirty years in exile in Europe until he was eventually pardoned by Nicholas I's successor, Alexander II (reigned 1855–81).

The Decembrist Revolt illustrated the influence of Western ideas on Russian intellectuals. Many participants were military officers who had marched with the Russian army as it pursued Napoleon across Europe after his failed 1812 invasion of Russia. What they saw in Western Europe convinced them of Russia's relative backwardness and of the need to reform their country in accordance with the most advanced model available. As one Decembrist, Matvei Muravyov-Apostol (1793–1886), put it, "The first notions of free thought and liberalism I acquired during our stay in Paris in 1814."[4]

In the years that followed, however much he tried, Nicholas I was unable to prevent Western ideas of historical development from creeping further into Russian society. Even people of a conservative and nationalist disposition often shared the belief that history was marching in a definite direction. Disagreements were perhaps more about the pace, and about the manner in which one should progress, than about the general concept or the ultimate destination.

Nicholas's minister of enlightenment (in effect, minister of education), Sergei Uvarov (1786–1855), is a case in point. Deeply conservative, Uvarov was tasked with reorganizing Russian education on patriotic lines, and in 1833 he unveiled the ideology of "Official Nationality." This consisted of three principles—"Orthodoxy, Autocracy, Nationality"—that were to be the basis of the moral education of Russia's youth.[5] The conservative tenor of Uvarov's policies has earned his Ministry of Enlightenment the moniker "Ministry of Darkness."[6] Yet Uvarov fully believed in progress. He had a deterministic view of history, in some respects in keeping with that of the Decembrists. But whereas the Decembrists wanted to make a great leap forward, Uvarov wanted to move forward one small step at a time.

Uvarov was a thoroughly Europeanized individual. He studied at Göttingen University in Germany (as did Nikolai Turgenev), was well versed in Western European history and philosophy, and read seven languages.[7] He viewed history as a progression toward ever-increasing freedom. As societies matured, he argued, their morality and form of government evolved to reflect their stage of development. In due course, this process would lead all societies to a state in which "human rights are recognized by everyone and citizens' rights are everywhere defined."⁸ "Pay attention to the voice of history!" Uvarov declared in an 1818 speech: "States have their epochs of birth, their infancy, their youth, their age of maturity and finally their decrepitude.... The wish to prolong one of these ages longer than the time designated by nature is as vain and reckless as the wish to confine a growing youth within the tight limits of a baby's cradle. The theory of government in this instance resembles the theory of upbringing.... All these great truths are contained in history.... Woe to those who do not follow its directions!"⁹

In Uvarov's eyes, Russia was still very much in its infancy. The path to maturity, he believed, came through education. As the benefits of education reached more and more Russians, the population would become fit for freedom, a process that Uvarov sought to enable by expanding access to formal education for Russia's upper classes. But Uvarov also felt that this process needed to move slowly and cautiously to avoid revolutionary disruptions. Along the way, the firm hand of the autocracy would be required to guide the still-youthful people toward enlightenment. Uvarov therefore believed both in progress and in the maintenance of autocratic rule. As he grew older, his caution grew as well, and his idea of the desirable pace of progress slowed. Nevertheless, Uvarov's biographer Cynthia Whittaker concludes that he "never altered his views on the direction of European development."¹⁰

Uvarov believed in the merits of an enlightened autocracy. So too did many of the first generation of moderate Westernizers, who emerged onto the Russian intellectual scene in the 1830s and '40s. But unlike Uvarov, they did not believe that the policies pursued by Nicholas I fitted the model of enlightened autocracy. While they did not challenge the emperor's absolute authority, they demanded a more rapid expansion of civil liberties.

To make their point, many of them turned to history. Interpretations of the past became the vehicle for policy recommendations about the future. Russian nationalists used history to argue that Russia was unlike Western Europe and therefore should not copy it. Westernizers used it to make the opposite point—that Russia and the West were both moving in the same direction and that talk of copying the West was therefore absurd.

Chief among the nationalist historians was Mikhail Pogodin (1800–75), who developed the "Norman theory of history," according to which Western European states were formed when foreign invaders conquered territories and formed a privileged ruling class. Consequently, they experienced a divide between the rulers, who were of one tribe, and the ruled, who were of another. In due course, this turned into a conflict not of tribes but of classes. By contrast, Russia came into being when the early Russians invited the Viking prince Rurik to take the throne of Rus'. Because their rulers were not conquerors but guests, Pogodin claimed, Russians managed to avoid the class conflict that bedeviled Europe and instead created a harmonious social order. According to Pogodin, other differences, such as terrain, weather, and patterns of historical settlement, further separated Russia from the West. The two were therefore entirely different, and it made no sense for the former to copy the latter.[11]

Westernizing historians countered by arguing that the path of historical development in Russia and Western Europe was the same, albeit with Russia lagging somewhat behind the West. One of the most influential of these historians was the Moscow University professor Timofei Granovsky (1813–55), who is said to have "adopted a centrist interpretation of Hegel to argue that recent European history offered a prototype of the process of individual emancipation from external authority and customary traditions, and implied that Russia too must develop in the light of the universal laws of reason."[12] Granovsky argued that "individualization of the masses through the power of ideas is the essence of historical progress. The goal of history is the moral, enlightened individual, emancipated from the fatalistic pressure of external determinations."[13] In a series of lectures in the 1840s, he laid out the theory that new social forms inevitably replace old ones in a progressive process, leading eventually to the liberation of the person.[14] This law of history applied equally to Russia and the West, he said.

Granovsky's lectures on history proved extremely popular among Moscow intellectuals. Moreover, the professor established close links with what have been called the "enlightened bureaucrats" in the government administration, many of whom went on to lead the process of reform that took place under Alexander II in the 1860s and 1870s. Also among those whom Granovsky influenced was Konstantin Kavelin (1818–85), who joined Granovsky as a professor at Moscow University from 1844 to 1848, after which he moved to St. Petersburg. From 1857 to 1858, Kavelin briefly acted as a tutor to the then heir to the throne, Grand Duke Nikolai Aleksandrovich (1843–65).

Like Granovsky, Kavelin used history to argue in favor of a Western-style liberal future. In 1847, he produced an essay titled "A Brief Survey of Juridical Relations in Ancient Russia," which has been described as "one of the defining statements of Russian Westernism."[15] Countering the nationalist historians, Kavelin wrote that "we are a European people, capable of perfection, of development, which does not like to repeat itself or to stand still in one spot for a countless number of centuries."[16] Kavelin argued that history involved the gradual development of the autonomous individual, or as he put it, the "principle of personality." Historical progress, he wrote, consisted of "the gradual formation and appearance of the principle of personality . . . and the gradual negation of an existence founded purely on blood, in which personality could not exist."[17]

According to Kavelin, Russian history had passed through various stages—communal, tribal, and family—before reaching the era of the state. In the earliest stages, he wrote, *"the person as a person* meant nothing."[18] Strong blood ties meant that people did not examine the differences between themselves and those around them.[19] With the advent of Christianity, ideas of the inherent dignity of all people began to spread, but it was only with the creation of the modern state that life was established on a principle other than bloodlines and so enabled personality to flourish.[20]

Kavelin argued that as this process unfolded, "the Russian and the foreign have merged into one to carry Russia forward. . . . The boundaries between the past and the present, Russian and foreign, are being destroyed."[21] This was not a matter of Russia copying the West. The process of moving toward the state and the principle of personality was a universal phenomenon, not something specifically Western. The fact that Russia was moving in that direction later than the West did not mean that it was copying the West and so ceasing to be Russian. Both Russia and the West were obeying the same rule of history; the West just happened to be further along the universal path.[22] Thus, concluded Kavelin, "The difference [between the West and Russia] lies solely in the preceding historical facts; the aim, the task, the aspirations, the way forward are one and the same."[23]

Kavelin's theory of history bears a striking, and by no means coincidental, resemblance to Hegel's. Like Hegel, Kavelin viewed history as a progress toward freedom, made possible through the mechanism of the state. Like Uvarov, therefore, he was in some respects quite conservative, in that he insisted on the retention of powerful, centralized state authority and expressed skepticism about Russia's suitability for representative government. Unlike Uvarov, though, he demanded that autocracy be combined with civil liberties. He thus wrote to Granovsky, "I believe completely in the necessity of absolutism in present-day Russia, but it ought to be progressive and enlightened."[24]

Kavelin's belief in the benefits of enlightened autocracy had some basis in reality during the reign of Alexander II, when the imperial government initiated a large series of economic, social, judicial, political, and military reforms. Under Alexander's successors, Alexander III (reigned 1881–94) and Nicholas II (reigned 1894–1917), the Russian government became far more conservative. This induced Russian liberals to move in a more radical direction, demanding the immediate enactment of a constitution, expanded civil rights, and the creation of a parliament directly elected by means of universal suffrage.

Underlying this radicalism was a perception that Western European democracies were the most advanced form of rational government and thus something that Russia should emulate. Perhaps the most important proponent of this belief was yet another historian, Pavel Miliukov (1859–1943), a convinced positivist who at the start of the twentieth century would become the leader of Russia's largest liberal party, the Constitutional Democratic Party (often referred to as the "Kadets" because of the party's initials, K.D.).

Miliukov earned a reputation among his enemies as an opportunist. In the First World War, for instance, he was an avid supporter of Russia's alliance with France and Britain against Germany, but after the Bolshevik revolution of 1917, he urged the anti-Bolshevik White armies to ally with Germany. Then, having supported the military dictatorship of the White generals during the Russian Civil War, after their defeat he denounced them as reactionaries, rejected armed struggle, and urged an alliance with the revolutionary left. But despite what one might generously call his tactical flexibility, Miliukov always remained firm about one thing: Russia was a European country, and the laws of history dictated that it was destined in due course to join civilization, an idea he identified above all with liberal democracy along British, French, and American lines. He told a conference of English historians several years after the Russian Revolution, "We believe that Russia is part of the civilized world: and so long as there is a civilized humanity, the leading principles of English and Anglo-Saxon political life cannot be extinguished. They are immortal."[25]

In his book *Outlines of Russian Culture*, Miliukov remarked that "in all spheres of life, our historical development proceeds in the same direction as it has proceeded everywhere in Europe."[26] Echoing Kavelin, he told an American audience that progress was not a matter of Russia copying the West but merely one of following the same inevitable path. "The Russian nation is itself European," he said, "and the process of it remolding itself originated, as much as elsewhere in Europe, in internal evolutionary causes and not in the fanciful pleasure of 'borrowing' new fashions."[27] "Civilization makes nations, as it makes individuals, more alike," he continued: "National self-consciousness clings to particular features of national existence, such as dress, dwelling, social habits, political institutions, and old forms of the popular creed. But in the long run these features cannot be preserved."[28]

It followed from this that as Russia's economy grew, its people became more educated, and its society as a whole became more civilized, Russia would inevitably adopt the same forms of government as other civilized states—in other words, those of Western Europe. As Miliukov put it, "Free forms of political life are as little national as the use of the alphabet or the printing press, steam or electricity. They are simply forms of higher culture. . . . They become necessary when social life becomes sufficiently complicated that it cannot find room for itself within the framework of a more primitive social order. When such a time arrives, when a new era of history knocks on the door, it is useless to place obstacles and delays in its way."[29]

By 1900, Miliukov and many other Russian liberals believed that the new era had arrived. Russia had no choice, they argued, but to adopt a constitutional form of government like those of Britain and France. Social Darwinist ideas contributed to this belief. Liberals argued that reform was needed to strengthen Russia. Without it, the country would be destroyed in the dog-eat-dog world of international competition that characterized late nineteenth- and early twentieth-century Europe. Confronted by the complaint that Western European models did not apply to Russia, Miliukov had a simple response: Russia had to obey "the laws of political biology."[30]

The problem with the laws of political biology was that different people had very different opinions as to what they were. Whereas Miliukov and his fellow liberals felt that the end of history was capitalist liberal democracy, many others followed Marx in believing that history had yet another stage beyond that—communism.

One of the first Russians to declare himself a Marxist was Georgy Plekhanov (1856–1918), who in 1895 published a book titled *The Development of the Monist View of History*. By "monist," Plekhanov meant that there was only one version of historical progress and that it was the same for all societies. In his book, he traced the development of the concept of dialectical materialism from the period of the French Revolution onward and defended Marx's understanding of the mechanism of historical change. "What did Marx have to do?" asked Plekhanov, answering, "The preceding history of social science and philosophy had piled up a 'whole Mont Blanc' of contradictions, which urgently demanded solution. Marx did precisely solve them with the help of a theory . . . [according to which] the historical progress of humanity is determined by the development of productive forces, leading to changes in economic relations."[31] "It is only the historical theory of Marx that . . . brings the argument to a satisfactory conclusion or, at any rate, provides the possibility of concluding it satisfactorily, if people have ears to hear and a brain wherewith to think," Plekhanov remarked.[32]

Plekhanov devoted much of the book to denouncing criticisms of Marxism by the Russian sociologist Nikolai Mikhailovsky (1842–1902), a leading member of the Populist movement. The Populists believed in a form of peasant socialism, founded on the Russian peasant commune, and looked very negatively on capitalism, arguing that Russia should seek a noncapitalist mode of economic development. Plekhanov contended that this was futile. "There are no data allowing one to hope that Russia will soon leave the path of capitalist development upon which it entered after 1861," he wrote.[33] This, though, did not mean that Russians should just sit back and submit to the iron laws of history. Plekhanov rejected what he referred to as "fatalism." Instead, he argued that knowledge of the laws of history provided people with a powerful tool. Ignorant of them, they could do nothing but submit. But once they became aware of them, they could mobilize themselves to overthrow capitalism and create a socialist future. As Plekhanov wrote,

> Just as the nature surrounding man itself gave him the first opportunity to develop his productive forces and, consequently, gradually to emancipate himself from nature's yoke—so the relations of production, social relations, by the very logic of their development bring man to realization of the causes of his enslavement by economic necessity. This provides the opportunity for a new and final triumph of consciousness over necessity, of reason over blind law. . . . Thus dialectical materialism not only does not strive, as its opponents attribute to it, to convince man that it is absurd to revolt against economic necessity, but it is the first to point out how to overcome the latter. . . . The individual personality is only foam on the crest of the wave, men are subjected to an iron law which can only be discovered, but which cannot be subjected to the human will, said Georg Büchner. No, replies Marx: once we have discovered that iron law, it depends on us to overthrow its yoke, it depends on us to make necessity the obedient slave of reason. I am a worm, says the idealist. I am a worm while I am ignorant, retorts the dialectical materialist: but I am a god when I know.[34]

After Russia's communists seized power in 1917, radical historical determinism triumphed over its more moderate variant, and dialectical materialism became one of the chief ideological supports of what became known as the Soviet Union. In 1938, Soviet leader Joseph Stalin (1878–1953) laid out the official understanding of historical progress in a chapter he wrote for a history of the Communist Party of the Soviet Union. Titled "Dialectical and Historical Materialism," the chapter also appeared as a separate booklet.

Stalin viewed himself as an intellectual. He read voraciously on a wide variety of topics. By far the largest number of books in his personal library were works by or about Vladimir Lenin (1870–1924), although he also owned many works by other Bolsheviks. Communist ideology and tactics were the most common topics, followed by history, economics, and military affairs.[35] Stalin did not read all this just for his own interest. Knowledge was meant to inform action, and a good understanding of Marxist-Leninist theory was deemed essential for any serious communist. Stalin used his reading to participate in intellectual debates and impose his own understanding of theory. Given that the theory of dialectical materialism played a vital role in legitimizing Soviet rule, it would seem that Stalin deemed it too important a matter to be left to others. Thus, whereas the rest of the 1938 history of the Communist Party was written by a committee, Stalin penned the chapter on "Dialectical and Historical Materialism" himself.

"Contrary to idealism," wrote Stalin, "Marxist philosophical materialism holds that the world and its laws are fully knowable, that our knowledge of the laws of nature, tested by experiment and practice, is authentic knowledge having the validity of objective truth, and that there are no things in the world that are unknowable. . . . Hence social life, the history of society, ceases to be an agglomeration of 'accidents,' and becomes the history of the development of society according to regular laws, and the study of the history of society becomes a science."[36] The fundamental social law revealed by Marxism-Leninism, according to Stalin, was that "the chief force of the development of society" was "the mode of production of material values . . . which are indispensable for the life and development of society. . . . The clue to the study of the laws of history of society must be sought not in men's minds, in the views and ideas of society, but in the mode of production practised by society."[37]

Stalin identified five historical modes of production, corresponding to Marx's social formations. These were "primitive communal, slave, feudal, capitalist, and socialist."[38] History consisted of a progression through these modes of production, ending with socialism. At each stage, the relations of production eventually came to contradict the mode of production, resulting in revolution and the beginning of a new mode. Capitalism, for instance, "by expanding production and concentrating millions of workers in huge mills and factories . . . undermines its own foundation, inasmuch as the social character of the process of production demands the social ownership of the means of production."[39] Under socialism, by contrast, "the relations of production fully correspond to the state of productive forces," ensuring the system's stability and thereby bringing the process of historical evolution to an end.[40] "Such is Marxist materialism as applied to social life, to the history of society. Such are the principles of dialectical and historical materialism," concluded Stalin.

Stalin's exposition of dialectical and historical materialism was a fairly orthodox Marxist account. In broad terms, the Soviet Union never moved far from it. After Stalin's death in 1953, however, Soviet thinkers did begin to modify it on the edges. In the process, the Soviet view of history became less radical over time, allowing for more possibilities of different modes of historical development.

From the 1950s onward, the process of decolonization led to the creation of a large number of newly independent states in what became known as the Third World. These soon became an important geopolitical battleground, with the West and the Soviet Union competing to win the new states as their allies. It soon became clear to the Soviets that most Third World countries lacked the prerequisites for a socialist revolution. According to the logic of dialectical and historical materialism, they would need first to pass through a stage of capitalism. This, however, would lead them naturally into the camp of the capitalist West, something that was obviously undesirable from the perspective of Soviet foreign policy. To get around this problem, Soviet theorists began to argue that former Western colonies should do something that Plekhanov had denied was possible—namely, follow a "non-capitalist path of development." With Soviet assistance, they argued, any progressive class could initiate the movement toward socialism by constructing state-owned industries and so creating a proletariat while skipping the capitalist stage of development.[41]

This constituted a major revision of Marx's historical theory. At the same time, Soviet philosophers began to tweak the orthodox view of dialectical materialism as laid out by Stalin. Some, for instance, suggested that societies could contain elements of more than one social formation at the same time, a concept known as *mnogoukladnost'* (having many structures).[42] Others proposed the existence of additional social formations beyond the five identified by Marx, while still others noted that historical progress depended on more than a given society's mode of production; it also varied based on external forces, such as the systems existent in other countries, as well as on what were deemed "economically neutral factors" such as language, geography, and social psychology.[43] Philosophers brought culture into the equation, arguing that culture was dependent on more than just the mode of economic production and that culture itself had a powerful impact on the ways societies developed. This opened up the way for a whole new trend of thought known as "culturology," discussed in more depth in chapter 7. In these ways, Soviet historical determinism became less and less dogmatic as time went along, allowing for more and more variables and painting a much more complex picture of history than that depicted by the likes of Plekhanov and Stalin.

Nevertheless, as long as the Soviet Union existed, the end of history was officially the same—communism. Dialectical materialism officially remained at the heart of Soviet ideology, being a compulsory topic in schools and universities, where until the very end of the Soviet Union students learned about Marx's five social formations. The result was several generations of Russians who were thoroughly indoctrinated in dialectical materialism. Eventually, by the late 1980s, most had begun to reject the communist idea of where the historical process was leading. But the belief that the historical process led in a definite direction and was driven by material factors remained strong in certain circles, especially among economists.

From the 1960s onward, a new generation of Westernizers emerged who felt that the Soviet Union had at some point gotten onto the wrong historical track. This small but influential group of intellectuals associated civilization with Western Europe and argued that the Soviet Union must "return to Europe" by ending the Cold War division of the continent into two. Proponents not of Western capitalism but of "socialism with a human face," they argued that in this way the Soviet Union would once again be able to go forward on the true path of history.

Initially concentrated in academic research institutes such as the Institute of World Economy and International Relations (IMEMO) and on the staff of journals such as the Prague-based *Problemy mira i sotsializma* (*Problems of Peace and Socialism*, published in English as the *World Marxist Review*), some of these intellectuals would come to occupy high-ranking positions in the foreign policy community under the Soviet Union's final leader, Mikhail Gorbachev (1931–2022). Examples include Georgy Arbatov (1923–2010), Georgy Shakhnazarov (1924–2001), and Anatoly Chernyaev (1921–2017). As advisers to Gorbachev, these men played an important role in bringing the Cold War to an end in the late 1980s.[44]

Arbatov, Shakhnazarov, and Chernyaev all worked at one point for *Problemy mira i sotsializma*. So did Georgian philosopher Merab Mamardashvili (1930–90), who later taught at Moscow State University, where his lectures attracted large audiences. Although he was Georgian, he lectured and wrote in Russian and had a major influence on late twentieth-century Russian thought. Mamardashvili argued that Europe was not a geographic entity but an idea embodied in values such as freedom, the rule of law, and self-determination.[45] To become truly European, Russia needed to adopt these values. "At one point this problem had already begun to be solved, but we were derailed and became feral," he said:

> Now if we really want to save or take part in saving civilization on earth, if we want to go back to our European house and have a right to talk about it as its defenders, we ourselves have to first become civilized— more civilized, or simply civilized people; in other words, to jump to

a new track altogether. . . . Speaking directly and succinctly, this state is simply monstrous—but, apparently, it couldn't have been otherwise. The people who jumped out of history and life (I have in mind all peoples within Russia's territory) could not have been avoided being sick as a result.[46]

Mamardashvili's comment about jumping "out of history" displays his view of history as moving in a single direction, toward "civilization," defined in terms of Western values and institutions. Other late Soviet thinkers shared his perspective. Historian Leonid Batkin (1932–2016), for instance, argued in a 1988 article that "we too are the 'West' . . . to the extent that we managed or have not managed to get rid of what Lenin liked to call Russian 'barbarism.' . . . [The West] is the general definition of the economic, scientific-technical and structural-democratic level without which it is impossible for any really modern society . . . to exist."[47] At the start of the twentieth century, Russia had had the chance to become Western, Batkin wrote, but "from the middle of the 1920s, and quite fatally in the 1930s, we completely rejected this vector. . . . We have dropped out of world history. . . . We must in our own way and in accordance with our own historical peculiarities and ideals return to the highroad of modern civilization"[48]

Initially, many of those propounding this point of view still believed that something could be salvaged from communism. But by the late 1980s, the situation had dramatically changed, and they were shoved to one side by a new generation of intellectuals who adopted a far more radical vision of historical progress.

The policy of perestroika (restructuring) pursued by Gorbachev after he became head of the Communist Party in 1985 led to a rapid unraveling of the Soviet Union. National minorities demanded independence, the Communist Party's authority collapsed, and the economy went into free fall. Faith in communism disintegrated, and many intellectuals shifted ground and looked to the one alternative model of which they were aware, that of the West. However, they retained their belief in historical materialism. History, in their eyes, still had a goal, and the economic mode of production was still the driving force. But the goal was now a Western-style state, and the preferred mode of production was capitalism. Economic liberalization, many believed, would automatically bring with it other beneficial changes. However, since liberalization would in the short term cause significant economic harm to a large part of the population, it would require those in authority to use undemocratic methods to push it through. The political and social superstructure (democracy, civil society, and so on) were a product of the economic substructure—capitalism. First, therefore, one had to create capitalism. Everything else would then, in theory, fall into place.

This logic was well expressed in a dialogue between two prominent liberal intellectuals, political scientist Andranik Migranian (b. 1949) and sociologist Igor Kliamkin (b. 1941), published in 1989 under the title "Do We Need an Iron Hand?" Both men viewed history as developing toward a free market and liberal democracy, but according to a given pattern that had to be followed if the process was to be successfully completed. Civil society had always come first, democracy second, Migranian claimed. The Soviet Union had no civil society, however, and therefore a period of transitional authoritarianism was necessary in order to move from Soviet totalitarianism to liberal democracy. "Yes, at present I am for a dictatorship, for a dictator," said Migranian.[49] Kliamkin, meanwhile, argued that markets necessarily preceded democracy. "Absolute regimes created national markets," he claimed.[50] "If we pretend that economic and political reforms advance in parallel, we know nothing (or don't want to know) about the entirety of world history," said Kliamkin.[51] Kliamkin claimed not to be saying that an authoritarian regime was desirable, merely that the laws of history meant that it was inevitable.[52] "Reality has its laws of development that carve their own path independently of my preferences and yours," wrote Kliamkin.[53]

This attitude was reflected in the policies pursued by the Russian government of President Boris Yeltsin (1931–2007) after the final collapse of the Soviet Union in December 1991. Under the direction of deputy prime minister Yegor Gaidar (1956–2009), the government embarked on a policy of rapid economic liberalization known as "shock therapy." The son of Soviet admiral Timur Gaidar (1926–99) and the grandson of famous children's writer Arkady Gaidar (1904–41), Yegor came from a high-ranking communist family and in the 1980s worked as an editor for the Communist Party's ideological journal *Kommunist*. In the eyes of his detractors, he and his colleagues just substituted capitalist orthodoxy for communist orthodoxy, earning them the derogatory label "Market Bolsheviks."[54] The difference was that whereas the Bolsheviks believed that the laws of history pointed toward communism, Gaidar and his colleagues claimed that they pointed toward free market capitalism. As one critic notes, "The Russian liberals were just as convinced bearers of an absolute truth [as the communists], and in the end their liberalism was no less utopian than the vulgarised Marxism of their opponents. . . . What was not changed . . . was the notion of history as a purposeful process. The Soviet *telos* was replaced by a liberal *telos*."[55]

Shock therapy's aim was to turn the communist system into a free market economy in the shortest possible time. When the policy ran into resistance from the Russian Parliament, Yeltsin issued an illegal decree dissolving it, to which Parliament responded by impeaching Yeltsin. The president then called on the army to bomb Parliament into submission, after which he issued a new constitution concentrating power in his own hands. Democracy took second place to economic reform. The logic was clear—economics was the substructure underpinning everything else. Anything standing in the way of economic reform had to be removed.

Gaidar and his colleagues have been called "probably the most radical Westernizers in Russian history."[56] They viewed the West as the exemplar of the universal path of development and firmly believed in the idea that Russia should "return to civilization"—that is, to Europe, or the West more generally. Thus, Gaidar said that the aim was to "enter the commonwealth of civilized nations."[57] "An important result of the changes of recent years is Russia's return to the modern world," wrote Gaidar, adding, "Before World War I the Russian intellectual and business elite was part of a Eurocentric world. The ties were broken in subsequent decades. . . . Over the last few years, we have started our return to the world."[58]

Russia's "return to the world" was seen as dependent on the adoption of free market economics. Liberal economic ideas were viewed as universal laws. "We proceeded from the fundamental laws of economic behavior of *homo sapiens*," said Gaidar, "and it turned out that these laws work in Russia, with our specific character, as well as they work in Argentina, Korea, the Czech Republic, Slovakia or Australia."[59] "There are no special countries. All countries from the point of view of an economist are the same," said Pyotr Aven, minister of foreign economic relations from 1991 to 1992.[60]

The idea that all countries follow the same path of historical development exerted a powerful influence on Russian thinkers for the best part of two centuries. Under Yeltsin in the early 1990s, it dictated state policy. But for reasons that I explore in chapter 7, its victory proved short-lived. By the late 1990s, few Russians accepted it. This put Russian intellectuals in a difficult position, needing to find a new vision of the world. They found it in the form of civilizational theory. In search of inspiration, Russian thinkers of the early twenty-first century turned to the likes of Spengler, Toynbee, and Sorokin. But even more than foreign sources, they also drew on a native Russian tradition of civilizational thought. It is to that tradition that we now turn.

CHAPTER 3

The Origins of Russian Civilizationism

The communist and liberal visions of the end of history have much in common. Both are founded on rationalism and materialism and display a decidedly optimistic belief in human perfectibility. But there is another long-standing trend in Russian thought. Resting on Christian faith and concerned with spiritual rather than material affairs, this imagines history as ending in a fiery apocalypse rather than in the arrival of an earthly utopia. It assigns a special task for Russia as the defender of the one true faith, Orthodoxy, against the forces of the Antichrist. Adherents of this philosophy believe that Russia is destined to play a crucial role in world history. Many of their ideas may seem decidedly strange to the average Western reader. Some of these ideas' proponents were also extremely eccentric. But they were often extremely intelligent and highly original thinkers. Dismissing them out of hand because their viewpoint is so at odds with that of Western postmodernity is perhaps unwise. Besides, their philosophies have inspired large numbers of Russians and today provide much of the language that is used to depict Russia and the West as separate civilizations. For better or worse, their thinking has shaped how modern Russians view the world.

For most of Russia's history, the great majority of the country's population were peasants, and to be Russian was to be Orthodox. According to the historian Leonid Heretz, prerevolutionary Russian peasants viewed history as leading toward the Final Judgment, which they conceptualized as a catastrophic event characterized by "all-consuming fire."[1] Rather than being the product of progress, the apocalypse would arrive after a period of moral decline that paved the way for the arrival of the Antichrist. According to Heretz, "Traditional Russians . . . applied piety/morality as the only relevant criterion for assessing change in the condition of the world, and by that measure they perceived accelerating decline from one generation to the next, from God-fearing ancestors down to the present corrupt race, and anticipated Judgment as the imminent end of the downward movement."[2] Modernization was perceived not as a positive thing but as a symptom of this downward movement, accelerating the breakdown of respect for God and traditional ways of life. To the average prerevolutionary Russian, therefore, what we nowadays like to call progress was nothing of the sort.

This mode of thinking was particularly strong among the Old Believers, a sect that broke away from the Russian Orthodox Church in protest at church reforms carried out in the seventeenth century. The Old Believers identified human reason as the weapon used by the Devil to undermine faith and encourage people to imagine that they themselves could understand the ways of the world. They rejected the import of Western customs, clothing, and foods and regarded Peter the Great's policy of Westernization as evidence of the imminent arrival of the Final Judgment.[3]

According to this viewpoint, the West was the home of Satan, and Russia was the home of the true faith. The world consisted not of one civilization but of two, and history was not a march toward universal perfection but a continuous battle between the forces of good and evil.[4] In this context, Russia was the *katechon*, the shield that held back the forces of the Antichrist and so saved the world from the apocalypse. The modern Russian conservative writer Yegor Kholmogorov (b. 1975) describes the *katechon* as follows: "This is how the Byzantine idea of *katechon* is refracted in our imperial consciousness, the idea of withholding the world. That which stands on the bridge between the Antichrist and the world and which does not let the Antichrist into the world. Now it is not a bridge but rather a manhole, the lid of which is removed from time to time, and some vampires or werewolves or murderers come out of this hole. The Russian tarpaulin [army] boot stamps on that lid and restores silence for some time."[5]

Elements of this worldview have long informed Russian reactions to Western concepts of the end of history. While discarding some of its more extreme apocalyptic and antirationalist elements, Russian intellectuals have built on it to construct a vision of the West as the home of godless rationalism, materialism, and individualism. At the same time, they have constructed a picture of Russia as a country that has succeeded in combining reason and modernity with continued religious faith, spirituality, and collectivism. This has given Russia a holy mission—to rescue the world from the errors of Western civilization.

The first group to articulate these ideas in the language of modern philosophy was a small collection of thinkers known as the "Slavophiles." As the first half of the nineteenth century rolled along, Russian intellectuals found themselves in a state of considerable angst. Their country was a great power, but somehow it was not as great as they felt it ought to be. In September 1812, the Russian army had temporarily abandoned Moscow to Napoleon. On March 31, 1814, it entered Paris, completing an enormous march of 2,900 kilometers in less than two years. Militarily, Russia was the strongest nation in Europe, perhaps in the world. Yet, culturally speaking, Russian intellectuals felt that their country was a desert. The great names of Russian literature, art, music, philosophy, and science had, with a few exceptions, yet to make their mark. Russia had not produced anything that could live up to the products of Western Europe. It had not contributed any big idea that might shape humanity's future. Its mark on the world was insignificant, or at least so many thought. As Moscow intellectual Pyotr Chaadaev (1794–1856) complained in a famous letter, "Recluses in the world, we haven't given anything to it, haven't taken anything from it, haven't introduced a single idea in the mass of ideas of humanity. . . . We haven't done anything for the common good of mankind, not one useful thought has grown on our barren soil, not one great truth has arisen among us."[6]

In the 1840s, the Slavophiles came up with a response to Chaadaev's complaint and formulated a holy mission for Russia that would, they thought, at last allow it to make its mark in the world. In the process, they also elaborated a theory of what made Russia different from the West. In this way, they laid the groundwork for the later development of Russian civilizational theory.

The Slavophiles' influence far outweighed their numbers. At the core of the Slavophile movement were just four men—Aleksei Khomiakov (1804–60), Ivan Kireevsky (1806–56), Konstantin Aksakov (1817–60), and Iury Samarin (1819–76)—although a few others, such as Ivan Aksakov (1823–86) and Aleksandr Koshelev (1806–83) also deserve mention. All were noblemen who owned sufficient property to devote themselves to intellectual pursuits. Brought up with a European education, they were fluent in multiple languages and well versed in Western, especially German, philosophy. By the standards of their times, they were progressive landowners, seeking to improve their estates by the introduction of modern machinery and new agricultural techniques.[7] Khomiakov even invented a steam engine, which he displayed at the

1851 Great Exhibition in London. In this sense, the Slavophiles can even be seen as modernizers. They believed in universal progress and strongly resisted the imputation that they wanted to stop time or even turn it back. They insisted that what they opposed was not progress as such but rather progress defined in a purely Western way. As Konstantin Aksakov put it, "The Slavophiles want to go, not only forward, but forward toward the truth. . . . The Slavophiles maintain only that their [the Westernizers'] path is mistaken, and that it is necessary to approach the truth by another path. . . . A path is endless movement. . . . Thus, there can be no talk of turning back."[8]

The Slavophiles drew heavily on German philosophy, above all that of Herder and the Romantic thinker Friedrich Wilhelm Joseph Schelling (1775–1854). From it, they took the idea that nations were organic beings, each growing gradually according to its own dynamic and each being of equal value. They also took the idea of the desirability of national diversity and the concept that each nation contributed to universal progress by developing what was unique about its own culture.[9] These influences lead some historians to conclude that there was very little that was genuinely Russian about Slavophilism and that it was merely a local variant of German Romanticism.[10] Others disagree and point to influences coming from Russian Orthodoxy. Indeed, the Slavophiles identified firmly as Orthodox and drew upon their understanding of Orthodoxy to develop their philosophy.[11] A fair conclusion might be that their thinking represents an adaptation of traditional Orthodoxy by means of late eighteenth- and early nineteenth-century Western Romanticism.

The Slavophiles did not reject Western thought in its entirety. In fact, while they often criticized the West, they were also keen to point out the great contributions that it had made to human progress. "The West has done much in the field of science. . . . The West hasn't buried in the earth the talents given to it by God!" exclaimed Konstantin Aksakov.[12] "In the West, science, art, industry and many other manifestations of human activity achieved significant development. . . . Let us study Europe and its enlightenment," agreed Koshelev.[13] "I still love the West. I am bound to it by indissoluble sympathies. I belong to it by education, habits of life, tastes, by the questioning make-up of my mind, even by the habits of my heart," said Kireevsky.[14] But this admiration of the West had its limits. According to the Slavophiles, the once-great West had lost its way. As Khomiakov noted, Western nations

> took advantage of divine grace and reached a high level of intellectual development, but blinded by their successes they became on the one hand (as is known) completely indifferent to the highest good—Faith,

and now stagnate in spiritual blindness; and on the other, they became not the benefactors of the rest of humanity (which was their calling), but its enemies, always ready to oppress and enslave other nations . . . throughout the whole world the ships of European nations are considered not the heralds of peace and happiness, but the heralds of war, and of greatest misfortune. . . . Fatal seeds produce fatal fruits, and the hostility of the Western nations . . . toward everyone gives rise to natural and just hatred of them among all nations.[15]

This passage presages similar denunciations of Western colonialism made by later generations of Russian civilizational theorists. But according to the Slavophiles, the West's problems went beyond its imperialism. In general, they felt, the West had fallen into decay; its great achievements were all in the past. As Khomiakov wrote in a poem titled "The Dream,"

How sad, how sad! Thick darkness falls
In the Far West, the Land of Holy Wonders:
. . . And how beautiful was that Majestic West!
How long has the whole world been kneeling before it,
And been wonderfully illuminated by its high glory.
The world was silent before it, humble and silent.
There the sun of wisdom met our eyes.
. . . But alas! The era has passed,
and the West is covered with the veil of death.
. . . Wake up, slumbering East![16]

Had the Slavophiles been alive when Francis Fukuyama published his "The End of History?" they would probably have agreed with him about one thing—namely, that Western philosophy had reached its end with Hegel.[17] But whereas for Fukuyama, Hegel was the end of philosophy, period, for the Slavophiles he was simply the end of *Western* philosophy. After Hegel the West had nothing new to add, they felt. But that did not mean that other, younger, cultures also had nothing to add. In fact, they did. And as they did so, human society would continue to progress. In the process, it would build on what the West had laid down, but the West would no longer be in the driver's seat.

The West having run to the end of its natural course, it fell to Russia to pick up the torch and make its mark on the world. The West's contributions to universal history had come in the realms of reason and science; Russia's contribution would come in the spiritual realm. This attitude reflected the Slavophiles' belief that the West's fundamental weakness was spiritual—namely, its allegedly overrationalistic, "one-sided" nature. This was a weakness that Russia, despite its material backwardness, had supposedly avoided.

Kireevsky dated the one-sidedness of Western thought back to early Catholicism, which, he said, made the mistake of allying itself with pagan reason. Over time, rationalism had come to dominate Western philosophy, driving out other ways of thinking, such as tradition and religious faith. He thought that the Orthodox Church had avoided this alliance and so preserved a "wholeness of spirit" that enabled Russians to maintain a spiritual outlook in an era when the West was replacing faith with aimless individualistic materialism. "In the West, theology became a matter of rationalistic abstraction, whereas in the Orthodox world it retained its inner wholeness of spirit," wrote Kireevsky, adding that "European culture has attained such a fullness of development that its special significance has become obvious to any thoughtful observer. . . . Yet the result of this comprehensive development and clarity of conclusions has been an almost universal feeling of dissatisfaction and frustrated hopes . . . because, despite all the brilliance and the convenience of life's exterior improvements, life itself has been drained of its essential meaning."[18]

The Slavophiles argued that as well as wholeness of spirit, Russia had preserved another key attribute that was lacking in the West—*sobornost'*. First coined by Khomiakov, the word *sobornost'* is one of the Slavophiles' most lasting legacies, being regularly used to this day to express the idea that Russia is bound together by a uniquely collectivist spirit. *Sobornost'*, wrote Khomiakov, was the opposite of the principles of individualism and rationalism that he said lay at the heart of Western Christianity.[19] The word has no exact equivalent in English but roughly speaking signifies a collectivity bound together by common traditions and beliefs, in which people reach decisions by consensus and then freely agree to abide by those decisions. Khomiakov claimed that due to its individualism, the West lacked *sobornost'*. In Russia, it was embodied in the peasant commune, the basic social structure of most Russians' lives. Likewise, Konstantin Aksakov argued that the commune was a "moral choir," in which the individual voice was not stifled but was "heard in harmony with the other voices."[20] "The principle of the commune, manifesting itself on earth as separate communes among the people, is still imperfect, even when enclosing all the people into one commune. The highest, true form of the commune is the church—the commune that encompasses all of humanity," he wrote.[21]

For the Slavophiles, Russia's holy mission consisted of resisting Westernization and preserving and developing wholeness of spirit and *sobornost'*. Russia could then bring the benefits that resulted from these to the rest of the world, in particular to the West, thereby saving the latter from itself. "History is calling Russia to take its place in the forefront of universal enlightenment," said Khomiakov.[22] He proclaimed, "In the course of centuries of intellectual development, the West did great and glorious things. But . . . the edifice of your faith is crumbling and sinking. We do not bring you new materials to reinforce this edifice. No! We do no more than return to you the cornerstone rejected by your ancestors, the mutual love of Christians and the divine graces attached to it. Put back the cornerstone of this building and . . . this building will rise in all the grandeur of its sublime proportions to be the salvation, happiness, and glory of all future generations."[23] The holy mission was thus a universal one, envisaging a future that Russia and the West would share.

These ideas had a powerful influence on the next generation of Russian thinkers. An example was writer Fyodor Dostoevsky, who combined criticisms of the West with calls for Russian-Western reconciliation.[24] In his *Winter Notes on Summer Impressions*, Dostoevsky commented that "everything, literally everything we can show which may be called progress, science, art, citizenship, humanity, everything, everything stems from there, from that land of holy miracles. The whole of our life, from earliest childhood, is shaped by the European mould."[25] But he also complained that "we [the Russian elite] are so wonderful ourselves, so civilized, so European that the common people feel sick at the very sight of us. We have now reached the point when the common people regard us as complete foreigners, and do not understand a single word of ours."[26]

According to Dostoevsky, there was a way out of this unfortunate situation. In his *Writer's Diary*, Dostoevsky described numerous stories of violent crime committed by ordinary Russians. At the same time, though, he said that the ordinary people retained something that the Westernized elite had lost—namely, "a warm-hearted knowledge of Christ and a true understanding of him. . . . The people know Christ, their God . . . because for many centuries they have endured many sufferings. . . . Believe me, in this sense, even the darkest layers of our people are far more educated than you, in your cultured ignorance of them, suppose."[27] To reconcile Russia's social classes, the elite would raise the masses out of their barbarity by providing them with the benefits of Western education and culture. In return, the masses would restore true religious faith.

Dostoevsky believed that the same logic applied to the international scene. Like the Slavophiles, he saw Russia as playing a vital role in bringing true Christian faith to the overly rationalistic West and so putting universal progress back on the correct track. Russia could do this, he felt, because of what he saw as its uniquely universalistic character. Whereas the West limited itself to its own ideas, Russia absorbed ideas from everywhere, reconciling them into a single whole. In an 1880 speech in honor of poet Alexander Pushkin, Dostoevsky declared that "of all peoples, perhaps the Russian heart is the most inclined toward the universal and towards the brotherly union of all humanity."[28] To carry out its holy mission, however, Russia needed to preserve its unique character. Dostoevsky wrote in a letter to the heir to the throne Grand Duke Aleksandr Aleksandrovich (later Alexander III), "Embarrassed and afraid that we have fallen so far behind Europe in our intellectual and scientific development, we have forgotten that we ourselves, in the depth and tasks of the Russian soul, contain in ourselves the capacity perhaps to bring new light to the world, on the condition that our development is independent. . . . All great nations displayed their great powers only to the extent . . . [that] they have remained themselves, proud and steady, arrogantly independent."[29]

Another late nineteenth-century advocate of the idea that Russia's distinctive nature gave it an exceptional role in world history was Vladimir Solovyov (1853–1900), to this day regarded by many as Russia's finest philosopher. Solovyov was somewhat eccentric, claiming to have seen a vision of the Divine Sophia (Wisdom) while working in the British Library in London. Sophia told him to go to Egypt, so he traveled to Cairo. There, he was mugged and left for dead by Egyptian brigands, whereupon he again saw Sophia, who, he wrote, "gazed at me, like the first rays of the universal day of creation."[30]

Solovyov believed in what he called *"vseedinstvo,"* which one might translate as "all-unity." To Solovyov, all things were related—faith, reason, art, science, and so on.[31] Likewise, all humanity was one, as were humanity and God. Just as Kireevsky had argued that Russia retained a wholeness of spirit that the one-sided, overly rationalistic West had lost, so too Solovyov believed that it was in Russia that the spirit of *vseedinstvo* could be found. He contrasted the Russian belief system with that of the East, which he said involved an "inhuman God," justifying human servitude, and also with that of modern Europe, which he described as being based on the idea of "the godless human principle," justifying "universal egoism and anarchy." Instead of the "inhuman God" and the "godless human," Russian faith united God and human in the principle of *"bogochelovechstvo"* (sometimes referred to as "God-manhood" or "the humanity of God").[32] The humanity of God, revealed in Jesus Christ, was, to Solovyov, the essence of Christianity, with Christ acting as a promise to humankind of the eventual "unity of God with creation."[33] "The historical process," he wrote, "is a long and difficult *transition* from the bestial man to the divine man. . . . The purpose of the world-process is the revelation of the Kingdom of God or the perfect moral order realised by a new humanity *which spiritually grows out of the God-man.*"[34]

In Solovyov's eyes, this was a universal process, as the good, he said, had a "universal character."[35] The objective of the historical process was "the cause of *universal salvation*."[36] "The modern world gravitates toward the idea of Spiritual Humanity, that is, toward the *imaging of Christ* in everyone," Solovyov wrote.[37] To this end, Solovyov believed that it was necessary to end division in the Christian world.[38] He therefore sought the reconciliation of Russia and the West, envisioning it as taking place under the spiritual guidance of the pope and the temporal leadership of the Russian tsar.

Solovyov was fond of threes, penning works with titles such as "Three Encounters" and "Three Forces." His final work was a book titled *War, Progress, and the End of History: Three Conversations, Including a Short Story of the Anti-Christ*. The book consists of imaginary debates taking place among a group of five Russians—the General, the Politician, the Lady, the Prince, and Mr. Z—at a resort somewhere in the Alps. In each of the three conversations, a different point of view dominates. In the first, it is that of the General, whom Solovyov describes in his preface as personifying "a religious conception of the everyday life, which is characteristic of past times."[39] The General argues that it is absurd to imagine that one can use words alone to deter evildoers. War was sanctioned by the church, he said, and at the end of battle his conscience was clear: "My soul was still in glory from the ecstasy of our fight. . . . I was feeling God, and there was the end of it."[40]

Against this, in the second conversation, the Politician represents, as Solovyov wrote, "the ideas of culture and progress prevailing in our time."[41] The Politician argues that war is becoming useless and will disappear as European civilization expands outward, a point of view closely reflecting Kant's concept of perpetual peace. "Now has arrived the time for peace and the peaceful expansion of European culture over all the world. All must become Europeans. The idea expressed by 'European' must become as all embracing as that expressed by 'person' and the idea of the European civilized world identical with that of humanity. In this lies the meaning of history," says the Politician.[42]

Finally, the third chapter belongs to Mr. Z, whom Solovyov says personifies a "third standpoint which is absolutely religious and which will yet show its decisive value in the future." "Personally," wrote Solovyov, "I unreservedly accept the last point of view."[43] Mr. Z objects to the Politician's concept of progress. What is its point, he asks, noting that progress has to have some objective. Beyond that, he casts doubt on whether it is truly progress at all, for in the Politician's concept of the end of history, everybody ends up just as dead as in any other social setup. Death, says Mr. Z, is the "extreme evil.... Were we compelled to recognize the victory of this extreme physical evil as final and absolute, then no imaginary victories of good in the individual and social spheres could be considered real successes."[44] The Politician's idea of progress thus counts for nothing. "The Kingdom of God is the kingdom of life triumphing through resurrection," claims Mr. Z: "The real victory over evil [is] in the real resurrection. Only this, I repeat, opens the real Kingdom of God whereas, without it, you have only the kingdom of death and sin and their creator, the Devil."[45] The end of history, in other words, is resurrection.

Having laid out his views on the end of history, Mr. Z completes the book by recounting an apocalyptic story about the Antichrist. This starts with an Asian army sweeping through Russia and conquering the whole of Europe. After fifty years, the Europeans overthrow their occupiers and form a United States of Europe. At this point a man of "exceptional genius, beauty, and nobility of character" appears, a man whose only fault is that "he believed in God, but in the depths of his soul involuntarily and unconsciously preferred himself."[46] The peoples of Europe appoint this genius emperor, after which he sets about enacting a series of reforms that bring peace and stability and successfully eradicate the continent's social and economic problems.

Next, the "Emperor Superman" decides to reunite the divided Christian churches and summons an ecclesiastical congress. When the congress meets, an Orthodox elder, John, challenges him: "Confess now and before us the name of Jesus Christ, the Son of God." The emperor refuses. "Little Children—it is the Antichrist!" shouts John, whereupon the pope declares to the emperor, "I cast you out forever foul dog, from the city of God, and deliver you up to your father Satan! Anathema! Anathema! Anathema!"[47]

Shortly thereafter, a rebellion breaks out against the emperor. The rebel and imperial armies meet, only for an earthquake to interrupt their battle. Solovyov wrote, "An enormous volcano, with a giant crater, rose up by the Dead Sea, around which the imperial army was encamped. Streams of fire flowed together into a flaming lake that swallowed up the Emperor himself, together with his numberless forces. . . . The heavens were rent by vivid lightning . . . and they saw Christ coming toward them in royal apparel. . . . For a thousand years, they lived and reigned with Christ."[48]

Exactly what Solovyov meant by this story has divided scholars ever since. But part of the message seems to be that evil comes in the guise of good. In the absence of faith in Christ, progress in the form of peace and prosperity is a chimera.

Solovyov's idea that resurrection is the ultimate aim of history bears the hallmark of the Moscow librarian Nikolai Fyodorov (1829–1903), often credited as the founder of the philosophy of cosmism. Fyodorov outlined his views in a book titled *The Philosophy of the Common Task,* which remained unpublished during his lifetime but which circulated in draft form in philosophical circles. Among those who read it was Dostoevsky, who so liked it that he showed it to Solovyov, who then wrote to Fyodorov, declaring, "I read your manuscript avidly and with a delight of spirit. . . . I can only recognize you as my teacher and spiritual father. Your goal is not to proselytize, however, or to found a sect, but to save all mankind by a common task, and for the sake of that it is necessary, first of all, that your project be made known and recognized by all."[49]

The illegitimate son of a Russian prince, Fyodorov was even more eccentric than Solovyov. After a spell as a teacher, he worked as a librarian at the Rumiantsev Library in Moscow (later the Lenin Library and now the Russian State Library). He lived in deliberate poverty, giving away all his money to the poor, wearing ragtag clothes, surviving largely on a diet of bread and tea, often going months without a hot meal, and sleeping on a humpback wooden trunk with a book as a pillow. Occasionally, admirers would buy him furniture and pay his landlord to feed him proper meals, only to find that Fyodorov immediately sold the furniture and instructed the landlord to revert to meals of tea and bread.[50] "He leads the purest Christian life," wrote one of his admirers, the great Russian writer Lev Tolstoy (1828–1910): "He is sixty, a pauper, gives away all he has, is always cheerful and meek."[51]

Like Tolstoy and Solovyov, Fyodorov had a very negative attitude toward sex, although unlike Tolstoy he seems to have followed his own preaching and remained abstemious. The problem with procreation, he argued, was that it encouraged people to look to the future. Instead of future generations, they should, he said, be looking toward those of the past. Instead of creating new people, humanity should be focusing on recreating people who were dead.[52] "The will to procreate," argued Fyodorov, "engenders wealth and leads the human race to demoralisation . . . whereas the will to resuscitate, when the problem of returning life is seen as the purpose of conscious beings, moralises all the worlds of the Universe."[53]

Fyodorov denounced the positivists' conception of progress, writing that "progress is a sense of superiority, (1) of an entire generation of the living over their ancestors, and (2) of the younger over the old. . . . It is the replacement of love by presumptuousness, contempt and the moral, or rather immoral, displacement of fathers by sons. . . . Progress is precisely the form of life in which the human race may come to taste the greatest sum of suffering while striving for the greatest sum of enjoyment. . . . Progress is truly hell."[54]

In contrast to the positivist view of progress, Fyodorov argued that true progress "demands that improvement should arise not through struggle and mutual annihilation but by the return of the victims of this struggle [in other words, the dead]. . . . Progress itself demands resuscitation. . . . The ideal of progress, according to the learned, is to enable everybody to participate in the production and consumption of objects for sensual pleasure, whereas the aim of true progress can and must be the participation in a common task, the work of studying the blind force that brings hunger, disease and death in order to transform it into a life-giving force."[55] True progress, in other words, is the resurrection of the dead.

Fyodorov looked to technology to solve humanity's social and economic problems so as to unite the world behind the common task of raising the dead. "Our task is to make nature, the forces of nature, into an instrument of universal resuscitation and to become a union of immortal beings," he wrote.[56] Resurrection, he felt, was not something that could be left to God. It was up to humans to achieve it: "Humanity must not be idle passengers."[57] Resurrection was humanity's "common task."

Fyodorov envisioned Russia as playing a leading role in this. "To carry out the natural task two unifications are necessary," he wrote, "an external one, which can be achieved by [the Russian] Autocracy, and an inner one to be achieved in Orthodoxy; it would be the union of all rational beings in the task of comprehending and controlling the irrational force which procreates and murders."[58] Under the "external regulation" of the Russian autocracy, "the inner psychophysiological force will tilt the balance away from sexual drive and lust towards love for the parents, and will even replace them, thus transforming the force of procreation into one of re-creation," wrote Fyodorov.[59]

But that was not all. "The destiny of the Earth convinces us that human activity cannot be bounded by the limits of the planet," he added.[60] Outer space would provide the "future dwelling places" for the resurrected.[61] "The ability to live all over the Universe, enabling the human race to colonise all the worlds, will give us the power to unite all the worlds of the Universe into an artistic whole," claimed Fyodorov.[62] Beyond that, once they mastered the science of resurrection, humans would "be able to live in any environment, take on any form and visit all generations in all the worlds, from the most ancient to the most recent, the most remote as well as the nearest."[63] In short, humans might finally cast off their mortal bodies and acquire an entirely different form.

Fyodorov's talk of overcoming death, of transforming humans, of conquering outer space, and of the almost limitless capacity of technology inspired the subsequent generation of cosmists. Among them was science fiction writer and rocket scientist Konstantin Tsiolkovsky (1857–1935), who met Fyodorov while studying at the Rumiantsev Library. The two often talked, and Fyodorov once bought Tsiolkovsky an overcoat after noticing that the student's was unsuitable for the cold weather.[64] Later, Tsiolkovsky would become the first person to solve many of the practical problems associated with building manned spacecraft.[65] His statue now stands outside the Cosmonautics Museum in Moscow, in recognition of his status as the father of space travel. In a roundabout way, via Tsiolkovsky, the Soviet space program thus had its origins in Fyodorov.

One of the most famous Soviet cosmists was the scientist Vladimir Vernadsky (1863–1945), who developed the theory of the "biosphere." Vernadsky described the biosphere as an envelope of life, charged by cosmic radiation, that covered the earth (the "geosphere") and then transformed it into something entirely different. In due course, according to Vernadsky, the human mind would develop so much as to create an envelope of consciousness—the "noosphere"—around the biosphere. Just as the biosphere transformed the geosphere, the noosphere would transform the biosphere. To ensure that this did not have catastrophic consequences, humanity would have to develop a new holistic way of thinking that, in line with Solovyov's concept of *vseedinstvo*, recognized the all-unity of humanity and the cosmos. The American academic George Young notes that "Vernadsky's spiritual and scientific vision was of a wholly interconnected cosmos. Man in Vernadsky is both a result of and an active participant in the ongoing evolution of the cosmos, in which nonmaterial as well as material realities operate. Like other cosmist thinkers, Vernadsky assumed that knowledge was whole, that scientific, spiritual moral, theoretical and practical approaches would not lead toward different directions and goals, but would in the end unite in ultimate truth."[66]

Another cosmist was fellow Soviet scientist Aleksandr Chizhevsky (1897–1964), whose theory of the cosmic origins of important historical events contradicted Soviet dialectical materialism's emphasis on the forces of production and led to "accusations of mysticism, occultism, and irrationality," and eventually to his arrest in the Great Terror of 1937 on charges of being "an enemy under the mask of a scientist."[67] Chizhevsky argued for the existence of "world-historical cycles," each of which reflected a different type of behavior by the masses. These were the periods of minimal, increasing, maximum, and decreasing excitability. Each was correlated with sunspot activity—minimal sunspot activity with minimal excitability, increasing sunspot activity with increasing excitability, and so on. The correlation was not exact, Chizhevsky, claimed; nor were sunspots the only variable. Nevertheless, there was a correlation, which Chizhevsky believed to be causal. He concluded,

> In an epoch of maximum sunspots, the most intense economic, political, and military forces drive the mass behavior of humanity across the Earth, exploding into revolutions, uprisings, wars, struggles, and migrations, creating new formations in the development of particular states and new historical era in the development of humanity. . . . In the epoch of minimum sunspots, the intensity of the military and political activity of all humanity gives way to creative activity and an all-around decline in political and military enthusiasm, peace and calm creative work in the sphere of organizing the foundations of government, international relations, science, and art. . . . The intermediary stages between the epochs of the cycle's maximum and minimum are characterized by respective intermediate sociopsychological characteristics.[68]

As we shall see in chapter 5, Chizhevsky's idea of solar activity as a driver of historical change was later taken up by Soviet ethnologist Lev Gumilyov, who combined it with Toynbee's concept of creative minorities to produce his own theory of how civilizations came into being.

Tsiolkovsky had some even stranger ideas than Chizhevsky. He declared, "I am a pure materialist. I acknowledge nothing but matter. I see only mechanics at work in physics, chemistry, and biology. The entire cosmos is merely an endless, complex machine."[69] Yet he qualified this by adding, "I am not only a materialist but also a panpsychist who acknowledges the sensitivity of the entire universe. . . . Everything is alive."[70] Every atom in the universe, he wrote, at some time exists inside the brain of a living thing, at which point "it lives their life and feels the joy of being conscious and serene."[71] After a long time, maybe billions of years, the atom then enters the brain of another being, but from the atom's subjective point of view, this happens instantaneously, and so "what exists is a single, supreme, conscious, happy life that never ceases."[72] But this happiness is only really possible in higher life forms: "The existence in the universe of imperfect animals such as our monkeys, cows, wolves, deer, hares, rats, and the like is of no benefit to the atom. Likewise, the existence of imperfect people and similar beings elsewhere in the universe is of no benefit."[73] The process of history thus involves the elimination of lower life forms and their replacement by "superior life." "Such, perhaps, is Earth's martyr-like honorable role," concluded Tsiolkovsky.[74] He explained what he had in mind: "Billions of billions of beings will grow and evolve around the Sun near the asteroids. A variety of breeds of perfected beings will be produced: breeds suited for living in different atmospheres, at different gravities, on different planets; breeds suited for living amid the vacuum or rarefied gas, for living with food or without it; breeds living only on solar radiation, capable of withstanding heat, cold, and abrupt, substantial temperature changes. The dominant breed, however, will be the most perfect type of organism, dwelling in the ether and nourished directly by solar energy like a plant."[75] Tsiolkovsky's vision of the end of history finds a reflection in the beliefs of modern Russian cosmists, many of whom promote transhumanism, the idea that humans can eventually transcend their current physical forms (by, for instance, downloading their consciousnesses into machines). Meanwhile, cosmism has also had a strong impact on Russian environmentalism and is sometimes connected to a form of anti-Westernism that maintains that the West is too individualistic to be able to recognize the all-unity of humanity and the earth and is therefore destroying the latter in pursuit of short-term material benefit. According to this logic, it falls upon the more collectivist-minded Russia to take up leadership in the common task of preserving the earth for the benefit of all.

The ideas expressed in this chapter have had a powerful effect on how Russians view themselves and what they consider to constitute their country's distinctive character. To a large degree, this character is described in spiritual terms. What makes Russia different from the West is that it has preserved a spiritual and collectivist nature, a wholeness of being, a *vseedinstvo*, that the increasingly irreligious West either always lacked or abandoned at some point in favor of narrow rationalism, materialism, and individualism.

Yet despite stressing Russia's difference, the thinkers analyzed in this chapter did not separate Russia entirely from the West. They viewed Russia as having an exceptional role in the advance of universal history, a viewpoint that is often described as messianic. But a corollary of this was that they also believed in universal history. The end of history that they imagined was not one based on the contemporary West, but it would be one that the West and Russia shared. They contributed to the eventual development of civilizational theory by establishing what it was that made Russia different, but they fell short of being civilizational theorists according to the definition provided earlier in this book. For civilizational theory to arrive, somebody had to make the decisive intellectual leap of denying universal history and the existence of any common future or common task. That person would be Nikolai Danilevsky.

Chapter 4

The Emergence of Russian Civilizationism

Russian civilizational theory came into being with two books that were published within seven years of each other during the reign of Emperor Alexander II: Nikolai Danilevsky's 1869 *Russia and Europe* and Konstantin Leontyev's 1876 *Byzantinism and Slavdom*. Danilevsky proposed that human history advances not in one direction but in many. Leontyev celebrated diversity in all its forms and created a three-stage model of civilizational development that included the notion "flowering complexity." Together, the two men laid the foundations on which all subsequent Russian civilizational thinking has built. This chapter looks at each in turn.

Largely ignored for the first 120 years after its publication, until recently *Russia and Europe* was not taken very seriously even by most of those who did read it. Danilevsky's one English-language biographer, Robert MacMaster, wrote in the mid-1960s that *Russia and Europe* "was a distinctly amateurish work, full of loose ends, weak in unity and coherence. . . . His eccentric, ambiguous, and delusionary book should not be thought of as 'important.'"[1] Much has changed in the past sixty years. Since the collapse of communism, *Russia and Europe* has enjoyed an enormous surge in popularity in Russia. As noted in the introduction, Russian international relations scholars consider Danilevsky the most influential of all Russian writers in their discipline. This reputation rests largely on *Russia and Europe*. Perhaps in another sixty years, the book will again be cast into the dustbin of history. But at this specific moment in time, contrary to MacMaster's conclusion, its influence is such that one may consider it the most important work ever published in Russian international relations theory.

Danilevsky's contribution to intellectual history was well summarized by one of his friends, journalist Nikolai Strakhov (1828–96), who wrote, "Danilevsky's main idea is incredibly original and incredibly interesting. He provided a new formula for the construction of history, a much broader formula than earlier ones. . . . Namely he rejected the single thread in the development of humanity, the idea that history is the progress of reason, or civilization, in general. There is no such civilization, says Danilevsky, but only individual civilizations, and the development of separate cultural-historical types."[2] By laying out this idea, Danilevsky can be seen as the originator of civilizational theory, predating Spengler by some fifty years.

Danilevsky was not an obvious candidate to produce what has become one of the canonical works of Russian philosophy. A biologist by training, in his youth he had dabbled in French socialist theory and joined what one might call a socialist book club and discussion group that met at the home of an interpreter in the Russian Ministry of Foreign Affairs, Mikhail Petrashevsky (1821–66). Known as the "Petrashevsky Circle," the group's members were for the most part followers of French socialist thinker Charles Fourier (1772–1837), though they differed somewhat in their attitudes. A few argued for immediate revolution, while others avoided taking a stance on the advisability of political action or felt that a long period of education and propaganda would be necessary before the Russian people would be in a position to overthrow the imperial regime.[3] In April 1849, after a meeting of the circle read aloud a letter from literary critic Vissarion Belinsky (1811–48) denouncing the Orthodox Church, the secret police decided that enough was enough. The circle's members were arrested, and twenty-one of them were sentenced to death by firing squad. Among them was one of the circle's regular attendees, novelist Fyodor Dostoevsky.

On December 22, 1849, Dostoevsky and the other condemned men were taken from their cells to the place where they were to be shot, in groups of three. The first three men, including Petrashevsky, were tied to stakes, and the order for their execution was read out. Then, at the very last second, a messenger arrived and announced that the emperor had commuted the sentences to long terms of imprisonment in Siberia. It would appear that Nicholas I had never intended for the men to be executed and that he staged the event in order to terrify them and to teach them a lesson that they would never forget. In Dostoevsky's case, the ploy seems to have worked, as the writer went on to become a loyal supporter of the Russian absolute monarchy. He would describe his prison experiences in his autobiographical novel, *The House of the Dead*.

Other members of the Petrashevsky Circle managed to avoid the horror of a mock execution. Among them was Danilevsky, who had at one point delivered lectures to the circle about Fourier. When he was arrested, he was able to convince his interrogators that his interest in Fourier was purely scientific, and that in any case Fourier's writings (which were not banned in Russia) were not revolutionary and that their implementation would actually reduce the chance of political discontent by alleviating poverty.[4] After one hundred days' imprisonment in the Peter and Paul Fortress in St. Petersburg, he was cleared of all charges. The authorities did not entirely trust him, however, and Nicholas I ordered that he be expelled from St. Petersburg and sent to work for the governor of Vologda province, some 450 kilometers northeast of Moscow.[5]

Subsequently, Danilevsky had a long career working as a government scientist, undertaking numerous expeditions across Russia to explore the country's fisheries. In the 1850s, he worked alongside the famous naturalist Karl Ernst von Baer (1792–1876), one of the leading figures in the history of embryology. Von Baer criticized Charles Darwin's theory of natural selection on the grounds that "I can find no probability that supports the idea that all animals have developed by transformation one from the other. . . . We have no experience of a very distinct type arising through reproduction and we are not able to picture on the basis of actual observation how, for example, a man may have arisen from an orang-utan."[6] Von Baer believed that there must be some purpose and direction in evolution, and he complained that Darwinism replaced purpose with chance.[7] He never, however, produced an adequate alternative explanation for evolution, in part perhaps because he also rejected the idea of creative intervention by an outside force such as God.[8]

Danilevsky was equally critical of Darwin. His objection was not so much to the concept of evolution as to Darwin's explanation of the mechanism by which it took place and the end toward which it was moving. Whereas to Darwin, there was no end, to Danilevsky evolution served a divine purpose. In 1885, he published a 1,200-page book titled *Darwinism: Critical Research* that summarized anti-Darwinian arguments made by other scholars. Danilevsky planned a second volume in which he intended to lay out his own views of the matter, but he was unable to finish it before he died on November 7, 1885.

Danilevsky's belief that the evolution of species moves in a specific direction stands in apparent contradiction to his ideas on the evolution of human civilizations and has therefore been described as "quite inconsistent" with the thesis laid out in his book *Russia and Europe*.[9] One explanation may be that his views changed over time. Another may be that he regarded natural laws and social laws as being very different. History, in Danilevsky's eyes, was a story of the revelation of the scientific laws of nature. At the same time, he rejected political historical determinism, claiming that laws of historical necessity applied only to scientific discoveries and not to anything else, especially politics. As he wrote, "Some historical events, namely those which can be called the practical realizations of the scientific activity of the development of thought, represent a completely logical sequence in their development. All external, political events are by their very nature accidental."[10] Danilevsky invited people to imagine the course of history as the average of two lines: on the one hand, the "line of scientific movement," which moved in a straight direction; and on the other hand, the "accidental-political" line, which moved around in completely random directions.[11] There was, in Danilevsky's eyes, no relation between scientific progress and political change.

Although he devoted most of his life to science, Danilevsky never lost his interest in political theory, and like Dostoevsky he moved in a conservative direction after his youthful dalliance with socialism. Nowadays he is best known not for his biological research but for *Russia and Europe*, which contains numerous biological comparisons. Danilevsky describes human societies as organic beings that are born, live, and die. As each eventually perishes, none can claim to be the end of human history.

Danilevsky began *Russia and Europe* by discussing Prussia's invasion of Denmark in 1864. He noted that this act of aggression went largely uncriticized in Europe. He then contrasted this lack of criticism with the virulent reaction when the Russian army marched into the Ottoman-controlled provinces of Moldavia and Wallachia in 1854. Britain and France demanded that Russia withdraw. After it did, they decided to go to war with Russia anyway and sent their armies to invade Crimea. The result was the Crimean War of 1854–56. Russia found itself entirely without friends during the Crimean War. Although Nicholas I had sent Russian troops to Hungary in 1849 to save Austro-Hungarian emperor Franz Joseph from revolution, even Franz Joseph refused to help Russia. Throughout Europe, Russia was viewed as a pariah.

To Danilevsky, the contrast in Europe's reactions to these two events revealed a striking double standard. German aggression was ignored. But Russia's actions led to wholesale condemnation and war. The accusation of double standards is one that can also be heard today, with Russians contrasting the more or less indifferent, or even supportive, reaction of Western states to the Anglo-American invasion of Iraq in 2003 with the outraged reaction to the Russian invasion of Ukraine in 2022. Danilevsky asked what caused this double standard. The answer, he said, was that "Europe does not recognize us as what we are. It sees something alien in Russia and in the Slavs in general, but at the same time something that cannot serve merely as material to extract for its own benefit, as it extracts it from China, India, Africa, the greater part of America, etc., . . . Europe therefore sees in Russia and Slavdom not just an alien but also a hostile principle. . . . In short, the most satisfactory explanation for this political injustice . . . consists in the fact that Europe sees Russia and Slavdom as something alien to it, and not only alien but hostile."[12]

Europe, said Danilevsky, had no geographic significance, as Europe was just a peninsula of greater Asia. The term "Europe" had meaning only in terms of culture. Russia, however, was not part of Europe in this cultural sense. "It has not fed on even one of the roots from which Europe drew nourishment," such as Catholicism and the feudal system, claimed Danilevsky.[13] Rather, Russia, along with its Slav cousins, formed a distinct cultural-historical type.

Danilevsky noted that many people believed that "that there is no salvation outside of the progressive, European, universal civilization—that there can be no civilization outside of it, because there is no progress outside of it."[14] He thoroughly rejected this point of view. Other civilizations, like China, also had great achievements to their names, and while Chinese civilization was in decline, that was the fate of all civilizations and in due course would prove to be the fate of Europe too. "All living things," wrote Danilevsky, "are given a specific amount of life, at the end of which they must die. . . . History says the same thing about nations: they are born, reach various degrees of development, grow old and decrepit, and die."[15]

History, according to Danilevsky, had witnessed ten different types of cultural-historical development, of which the West (which Danilevsky referred to as "Romano-German" civilization) was merely the latest. He argued that "the principles of civilization of one cultural-historical type cannot be transmitted to peoples of another type." To this he added, "The development of cultural-historical types may be likened very closely to those perennial single-fruited plants whose growth period is indefinitely long, but whose period of flowering and fruiting is relatively short."[16] In line with this, "Progress . . . does not consist of everything going in the same direction (in that case it would soon stop) but of covering the entire field that constitutes humanity's historical activity, in all directions. Therefore, no single civilization can take pride in being the highest point of development."[17] Whatever the reasons that "made people mix up the European-national with the universal," doing so was a mistake.[18] Danilevsky wrote,

> Not only is there no universal humanity, but to want one is to be content with the commonplace, with colorlessness, and with a lack of originality. . . . The relationship of the national to the universal . . . can be likened to streets that intersect each other and by their intersections form a square, of which each street is only a part and which belongs equally to them all. . . . In order to promote the development of a city, that in our model represents all of humanity, there is nothing to do but build one's own street according to one's own plan, and not crowd into the common square and not continue building someone else's street . . . and thereby deprive the city of its proper diversity. . . . A universal civilization does not and cannot exist. . . . All historical analogies tell us that the Slavs . . . can and must form their own original civilization.[19]

This last point, according to Danilevsky, gave Russia an important political task. The West was at its apogee; "its brilliance reaches all ends of the earth, illuminates and warms everything with the light and heat emanating from it." But, he added, "No culture can be eternal," and the West had reached its peak and was headed for decline and eventual death.[20] Thus, he concluded, "the development of an original Slavic culture is not only necessary, but also in fact timely."[21]

Danilevsky argued that "Russia cannot be considered an integral part of Europe either by origin or by adoption, and so it has only two possibilities: either form a special, independent cultural unit together with other Slavs or lose all cultural and historical significance."[22] Danilevsky argued for the former, writing that "the Slavs must indeed form a federation . . . [that] should embrace all countries and peoples—from the Adriatic Sea to the Pacific Ocean . . . under the leadership and hegemony of an integral and unified Russian state."[23] This would inevitably cause conflict with Western Europe, but Russia should not flinch from this: "If storms and thunderstorms are necessary in the physical order of nature, then direct clashes of peoples are no less necessary."[24] "It is both possible and necessary for Slavdom to fight against Europe, a struggle that will be resolved, of course, not in one year, not in one campaign, but over an entire historical period," Danilevsky wrote.[25] Its outcome would determine whether Russia was "destined to form one of the self-contained cultural types of world history, or destined for the secondary importance of a vassal tribe."[26] Russia's victory was in fact necessary not only for Russia's sake but also for the wider good of humanity, as such a victory would protect the world from assimilation into Western civilization and thereby ensure the continuance of a diversity of cultural types. As Danilevsky concluded,

An All-Slavic Union would result not in world domination, but in an equal and just division of power and influence among those peoples or groups of peoples who in the present period of world history can be considered its leaders. . . . A worldwide monarchy, a worldwide republic, the worldwide domination of one system of states or of one cultural and historical type are all equally harmful and dangerous for the progressive course of history, in the only just sense of the word, because the danger lies not in the political domination of one state, but in the cultural domination of one cultural and historical type, whatever its internal political structure may be. The real, deep danger lies in the realization of the order of things that constitutes the ideal of our Westernizers: in the reign not of the imaginary but of the actual universal civilization that they so desire. This would be tantamount to stopping the very possibility of any further prosperity or progress in history through the introduction of a new worldview, new goals, or new aspirations. . . . One should therefore be afraid not so much of the political consequences of world domination as of the cultural ones. What is to be feared is not a world state, be it a republic or a monarchy, but the domination of one civilization, one culture, for this would deprive the human race of one of the most necessary conditions for success and perfection—the element of diversity.[27]

Another figure who praised the value of civilizational diversity was Konstantin Leontyev. In some respects a decidedly reactionary character, Leontyev opposed equality of every type, regarding the spread of equality as a sign of civilizational decay. A man who fell short at almost everything he put his hand to, he has been described as "a failed writer, a bad husband, a sinful man of God, but never a mediocrity, never part of the grey herd."[28] Indeed, it would be difficult to find anyone more extraordinarily out of sync with his times. Yet despite his lack of success during his own lifetime, he has, like Danilevsky, enjoyed a sudden upsurge of popularity in Russia in the past thirty years, even finding his way into the speeches of Vladimir Putin.

The son of a minor nobleman, Leontyev studied medicine at university in order to please his mother, who wanted him to become a doctor. He graduated just in time to serve in the Crimean War but did not find this a pleasant experience. After a couple of years as a family physician after the war, he quit medicine and decided to take up life as a writer, publishing his first novel in 1861. This, however, was a critical flop.[29] Unable to earn a living by writing, he joined the diplomatic service in 1863 and was posted initially to Crete, where he caused a scandal by whipping the French consul after he made derogatory statements about Russia. Transferred to Romania and then to Salonika, he subsequently pursued a mostly uneventful diplomatic career while continuing to publish largely unacknowledged works of fiction.[30] In 1871, he fell seriously ill with what he thought was cholera but what was probably a severe outbreak of malaria. Believing that he might die, he made a pledge to the Virgin Mary that if he survived he would go to the nearby monastery on Mount Athos, repent of his sins, and become a monk. Once he recovered, he fulfilled his promise and spent a year at Athos. However, the monks refused to accept him into their ranks, saying that he was of "too passionate a nature."[31] Having failed at being a monk, Leontyev then spent several years living near Constantinople, earning a small amount of money by writing articles about Eastern affairs for the conservative Russian journal *Russkii Vestnik* (*Russian Messenger*). It was in this period that he wrote the work for which he is most famous, the book *Byzantinism and Slavdom*.[32] In 1880, he finally managed to achieve some professional success by becoming editor of the journal *Varshavskii Dnevnik* (*Warsaw Diary*), only for the journal's owners to close it down several months later. For the next few years, Leontyev worked for the Russian government's censorship department, before in 1887 he decided to have another go at being a monk and decamped to the Optyna Monastery, 250 kilometers southwest of Moscow. This time he gained acceptance, and after being ordained he moved to the Holy Trinity Monastery at Sergeev Posad near Moscow, where he died four years later on November 24, 1891.

One may identify three main currents of thought in Leontyev's writings. The first is an assertion of the primacy of aesthetics over other considerations. The second is a commitment to what Leontyev called "Byzantinism." And the third is a theory concerning the cyclical rise and fall of civilizations.

The prevailing intellectual current in late nineteenth-century Russia dictated that aesthetics should take second place to ethics, in particular social justice. People felt that one should judge art and literature not on whether they were aesthetically pleasing but rather on the contribution they made to improving society. In short, the political message of a work of art was more important than the quality of its execution. This was the thesis expounded most famously by socialist writer Nikolai Chernyshevsky (1828–89) in his 1855 work *The Aesthetic Relationship of Art to Reality*. Leontyev rejected this point of view, earning the contempt of most of the Russian intelligentsia of his era. Sergei Bulgakov (1871–1944), whose career moved from Marxist economist to liberal politician to conservative theologian, denounced Leontyev as an "ethical monster."[33]

Leontyev wrote that "the aesthetic criterion is the most trustworthy and general, for it is uniquely applicable to all societies, to all religions, and to all epochs."[34] Leontyev's view of aesthetics relied greatly on the concept of diversity. What was aesthetically pleasing was what was diverse. For this reason, he valued what nowadays one might call "multiculturalism"—that is to say, the existence within society of a diverse collection of races, languages, cultures, and mores. He also valued diversity in the form of inequality—an aesthetically pleasing society, in Leontyev's eyes, was one with rich and poor, weak and strong, and clear hierarchies. Only such societies, he believed, were capable of great achievements. He wrote, "In order to have a variety of individuals with strongly developed character, there must be *separation*, a division of society into groups and strata. The more sharply separated these groups and strata are . . . the richer will be the moral and even the intellectual fruits of a given social stratum. They will not be richer *in spite* of the uneven diffusion of knowledge, but precisely *because of it*—because of the diversity of attitudes, customs, tastes, and needs."[35] The fact that such societies might be full of injustice and prone to conflict and war was not, in his mind, a bad thing. It was a necessary price for greatness, besides which dramatic events such as war had an aesthetic appeal of their own. What was to be avoided, according to Leontyev, was bland homogeneity of any sort.

Thus, in Leontyev's novel *A Place of One's Own*, the character Vasily Milkeyev, who in many ways represents Leontyev himself, states that "Beauty is unity in variety."[36] "Why fear struggle and evil?" says Milkeyev: "Don't you see, evil given its head will generate good! . . . If for the sake of Cordelia at one pole, a Lady Macbeth is unavoidable at the other, then bring her on! But preserve us from debility, slumber, indifference, turpitude and mercantile caution."[37] "We should be guided by nature, which worships luxuriousness of forms," claims Milkeyev: "The chief constituent of diversity is the individual who stands above his creations. More than anything else the goal of history is to develop the manifold potency of the individual and drive his fearless determination to achieve his goals."[38]

This attitude led Leontyev to despise Western liberalism and the spread of bourgeois society. The desire to make all people equal had the effect, he argued, of producing an aesthetically dull homogeneity. "I'm not speaking about the Europe of Byron and Goethe, Louis XIV, and even Napoleon Bonaparte," he wrote, "but about that Europe that *came after*, the Europe of railways, banks, chambers of deputies, in a word about the present caricature of Europe with its self-delusion and prosaic fantasies of universal welfare. . . . We don't need to fear the decay of Europe . . . decay is horrible, but can be fruitful. Europe is threatened by necrosis via a different route: ossification of the soul."[39] As he argued further in an essay titled "The Average European as an Ideal and Instrument of Universal Destruction," in Europe "the homogeneity of individuals, institutions, fashions, cities, and in general of cultural ideals and forms is spreading . . . and . . . the interfusion or mixing of homogeneous component parts . . . leads not to greater solidarity but to ruin and death."[40]

Fortunately, claimed Leontyev, Russia could avoid this fate because it was a distinct civilization from the West founded on the ideas of Byzantinism, a thesis that he outlined in *Byzantinism and Slavdom*. Published just a few years after *Russia and Europe*, parts of the book bear a striking resemblance to Danilevsky's work, although the extent to which Leontyev drew on Danilevsky and the extent to which developed his ideas independently are matters of some dispute. While the two men had much in common, they also disagreed on certain points.

Byzantinism, Leontyev wrote, was founded on the principles of autocracy and Christianity, albeit a different Christianity from that of the West. "We know," wrote Leontyev, "that Byzantinism . . . rejects all hope of the universal well-being of peoples; that it is the strongest antithesis of the idea of humanity in the sense of universal worldly equality, universal worldly freedom, universal worldly perfection and universal contentment."[41] According to Leontyev, "Byzantine spirit, Byzantine principles and influence, like a complex cloth . . . penetrate the entire Great Russian social organism."[42] Russia needed to remain loyal to this spirit, he wrote: "Byzantine ideas and feelings consolidated semi-wild Rus' into one body, gave us the strength to survive the Tatar pogrom . . . gave us all our strength in the fight with Poland, Sweden, France, and Turkey. If we remain faithful, under its flag, we will have the strength to resist the attack of international Europe in its entirety."[43]

Like Danilevsky, Leontyev denied the existence of a universal good. "The idea of the universal good, the religion of the common interest, is the coldest, most prosaic, and also the most improbable, most unfounded of all religions," he claimed.[44] He continued, "The equality of people, the equality of social estates, the equality, that is to say the homogeneity, of provinces, the equality of nations, all this is one and the same process: in essence, the same general equality, general freedom, general interest, general good, general anarchy, or general worldwide boredom."[45] Russia needed to avoid going down this path. Leontyev wrote, "If we get carried away by the cold and deceitful shade of the boring common good . . . we may incurably and prematurely upset the organism of our Kingdom . . . [leading] to disease and even dissolution."[46]

In *Byzantinism and Slavdom*, Leontyev explained why the pursuit of equality and the common good were associated with civilizational dissolution. All living things, he explained, began very simple, then grew increasingly complex, and then in the final stage decayed, lost their complexity, and returned to simplicity.[47] There were, therefore, three stages of development: "primary simplicity," "flowering complexity," and "secondary simplicity."[48]

Exactly the same rule applied to social organisms, such as civilizations, claimed Leontyev. They began very simple, with little economic or social stratification, little economic or cultural development, and so on. Over time, they became more complex, with the society being divided into different social classes, with the growth of the economy, and with the flowering of arts and science. Then, in the final stage of their life, they adopted liberal ideas of equality and became increasingly homogeneous and uncreative, thereby descending into secondary simplicity and ultimate death. Thus, wrote Leontyev, "movement in an egalitarian-liberal direction has no logical connection with the idea of development, on the contrary the egalitarian-liberal process is the antithesis of the process of development.... A process that struggles against despotism, social estates, guilds, monasteries, even wealth, and so on, is a process of dissolution, a process of the secondary simplification of the whole."[49] In short, liberalism and egalitarianism accelerated the process of secondary simplification and so brought any civilization that adopted them closer to its demise.

Leontyev argued that all civilizations went through this same three-stage process, which in general lasted 1,000 to 1,200 years.[50] European civilization had been in existence for roughly 1,000 years and so was entering its period of secondary simplicity and nearing the end of its life.[51] European states were becoming more and more alike, all adopting the same ways of life and the same political and social institutions. "Instead of organized diversity, dissolution in simplicity is becoming more and more widespread.... Everything is merging and everything is dissolving," claimed Leontyev.[52] At the end of this process, European countries would merge, he predicted: "France, Germany, Italy, Spain, etc. will fall; they will become regions of a new state."[53] Russia had a choice: either subordinate itself to the dying Europe or preserve its independence. To Leontyev, it was clear that Russia should pick the second option. Either way, he concluded, "We must strengthen ourselves, think less about the good, and more about force.... Fewer so-called rights, less of the imaginary good! That's what's important!"[54]

One should not imagine that those who nowadays cite Leontyev share all of his views. Instead, it tends to be the expression "flowering complexity" that is remembered, while much of the surrounding material is ignored. Similarly, Danilevsky's Pan-Slavism is hardly in vogue, even among those who appeal to Danilevsky to explain the nature of the international order. Nevertheless, we can observe in Danilevsky and Leontyev direct forebears of the rhetoric of the modern Russian government's complaints of Western double standards, of the idea that Russia is a distinct civilization from the West, of the insistence that Western civilization is not universal and that each civilization should develop in its own way, of the belief that civilizational diversity (flowering complexity) is preferable to the civilizational homogeneity that is thought to be the inevitable product of Westernization, and from all this, of the determination to resist the West, a resistance that is seen as benefiting not just Russia but humanity as a whole. Before taking on their modern form, however, Danilevsky's and Leontyev's ideas would undergo further development from a second generation of civilizational thinkers. These were the Eurasianists.

CHAPTER 5

The Eurasianist Strand of Russian Civilizationism

Determining that Russia was a separate civilization from the West was one thing; deciding what sort of civilization was another. Danilevsky envisaged Russia forming the nucleus of a Pan-Slav civilization that would stretch westward into central and southern Europe. Leontyev rejected Pan-Slavism and saw Russia as a distinct civilization founded on the principles of Byzantinism. In the 1920s, a new strand of philosophy emerged with yet another vision. This was Eurasianism.

The Eurasianists looked eastward. They argued that Russians formed a common civilization with the peoples of the Caucasus and central Asia. Their civilizational boundaries roughly coincided with those of the former Russian Empire and later of the Soviet Union. The Eurasianists also resurrected the Slavophile conception of holy mission. But whereas the Slavophiles imagined Russia saving the West from itself, Eurasianists tended more to imagine a future Eurasia saving the rest of the world from the West.

Eurasianism has become an important element of how post-Soviet Russians see the world. It is far from being a uniform ideology. All its variants, however, tend to be deeply suspicious of the West and to consider it essential to resist Western hegemony and build a polycultural world.

As seen in chapter 1, the First World War shattered many Europeans' faith in the relentless march of progress and induced the likes of Spengler, Toynbee, and Sorokin to jettison the idea of history as a unilinear process. For Russians, the shock of the early twentieth century was even greater, involving not just the First World War but also the Russian Revolution and the subsequent Russian Civil War (1918–21). Driven into exile by the communists, many Russian intellectuals reassessed their view of the world. One of the outcomes was the philosophy of Eurasianism, first outlined in a book titled *Exodus to the East*, published in Sofia in 1921.

The book's authors—Georgy Florovsky (1893–1979), Pyotr Savitsky (1895–1968), Nikolai Trubetskoi (1890–1938), and Pyotr Suvchinsky (1892–1985)—laid out Eurasianism's basic theses in their introduction. They wrote, "History for us is not an assured ascent to some prehistorically preordained absolute aim. . . . We sense that we are in the midst of a cataclysm . . . separating one epoch of world history from the next. . . . We do not doubt that the replacement of the Western European world will come from the East. . . . Russians and those who belong to the 'Russian world' are neither Europeans nor Asians. Merging with the native element of culture and life which surrounds us, we are not ashamed to call ourselves *Eurasians*."[1]

Already in the second half of the nineteenth century, Russian thinkers such as art critic Vladimir Stasov (1824–1906) had put forward the thesis that Russian culture and institutions were not purely European but also had important Asian elements. Meanwhile, others, such as Esper Ukhtomsky (1861–1921) and Sergei Syromiatnikov (1862–1933), propounded the idea that the world's future lay in the East and proposed that Russia form an alliance with countries of the East against the West.[2] Eurasianism built on this foundation.

The Eurasianists were exiles, having either fled or been expelled from Russia in the aftermath of the revolution. They never assimilated into the countries in which they subsequently lived, and, like many other Russian émigrés, they felt themselves to be decidedly different from the Europeans among whom they found themselves. Their Russian identity remained strong, as did their hope that the communist regime would soon fall. Anti-Europeanism, a belief in Russia's distinctiveness, and a fervent faith in Russia's spiritual purpose were key elements of their worldview.

In 1920, one such exile, the linguist Nikolai Trubetskoi, published a short book, *Europe and Humanity*, proposing that the fundamental conflict in the world was between "the Romano-Germans and all the other peoples of the world, between Europe and Humanity."[3] "The Great War and especially its subsequent 'peace' . . . shook peoples' faith in 'civilized humanity' and opened the eyes of many," he wrote.[4] Europeans' sense that their civilization was superior to others simply proved their "egocentric psychology," Trubetskoi claimed, noting that "European culture is not humanity's culture. It is the product of the history of a distinct ethnic group."[5] But, he continued, "we don't know of any Europeans who might recognize the cultures of so-called 'savages' as of equal value to that of the Germano-Romans. It seems that such people simply don't exist."[6]

Trubetskoi argued that "it is not that the 'savages'' level of development is lower than that of Europeans, but that the Europeans' and savages' development have gone in different directions.... There is no objective proof of the superiority of Europeans over savages, nor can there be."[7] European anthropology and ethnology, by propagating the idea of "higher" and "lower" civilizations, justified "the imperialist colonial policies and vandalistic civilizing missions of the 'great powers' of Europe and America."[8] Trubetskoi considered that efforts to Europeanize other peoples generally produced negative results. In particular, it divided societies between younger, more Europeanized generations and older, less Europeanized ones, as well as between the more Europeanized urban elites and the less Europeanized lower classes, thereby producing "a sharpening of class conflict."[9] In addition, the belief that European culture was superior undermined peoples' confidence in their own countries, thereby weakening patriotism and so weakening the people in the international struggle for survival.[10] Overall, concluded Trubetskoi, "the consequences of Europeanization are so severe and terrible that one must consider Europeanization not a benefit but an evil."[11]

It was unthinkable that Europeans would correct their own egocentric psychology, Trubetskoi wrote. The only solution was for the peoples of non-European countries to reject the idea that European culture was superior and needed to be copied. As such ideas tended to flow from the top down, from the intelligentsia to the wider masses, it followed that "the center of gravity must shift to the psychology of the intelligentsia of the Europeanized peoples. This psychology must be reformed in a fundamental manner. The intelligentsia of the Europeanized peoples . . . must liberate itself from the delusion of the Romano-German psychology."[12]

While Trubetskoi clearly had Russia in mind, his argument had broader anticolonial ramifications.[13] Russia, in Trubetskoi's eyes, could find a new role for itself as a leader of the anticolonial movement. By itself abandoning Europeanization, it would set an example for the rest of humanity to follow.[14]

An obvious retort to this would be that Russia should then decolonize along with the European powers. The Eurasianists got around this objection by arguing that Russia was unlike other empires because its peoples and territories formed an organic unity, bound together by a common history, common geography, a common linguistic heritage, common botany, common folklore, and so on. Thus, in *Exodus to the East*, Trubetskoi argued that there was "an especially close bond between the Proto-Slavic and Proto-Indo-Iranian dialects"; that Russian folk songs used the five-tone Indo-Chinese scale but were different from both European and Asian songs in being polyphonic; that Russian dance bore similarities to the dances of Finns, Turks, and Mongols; that Russian woodwork and ornaments had "connections . . . with the East"; and so on.[15] All this meant that "from an ethnographic point of view, the Russian people are not purely Slavic. The Russians, the Ugro-Finns, and the Volga Turks form a cultural zone" that is neither European nor Asian but distinctly its own.[16] As Pyotr Savitsky commented, "Russia is not merely the 'West' but also the 'East,' not only Europe but also 'Asia,' and even not Europe at all, but 'Eurasia.'"[17]

The Eurasianists explained that this Eurasian civilization was in no way inferior to that of Europe or the West more generally. Indeed, like the Slavophiles before them, they imagined that Western civilization had reached the end of its line. The world needed a spiritual "rebirth," claimed Florovsky, but "this kind of rebirth does not happen in the West. . . . The 'blowing' of the liberated spirit . . . is heard in our time only outside the limits of 'European' thought."[18] The duty of every non-European nation was "to protect itself against the deception of 'universal human civilization' and against all efforts to become 'genuinely European' at all costs," wrote Trubetskoi.[19] He concluded,

> If the highest earthly ideal for a human being is self-awareness, then it follows that the authentic culture is one that facilitates such self-awareness. . . . In other words, the only authentic culture is a completely unique national culture, because it alone can fulfill the ethical, aesthetic, and even utilitarian requirements incumbent upon every culture. . . . Thus the cultures of all nations should be different . . . a universal human culture, identical for all nations, is impossible . . . it would bring true happiness to no one. Therefore, efforts to achieve a universal human culture must be repudiated, and conversely, the efforts of any nation to create its own distinctive culture are fully justified, while cultural cosmopolitanism and internationalism merit universal condemnation.[20]

Banned in the Soviet Union and not much read in the West, the Eurasianists languished in obscurity for many years, a topic of minor academic interest for those interested in the comings and goings of interwar Russian émigrés, and as such little more than a footnote in the history of Russian political philosophy. Nevertheless, from the 1960s onward, a few Soviet citizens did manage to acquaint themselves with Eurasianist thought. One of these was Lev Gumilyov.

Gumilyov was the son of the famous poet Anna Akhmatova (1889–1966) and the less well-known poet Nikolai Gumilyov (1886–1921). Twice convicted of anti-Soviet activity, Lev Gumilyov spent about ten years in the Gulag between 1938 and 1956, with an interval of freedom in which he fought in the Soviet army during the battle for Berlin. Akhmatova wrote of anguish at her son's arrest in her poem "Requiem":

> You were taken away at dawn. I followed you
> As one does when a corpse is being removed.
> Children were crying in the darkened house.
> A candle flared, illuminating the Mother of God.
> The cold of an icon was on your lips, a death-cold sweat
> On your brow; I will never forget this.[21]

In prison, Gumilyov noted the tendency of humans to form groups. From this he drew the conclusion that social groupings were a natural, biological phenomenon, not, as communist theory would have it, a product of economics. He also came up with the idea that the drive to achieve great things is similarly a natural phenomenon, arising from some inner biological impulse. Observing the great wealth of the Germans during his march on Berlin, he concluded that the Soviet victory in the Second World War was due not to material factors but to the presence of such an impulse among the Soviets and its absence among the Germans.[22] These ideas would later come together to form the basis of his theory of ethnogenesis.

Following his final release from the Gulag in 1956, Gumilyov devoted himself to his true passion—the history of the steppe peoples of eastern Russia and central Asia. A huge admirer of those peoples, he earned the wrath of Russian nationalists, who denounced him as a "Tatar lover."[23] Gumilyov set about rewriting Russian history to portray the Russians and the steppe peoples not as enemies but as allies. For instance, he described the Battle of Kulikovo Field in 1380 not, in accordance with the normal narrative, as the first step in the liberation of Russia from the Mongol yoke but rather as a struggle between Moscow and Western European Catholic powers, with Mongol factions fighting on both sides. Far from being an oppressive force, Gumilyov argued, the Mongols had helped protect Russia against the West, and the Russians and Mongols had interbred, as a result of which they had created a common civilization.[24]

Gumilyov's critics complained that he had a rather flexible attitude to historical facts. Others, though, felt that the story he told was far more important than any imperfections in the telling. As a fellow ethnologist explained, "Gumilev's whole conception was basically poetry. Maybe he inherited this talent from his father, but it was very effective. The simpler and more elegant, the easier it is for people, dilettantes in this case, to grasp. Gumilev was very popular among the technical intelligentsia, the creative intelligentsia. . . . Gumilev was fun. It was utter, unprovable nonsense. But it was good to read. Like a novel."[25]

Asked near the end of his life which philosopher he felt closest to, Gumilyov said, "Konstantin Leontyev. I am attracted by the truth of his utterances on the subject of historical processes . . . Leontyev was the first to work out the natural lifespan of a people's development, although naturally he didn't have a full understanding of the matter. I tested his theory and it turned out to be correct. Leontyev left out of the account only the incubation period and the memorial phase. This is easily explained: he was a political scientist and I am an ethnologist."[26] Besides Leontyev, Gumilyov relied on Eurasianist thinkers to provide a theoretical framework for his study of history. Particularly important was Pyotr Savitsky, with whom Gumilyov corresponded and whom he met on a visit to Prague in the mid-1960s. Gumilyov also read the works of Arnold Toynbee and was acquainted with the writings of the Russian cosmists, having read Vladimir Vernadsky's book *Chemical Composition of the Earth's Biosphere*.[27] Together these helped shape what was possibly Gumilyov's most important work, titled *Ethnogenesis and the Biosphere*.

Gumilyov preferred to talk about ethnic groups (*ethnoi*) rather than civilizations, and in *Ethnogenesis and the Biosphere* he sought to explain how *ethnoi* came into being, expanded, and in due course decayed. An *ethnos*, said Gumilyov, "is a natural phenomenon . . . not a social phenomenon . . . a collective of individuals opposing themselves to all other collectives . . . on the one hand, a product of history . . . and on the other hand linked . . . with the biocoenosis of the landscape and country in which it was formed."[28] Each ethnos developed a "behavioral stereotype" suited for its landscape, but landscape alone could not create an ethnos. For that, there needed to be "an external influence,"[29] which Gumilyov saw as coming from a surcharge of cosmic energy in the biosphere. In due course, "the original charge of energy in such a system is gradually expended, and entropy continually increases," leading to the ethnos's decline.[30]

Gumilyov commented that "the forming of a new *ethnos* always starts with an irresistible urge to purposive activity. . . . This attribute has even been known as passion."[31] An ethnos thus arose when cosmic energy, channeled through the biosphere, created a group of "passionaries" charged with a drive to achieve great things ("passionarity"). As Gumilyov put it, "Any process of ethnogenesis begins with the heroic, sometimes sacrificial feats of a small group of people, to whom the masses then rally.... One can now say that the 'take-off moment' is the sudden appearance of populations with a certain percentage of people with drive."[32]

Gumilyov's mention of "take-off" perhaps suggests an acquaintance with American modernization theory of the 1960s, although, if so, it is unlikely that he viewed it positively. More obviously, his theory bore the marks of Toynbee's concept of a creative minority combined with Vernadsky's theory of the biosphere and Chizhevsky's thesis that historical cycles were linked to solar activity. Passionarity, Gumilyov claimed, was "equated... with a micromutation," but exactly what was this was, and how it all worked, he never satisfactorily explained.[33] Regardless, Gumilyov's view that ethnic groupings were natural, not social phenomena, each with its own behavioral stereotype suited to its own particular environment, led him to the conclusion that humanity could never merge into a single ethnos with just one behavioral stereotype. Some *ethnoi* had sufficient complementarities that they could combine into a "*superethnos*," but *superethnoi* could never combine and would always be opposed to one another. "With such an approach to the study," wrote Gumilyov, "the Eurocentric idea of the superiority of technical civilization over the development of other types, it goes without saying, loses its validity.... Anyone starting to study the global patterns of ethnic history must immediately disavow the principle of Eurocentrism."[34] In any case, ethnic diversity was a necessary condition for human flourishing. "If everyone merges and becomes the same, then there will be no movement, no cultural development, and life will simply cease to exist," Gumilyov argued.[35]

In the late 1980s, Gumilyov opposed Soviet leader Mikhail Gorbachev's concept of a "common European home," on the grounds that such a common home would not combine elements of both the European and Soviet *superethnoi* but could be achieved only by the destruction of the latter in favor of the former. As he wrote, "It would be a great error to think that the construction of a 'common European home' will be the mutual victory of common human values. The entry into a foreign *superethnos* always involves a rejection of one's own ethnic *dominanty* [dominant ideals] in exchange for the system of the new *superethnos*. It is highly unlikely that this will be any different in our case. The price for joining civilization [i.e., the West] will be the domination of Western European behavioral norms and psychology ... [resulting in] the destruction of our national traditions."[36] Russians therefore needed to avoid Westernization and look instead to the East and to the steppe peoples with whom, Gumilyov believed, they enjoyed a natural complementarity.

It is easy to dismiss Gumilyov's ideas as pseudoscientific gobbledygook, but it is probably fair to say that most of those who nowadays cite him are not thinking of his most farfetched theories, such as the link between passionarity and cosmic radiation. Instead, he is taken to stand for certain simple ideas: that Russians share much in common with the peoples of the East, that Russia and the West are bound to collide, and that the success of any society depends on moral factors, above all the determination of its people to achieve great things (in Gumilyov's words, on the presence within it of a sufficient number of passionaries). In this vulgarized form, Gumilyov provides a link between the original Eurasianists and the so-called neo-Eurasianists who emerged after the collapse of the Soviet Union.

One of the most prominent neo-Eurasianists was Aleksandr Panarin, who nowadays is among the most commonly cited authors in Russian writings on international affairs, is the topic of a huge number of books and articles, and is the inspiration for a set of annual conferences known as the "Panarin readings" that cover subjects such as "Traditionalism and the Civilizational Choice" and "Global Threats and the Solidarity of Civilizations."[37] Panarin is probably the leading light of contemporary Russian civilizationism.

Panarin began his intellectual career as a fervent anticommunist, a fact that led to his expulsion as a student from the philosophy department at Moscow State University. In the late 1980s, during Gorbachev's perestroika, he advocated reform along free market and democratic lines, thereby aligning himself with the liberal camp. The experience of the 1990s, however, left him thoroughly disillusioned and convinced him that Western ideas and institutions had been transferred onto Russian soil "without any consideration of the difficulties and the accompanying sociocultural barriers."[38] From this he concluded that it was necessary to reject the unilinear historical philosophy of Western liberalism in favor of multicivilizational diversity. Thereafter, he moved further and further in a conservative and radically anti-Western direction, becoming an advocate of Russia's reintegration with other states of the former Soviet Union.[39]

Western scholars have noted similarities between Panarin's philosophy and that of Alain de Benoist and the French Nouvelle Droite (see chap. 1). Indeed, Panarin on occasion drew inspiration from them.[40] But he also drew on other sources. For instance, his book *The Russian Alternative*, which devotes considerable space to theories of history, cites many of the authors mentioned in this work, such as Toynbee, Dostoevsky, Solovyov, Danilevsky, Leontyev, Vernadsky, Chizhevsky, and Gumilyov. Panarin fits well into the broad tradition of civilizational theory.

According to Panarin, the world in the 1990s and early 2000s was at a crucial juncture between the industrial and the postindustrial eras. Western liberalism's materialism and individualism meant that it was incapable of dealing with the challenges posed by postindustrialism. For instance, Western consumerism made it unable to deal with ecological problems. This was a moral rather than a practical failure. As Panarin wrote, "The turning point that has matured in Russian and world affairs, a turning point produced by the decisions of the ruling Westernism that have driven the world into a dead end, is not a matter of technical-productive or economic factors, but of our spirituality, our view of how the world is constructed, our values."[41] This provided an opportunity for Russia to lead the world in casting off Western values in favor of an alternative. To do this, though, it was first necessary to dismiss the notion that Westernization was an inevitable process and that the West constituted the end of history. That meant the construction of an alternative vision of history, one more in line with Danilevsky's model of multicivilizational progression.

Panarin argued that while the unilinear concept of history made sense if one viewed progress solely in technical-economic terms, it did not if one regarded it through a different perspective. "If you consider humanity's fate from the point of view of spiritual, moral, and psychological measurements, then our century has been one of the very worst in all human history," he wrote.[42] Progress, claimed Panarin, "depends on a dialectic of action and counter-action, on the existence among humans of alternative variants and of bearers of these variants whose calling is to neutralize each other's dangerous extremes and thereby prevent a murderously homogenous march of history."[43] "Creating a world with a single variant means putting all your eggs into one basket: the failure of the one path in such circumstances would mean the failure of all humanity," he wrote.[44] Given this, "more than anything else, humanity should be afraid of the 'final victories' of anything—everything earthly is marked with the seal of original sin, and therefore the triumph of any of its varieties needs a certain limit."[45] According to Panarin,

> No less important than the principle of political pluralism and tolerance of those who think differently within the European system is the *principle of pluralism of world cultures*, each of whom should be viewed as the bearer of salvational diversity, as the embodiment of this or that alternative variant in the spirit not of exclusion but of complementarity. Therefore, it is clear that the main danger facing humanity today is the theory of a single variant of the future, viewing all non-Western

cultures as survivals of the past and hindrances to modernization and Westernization.... Humanity's greatest wealth is not the resources of the land, or technical-economic achievements and their corresponding infrastructure, but the rich pantry of cultures that contain within themselves the sources of various alternative practices, that are held in reserve and then revealed when required for salvation.[46]

Westernization had proved to be enormously destructive, said Panarin, noting that "the very concept of Westernization supposes only one true subject of history—the West.... 'Universal history' therefore contains within itself the task of strengthening Western European identity ... and destroying everything else."[47] Paradoxically, therefore, Western universalism was actually anti-universalistic, since instead of promoting the universal good, it served to promote the interests of the West while undermining those of everybody else, dividing the world into the West and the rest.[48] The West wanted to bring history to an end, so as to prevent anything from destabilizing the world and threatening its dominance.[49]

Referring to Toynbee's concept of challenge and response, Panarin asked how the rest of the world should respond to the challenge of the West and thereby enact the "revenge of history." He rejected the idea of retreating into isolation and creating an "Island Russia" (a concept that I discuss in chapter 6).[50] Instead he proposed responding by means of a moral revolution based on three ideas—"the ecological idea," "the idea of the cultural diversity of the world," and "moral-religious fundamentalism."[51] This would involve "the union of the posteconomic person of the most developed countries of the world with the preeconomic person of the still unwesternized East."[52] Russia, claimed Panarin, was ideally suited to lead this spiritual revolution, as its culture combined "three powerful tendencies" that challenged the Western viewpoint.[53] The first was Russian cosmism, as "an alternative to the sociocentrism that separates humanity from nature." The second was "the philosophy of all-unity (*vseedinstvo*)," which encouraged people to view "nature as a temple." And the third was a distinctive "natural philosophical organicism," which embodied the vision of the "living Mother-Earth and the living Cosmos."[54]

In Panarin's eyes, the political instrument for enacting this moral revolution was Eurasian integration. "The idea of Eurasian federalism is necessary," he wrote, adding that "Moscow as the capital of the United States of Eurasia ... should embody not only the great written traditions of Slavdom but also the great written traditions of the Muslim peoples.... In both cultures *sobornost'* dominates."[55] "For Russia," wrote Panarin, "asserting its responsible presence in Eurasia as an in-gathering, integrating, and consolidating center means shaming Huntington's barbarian prediction and proving that confessionally diverse regions (in this instance, Slavic-Orthodox and Turkic-Muslim) can form a stable civilizational federative body."[56] Beyond this, Panarin claimed that Russia's history and geography meant that it had little choice but to follow its fate to be a continental power. "The Eurasian space has its own geopolitical logic that one cannot ignore," he wrote.[57]

Panarin declared that "there is no doubt that, asserting its rights and status as a subject in the reintegrating process in the post-Soviet space, Russia will meet resistance from the West." But he argued that Russia should not flinch from this, for "Russia's Eurasian identity is the only way to mobilize the national spirit (in a political, not an ethnic, sense) for the purpose of the civilizational assimilation of the great space of the Russian north, eastern Siberia, and the Far East."[58] Ultimately, this would benefit everybody. Panarin concluded, "I am talking about the revenge of history, not about the revenge of Russia or the East. What I am saying is that the West needs the approaching change in phases of the historical cycle no less and perhaps even more than the Eastern pole of human civilization. I am convinced that the East's response to the West's challenge will purify the West and give it new strength, new impulses of historical dynamism."[59]

This last remark reveals that despite his civilizational rhetoric, Panarin retained a universalistic outlook, believing that a multicivilizational order would serve the universal good of humanity. He hoped for a dialogue, not a clash, of civilizations. This idea has found some support among Russian elites. In 2016, for instance, the former head of the Russian railways, Vladimir Yakunin (b. 1948), established a Dialogue of Civilizations Research Institute in Berlin. This appears to have ceased activity, however, following Russia's 2022 invasion of Ukraine.

In recent years, civilizational theorists have begun to replace the world "dialogue" with "polylogue," indicating their desire for a civilizational conversation involving multiple parties. Moscow State University professors Ilya Ilyin and Olga Leonova explain the concept as follows:

> In the conditions of globalization and ever closer mutual relations of countries and peoples, a need has developed for communications not only of the one-sided, monological type that were characteristic of the unipolar world . . . but also of a two-sided, dialogical type, in which both sides are equal partners in the communication process. . . . With the arrival of a multipolar and polycentric era, another tendency is become ever clearer, namely the desire of nations, especially those on the global periphery who previously made up the silent and obedient

majority, to talk out loud about their national interests and to be heard. These tasks can be carried out only in the format of the so-called polylogue . . . a format in which all sides are simultaneously communicators and recipients."[60]

According to Ilyin and Leonova, a transition to polylogue "has become a political necessity." The problem, however, is that "Western global leaders are still not ready for respectful cooperation and participation in polylogue on an equal, not privileged, basis . . . [and] are not prepared to renounce their habitual format of political monologue."[61]

The word "polylogue" also appears on the website of the Moscow-based Katehon think tank, whose high-ranking supervisory board includes the conservative millionaire Konstantin Malofeev (b. 1974), former presidential economics adviser Sergei Glazyev (b. 1961), and retired intelligence general Leonid Reshetnikov (b. 1947). According to the website, "We at *Katehon* view the world as a global space in which there will always be permanent and distinct civilizations or 'civilizational spheres.' These polylogue spheres of influence are not going to disappear in the near future, nor should they. . . . We are obliged to recognize the great diversity of values, traditions, interests, and visions which exist among all of the world's civilizations. . . . This demands a new multipolar approach to studying each civilization and the many subtle distinctions that exist within them."[62]

Among those who have written for Katehon is the philosopher Aleksandr Dugin (b. 1962), who outside Russia is by far the best-known neo-Eurasianist thinker. In an April 2022 article for Katehon, Dugin defended Russia's war in Ukraine in language that echoed the apocalyptic thinking described at the start of chapter 3. In this, he wrote that "we have become not just witnesses, but active participants in the Apocalypse. Not only the fate of the Heartland, but also the fate of the Spirit depends on who controls Ukraine. Either this world will come under the omophorion of Christ and His Immaculate Mother, or it will remain under the dominion of Satan. . . . The fight for Donbass, for Odessa, for Kiev, and even for Lviv is part of the great eschatological battle."[63] The war in Ukraine, claimed Dugin, was between Russia acting as the *katechon* on the one side and the "world of the Western Antichrist" on the other—"It is not us Russians who need Ukraine. It is Christ who needs it. And that is why we are there."[64]

As this article shows, compared with Panarin, Dugin puts far more emphasis on the need for political, and more recently even military, struggle against the "Western Antichrist."[65] His anti-Western rhetoric is much sharper than Panarin's, although he on occasion denies being anti-Western, saying that he is merely antiliberal and anti the direction that the West has taken in the past few decades.[66] He also differentiates between the West as a whole and its "Atlanticist" and "Anglo-Saxon" elements (primarily the United States and the United Kingdom), and it is mostly against the latter that he directs his wrath. Russia's aim, he writes, should be the "liberation of Europe from the Atlantic occupiers."[67]

Dugin describes his intellectual journey as having passed through three stages. According to his own account, in the first stage, in the early and mid-1990s, he endeavored to unite the antiliberal right and the antifascist left under the umbrella of the National Bolshevik Front, an organization led by the well-known writer Eduard Limonov (1943–2020). At this time, he struck up a friendly relationship with de Benoist, who has been described as having been "Dugin's main ideological ally" in the early 1990s.[68] After the National Bolshevik Front failed to gain much traction, Dugin moved to what he called a "more moderate version of Eurasianism," which "was based on radical antiliberalism, anti-Americanism, but gave a priority to geopolitics, Russian Civilization, continental identity and the principle of Empire."[69] In this period, he drew heavily on the work of the British geographer Halford Mackinder (1861–1947), in particular Mackinder's distinction between maritime and continental powers and the inevitability of struggle between them. Finally, in the third stage, Dugin began to develop what he calls the "fourth political theory," in opposition to the three previous political theories of liberalism, fascism, and socialism. This remains a work in progress but is meant to serve as a rebuttal to claims that liberalism represents the final stage of humanity's ideological evolution. To develop the fourth political theory, Dugin turned for inspiration to German philosopher Martin Heidegger (1889–1976), arguing that Heidegger provides the key to understanding how Russia can free itself from the ideological pull of the West.[70] Dugin argues for the importance of authenticity, of staying true to one's being (what Heidegger called "Dasein"). For Dugin, this principle applies to peoples as much as individuals: peoples must be authentic in order to have a meaningful existence.[71] Internationally, he says, this implies that the world must be founded on plurality of different civilizations.[72]

Dugin draws on a wide and eclectic range of sources for his philosophy, including not only Western writings but also those of Eastern civilizations, including Iran and India. He says that "being a total anti-racist, I consider that you can't compare peoples with one another. We must accept them as they are. We can never evaluate one people from another's point of view. . . . Thus, if we look at Asia, at the East, not through the eyes of a Westerner, but through the eyes of a Russian, an open-minded person, we see a spiritual treasure there. We will not oppose European culture to Asian culture, but we see a deep world of variety and polyphony of East and West."[73]

Dugin is a master of self-publicity who has published scores of books. In the early 1990s, he lectured for a few years at the Russian General Staff Academy, which gave him an opportunity to spread his ideas to the future leaders of the Russian army. In 2009, he gained another important platform when he was appointed head of the Department of Sociology of International Relations at Moscow State University. This led some observers to consider him to be one of the most important intellectuals in Russia, even going so far as to describe him as "Putin's brain."[74] In reality, there is no evidence that Dugin has ever exerted any influence either on Putin or on other senior members of the Russian government, none of whom have ever cited him. Indeed, it would appear that Dugin's belligerence eventually became too much for the Russian authorities. In 2014, he lost his job at Moscow State University and thereafter disappeared off the screens of mainstream TV stations. In August 2022, his daughter Darya was murdered in an operation that the Russian police claim was orchestrated by the Ukrainian secret services. But despite the sympathy that this attack generated, Dugin has not been officially rehabilitated and remains on the fringes of Russian politics.

Asked about his influence, Dugin replied in a 2017 interview that "those who think that I stand on the periphery of power are correct. I have no influence. I don't know anybody, have never seen anybody. I just write my books and am a Russian thinker, nothing more."[75] It would be a mistake, therefore, to view Dugin as somebody who has had a direct impact on government policy. Instead, his impact has been indirect, as one of many figures who have contributed to the general intellectual atmosphere now prevalent in the Russian Federation. His works have reached a large audience and thus are worthy of attention as an extreme example of the kind of thinking that has come to the fore in post-Soviet Russia.

One thing that Dugin is very good at is listing what he is against. He writes, "I am radically against liberalism in all its versions, against capitalism, against Atlanticism and global financial oligarchy, against the USA and American hegemony, against contemporary democracy (as the power of the minority), against the ideology of 'human rights' (which are founded on the Western person), against the myths of the 'free market,' against individualism in all spheres, etc. But I am also against materialistic atheistic communism and fascist racism, chauvinism and xenophobia."[76] What Dugin is *for* is less clear, except for struggle with all of the above, but especially with liberalism and Atlanticism. "Liberalism," he writes, "is a totalitarian ideology."[77] He reiterates more emphatically, "Liberalism is an absolute evil."[78] Other powers must unite to resist it, he says: "Contemporary Eurasians have only one way out—forging an alliance with those countries and nations of the East who are struggling for geopolitical autarky and for the restoration of traditional values against the contemporary world and Atlantic American aggression."[79] Dugin argues in his book *The Fourth Political Theory*,

> The very ideology of progress is racist in its structure. The assertion that the present is better and more fulfilling than the past, and continual assurances that the future will be even better than the present, are discriminations against the past and the present, as well as the humiliation of all those who lived in the past. . . . Undoubtedly racist is the idea of unipolar globalization. It is based on the idea that the history and values of Western, and especially American, society are equivalent to universal laws. . . . [In fact] these values are local ones . . . and globalization is trying to impose them onto all of humanity. . . . Globalization is thus . . . the purest manifestation of racist ideology. . . . Societies can be compared, but we cannot state that any one of them is objectively better than the others. . . . Instead of a unipolar world, the Fourth Political Theory insists upon a multipolar world, and instead of universalism, on pluriversalism.[80]

"The Fourth Political Theory must be rooted in the fundamental rejection of the monotonic process," writes Dugin—in other words, in a rejection of the unilinear model of progress.[81] Instead, his theory gives central importance to the idea of civilizations, an idea that he claims will allow for "regional globalization" in the form of "large spaces . . . built on the foundation of a common value system and historical kinship."[82] In this model, "there will be no universal standard. . . . Each civilization will at last receive the right to freely proclaim that which is, according to its wishes, the measure of things."[83] Dugin concludes,

> Globalization is the equivalent of the end of history. . . . The common future is no future. . . . When we construct the future, it should not be global in scope. It cannot be just one future, we must have many futures. . . . The common history must be a symphony of the different music of local histories being created by the unique chronological rhythms of time, and not one part attempting to drown out and overwhelm the rest until it is the only sound that can be heard. . . . Modernity and its ideological basis . . . [are] the cause of the future

catastrophe of humanity, and the global domination of the Western lifestyle is the reason for the final degradation of the Earth. The West is approaching its terminus, and we should not let it drag the rest of us down into the abyss with it.[84]

Eurasianist thinkers share certain characteristics with their Slavophile forebears, including a rejection of the universality of Western models and a powerful sense of mission. But whereas the Slavophiles saw Russia as part of a Christian civilization that included the West, Eurasians view it as part of a separate, Eurasian civilization that looks east.

Not everyone accepts that Russia has an external mission. Indeed, some civilizational theorists regard the concept as dangerous. While they share the Eurasianists' belief in the necessity of spiritual renewal, they also tend to the view that Russians should be less concerned about saving the world and more concerned about saving themselves. As the next chapter explains, they call for Russia to avoid foreign entanglements, to cut itself off from the West, and to look to its own spiritual salvation as a separate civilization safe in the confines of "Island Russia."

Chapter 6

The Isolationist Strand of Russian Civilizationism

For Eurasianists, Russia is just one part of a much broader civilization incorporating the peoples of a territory that is much larger than the current Russian Federation. Many Russian nationalists disagree with this. Russians, they say, are not the same as Georgians or Kazakhs or Uzbeks. There is no Eurasia, only Russia. If Russians want to establish a truly self-contained civilization, their logic goes, then they are better off living alone than constructing an empire that includes other peoples. For adherents of this branch of civilizational theory, the preferred policy is thus one of isolation within the boundaries of "Island Russia."

For several centuries this was the policy followed by the rulers of medieval and early modern Muscovy. Cut off from the rest of Europe by the mid-thirteenth-century Mongol invasion, Russia's rulers continued to view Europe with suspicion even after the Mongols were driven back. While there were some contacts between Russia and Europe, they were few. For the most part, Russians were not allowed to leave their country. Likewise, only a few Europeans were permitted entry, and those who were, were largely confined to Moscow and closely supervised while there. The conquest of Siberia in the seventeenth century substantially expanded Russia's borders and led to the absorption of some non-Russian peoples, most notably the Tatars, but Russians remained the overwhelming majority of the population. It was only with the conquest of the Baltic region, Ukraine, the Caucasus, and central

Asia from the early eighteenth century onward that this ceased to be the case. For some modern civilizational thinkers, this final step of expansion was a mistake. Russia, they argue, is better off in its current boundaries, without the people it conquered after the year 1700. The collapse of the Soviet Union was not a tragedy, as Putin has called it, but an opportunity, a chance to return to the borders of Muscovy before Peter the Great and for Russians to live in peace, separated from the rest of the world and thereby protected from undesirable foreign influences.

There is a tendency in the West to associate Russian civilizational thinking only with Eurasianism and, as often as not, with its more extreme advocates, such as Dugin. This paints a picture of civilizationists as inherently bent on conflict with the West. But the isolationist strand of thought reveals a different possible future—one in which Russia and the West are not in conflict but live side by side in a state of mutual "civilizational indifference."

In 2006, Russian businessman Mikhail Yuriev (1959–2019) published a novel titled *The Third Empire: Russia as It Ought to Be*. The book describes a future in which Russia invades Ukraine in support of pro-Russian uprisings. War then follows between Russia and the West, ending in a Russian victory due to the existence of secret weapons that render Russia immune to nuclear attack. Writing in the *Atlantic* magazine in March 2022, a month after Russia's real-life invasion of Ukraine, author Dina Khapaeva described the book as "a utopian Russian novel that predicted Putin's war plan . . . an expression of post-Soviet neo-medievalism, a far-right, and antidemocratic ideology that assigns 'Russian Orthodox civilization' a dominant role over Europe and America."[1] "Putin and Yuriev knew each other," noted Khapaeva, adding that *The Third Empire* is rumored to be popular and highly influential in the Russian leader's circle; one Russian publication described it as 'the Kremlin's favorite book.'"[2]

This all sounds very alarming. It is also a bit misleading. Much modern-day Kremlinology tends to seize a single thing that some person wrote, take it out of context, add in an alleged connection to Putin, and then draw sweeping conclusions about what is going in the Russian president's mind. Yuriev is a case in point. For in reality, the businessman was less an imperial expansionist than an extreme isolationist, who wanted not to conquer the world but to cut Russia off from it entirely.

Yuriev laid out his ideas in this regard in an article titled "Fortress Russia," published in 2008, two years after *The Third Empire*. Yuriev began as follows:

> Amidst all the differences of opinion in our society about Russia's fate, everybody agrees on one thing: Russia must be an active member of

global society. . . . Some think that we should merge in ecstasy with the West. Others think not, that instead we must engage in a bitter struggle against it. . . . Only very rarely does some politician or publicist say what goes without saying, namely that for Russia isolation from global civilization (by which they mean exclusively Western civilization) is the equivalent of death. . . . The silence on the issue suggests that such a policy is impossible. But in reality it is possible, not only in relation to West, but to everybody else as well—such a policy, indeed not so much a policy as an all-round worldview, is called "isolationism." Here I will endeavor to show why it is not only possible but vitally necessary for Russia's survival.[3]

Yuriev argued that Russia could not achieve rapid rates of economic growth if it remained integrated into the global economy. Instead, the country needed a "private but closed market," founded on import substitution. To wean Russians off their dependence on the West, he proposed banning all foreign nongovernmental organizations, prohibiting Russian citizens from receiving grants from foreigners, and developing specifically Russian forms of sport, so that Russian citizens would no longer look to the West for entertainment. As for foreign policy, he wrote that "for the last half century Russian foreign policy has known two types of morality: sharp confrontation with the West . . . and the policy of 'universal values,' that is complete capitulation and servility to the West. . . . Earlier, in the eighteenth and nineteenth centuries, there was a third morality: active participation in European politics on the basis of equality. Needless to say, not one of these fits within the parameters of isolationism."[4] "In general," wrote Yuriev,

> there is no need for any foreign policy. . . . We will not support any countries in resisting the West, nor will we support the West in resisting them. We will not support international terrorism, nor will we support the struggle against international terrorism. We will not support breaches of human rights, nor will we support the struggle against such breaches. . . . We will start the process of quitting all multilateral organizations, both European and global, a process we shall complete by leaving the UN. . . . We can rely entirely on ourselves. . . . We must stop the endless anti-Western and especially anti-American rhetoric. . . . Using the principle "You do as you want, and we will respond as we must," we need to avoid the mistakes of the Cold War.[5]

Yuriev represents a strand of Russian thought that wishes to avoid Westernization but sees the best way of doing so not as involving spiritual or political struggle against the West but rather as Russia and the West living entirely separate lives. This strand of thought also tends to eschew ideas of Russia having an imperial or global mission. It urges Russians not to look outward but to focus inward, on their own development. For adherents of this isolationist viewpoint, meddling in the affairs of others does nobody any good and should be avoided.

In the modern era, this mode of thought has often been associated with a Russian cultural and ethnic nationalism that emphasizes the primacy of the interests of the Russian people within the Russian Empire/Soviet Union/post-Soviet Russian Federation, and that demands that Russian national interests not be sacrificed on behalf of other countries. In the 1860s, for instance, the Russian newspaper *Vest'* (*News*) published under the banner "Russia for the Russians." This was not an appeal for an ethnically pure Russia but rather a foreign policy statement aimed at countering the views of Pan-Slavists such as Danilevsky who wanted Russia to liberate the Slavic peoples said to be suffering under the imperial yoke of the Habsburgs and the Ottomans. "Sacrificing Russian interests for the Slavs? No, and a thousand times no! *Russia for the Russians*! That is our banner," the newspaper declared.[6] "Russia for the Russians . . . means . . . that valuable Russian blood should only be shed for Russia."[7]

In the twentieth century, the most notable proponent of this mode of thought was the Soviet dissident Aleksandr Solzhenitsyn (1918–2008). Solzhenitsyn came to fame with his novel *One Day in the Life of Ivan Denisovich*, which described daily life in a Stalin-era prison camp. Thereafter, he became a thorn in the Soviet authorities' side, cataloging the abuses of communist rule and writing public letters calling on the Soviet Union to change direction. In 1974, the Soviet authorities lost patience and expelled him from the Soviet Union. On arriving in the West, Solzhenitsyn then dismayed many of his admirers when it turned out that his dislike of Soviet communism did not translate into uncritical admiration of Western democracy and capitalism. In a 1978 speech at Harvard University he denounced the unilinear concept of historical development so prevalent in the West. Expecting Solzhenitsyn to tell them about the horrors of communism, the Harvard audience was shocked to hear him say instead,

> Any ancient and deeply rooted self-contained culture, especially if it is spread over a wide part of the earth's surface, constitutes a self-contained world, full of riddles and surprises to Western thinking. . . . For one thousand years Russia belonged to such a category, although Western thinking systematically committed the mistake of denying its special

character and therefore never understood it. . . . The persisting blindness of superiority continues to hold to the belief that all the vast regions of our planet should develop and mature to the level of contemporary Western systems, the best in theory and the most attractive in practice; that all those other worlds are but temporarily prevented (by wicked governments or by severe crises or by their own barbarity or incomprehension) from pursuing Western pluralistic democracy and adopting the Western way of life. Countries are judged on the merit of their progress in that direction. But in fact such a conception is a fruit of Western incomprehension of the essence of other worlds, a result of mistakenly measuring them all with a Western yardstick. The real picture of our planet's development bears little resemblance to all this.[8]

Solzhenitsyn thus both viewed Russia as a distinct civilization and rejected the idea that the West represented the end of history. But his understanding of Russian civilization was very different from that of the Eurasianists. Solzhenitsyn was a distinctly *Russian* nationalist who rejected imperial schemes and envisaged a Russia that shed its non-Russian territories and was thereby reduced to its ethnically and culturally Russian core. He also rejected the idea that Russia had some holy mission in the world. "The goals of the true Russia are not compatible with military occupation or interference in the affairs of other countries," he declared.[9]

Solzhenitsyn believed that instead of dreaming imperial dreams, Russia should focus on its own internal spiritual development.[10] This did not imply total isolation of the sort later demanded by Yuriev, but it did imply the breakup of the Soviet Union into its constituent national parts and the creation of a smaller, nonimperial Russian state. In his 1973 *Letter to Soviet Leaders*, he warned of impending ecological disaster and rejected the idea of progress. He wrote,

> If the earth is a finite object, then its expanses and resources are finite also, and the endless infinite progress dinned into our heads by the dreamers of the Enlightenment cannot be accomplished on it. . . . All that "endless progress" turned out to be an insane, ill-considered, furious dash into a blind alley. . . . Society must cease to look upon "progress" as something desirable. "Eternal progress" is a nonsensical myth. . . . There is one way out for us . . . namely, for the state to switch its attention away from distant continents—and even away from Europe and the south of our country—and make the North-East the centre of national

activity.... The demands of *internal* growth are incomparably more important to us, as a people, than the need for any external expansion of our power. The whole of world history demonstrates that the people who created empires have always suffered spiritually as a result.¹¹

Solzhenitsyn wrote that the mark of a nation was its "inner"—in other words, spiritual—development. Solzhenitsyn argued that this required Russians to "acknowledge our *external* sins" against other peoples, adding that "just as a family, in which there has been a great misfortune and shame, tries to isolate itself from everybody for a bit, and to work out its grief on its own, so too must the Russian people be alone with itself, without neighbors and guests; concentrating on its inner tasks; on healing its soul, educating its children, and sorting out its own house."¹²

In a 1990 essay titled "How Can We Rebuild Russia?" Solzhenitsyn described what this meant in practice. He called for dismantling the Soviet Union and leaving a Slavic rump consisting of Russia, Belarus, and the Russian-speaking northern part of Kazakhstan, along with whatever regions of Ukraine wished to remain with Russia (something that Solzhenitsyn said should be determined on a region-by-region basis). "We do not have the strength for an empire, we don't need it," wrote Solzhenitsyn.¹³

There is a tendency in the West to conflate different types of Russian nationalism, ignoring the wide differences between Slavophiles, Eurasianists, state nationalists, ethnonationalists, imperialists, isolationists, and the like. Even among those who talk of "Russia for the Russians," there are variations—between, for instance, those like Solzhenitsyn who believe in the need for repentance and inner rebirth and those of a more assertive, chauvinistic variety. An example of the latter was Konstantin Krylov (1967–2020), who, as well as political and philosophical works, published fantasy novels under the pseudonym Mikhail Kharitonov. In his 1997 book *Behavior* (*Povedenie*), Krylov made his own unique contribution to civilizational theory.

Like National Bolshevik leader Eduard Limonov, Krylov belonged to a category of thinkers whose extreme political views put them well beyond the comfort zone of most of their peers but whose intellectual brilliance was so obvious that they nevertheless retained a degree of social respectability. Conservative writer Yegor Kholmogorov remarked that "Krylov was the most intelligent Russian of our era. At some times it seemed to me that he was the most intelligent person on the planet."¹⁴

Krylov described the "Russian idea" as having three elements. First, all property in Russia had to be owned by Russians. Second, "Russians... cannot allow the existence anywhere in the world of non-Russian power. This doesn't mean that all power in the world has to be in the hands of ethnic Russians. It means only that all power in the world . . . must in one way or another be controlled by Russians." And third, Russians must control the interpretation of all ideas in the world: "Dominance of the ideological field is necessary . . . not because Russians think faster than others, but because they are right."[15] Kholmogorov wrote that "Krylov said something very important . . . Russians have enemies, and they hate us. . . . We shouldn't apologize for our existence . . . should be ourselves, do what has to be done, remember evil, and above all not permit further evil in the future."[16]

Such ideas put Krylov at odds with Russia's pro-Western liberal intelligentsia. Nevertheless, he and they made common cause against the government of Vladimir Putin, with Krylov joining the liberals in protesting against Putin's reelection to the presidency in 2012 and in demanding a more democratic political order. For Krylov, Putin's government was antinational. Nationalism and democracy went together, and a more democratic Russia would no doubt also be a more nationalistic one.

Krylov defined nationality in social rather than racial terms, writing that "the national is a system of unconscious evaluations of human behavior (both others' and one's own) transmitted by hereditary means."[17] In *Behavior*, he laid out his conception of the ethical nature of different civilizational types.

According to Krylov, the world contains three "civilizational blocks," each of which "functions on one, and only one, ethical system."[18] These are the South, the East, and the West. Each block contains individuals that dissent from their civilization's core ethical principle, but each nevertheless has such a principle that is "generally accepted" and that determines interpersonal relations.[19]

Southern civilization, according to Krylov, follows the principle "I should behave toward others as others behave towards me." Eastern civilization follows the idea "I should not do to others what others do not do to me." And the West obeys the formula "Others should behave toward me as I behave toward them."[20] According to Krylov, each of these principles is in constant struggle with a vulgarized, distorted imposture of itself. In the case of Western civilization, for instance, the ethical intuition "Others should behave toward me as I behave toward them" becomes simplified into "Others should behave as I behave."[21]

Krylov argued that Russia was a hybrid nation, part Western, part Eastern. He believed, however, that Russia could in due course create a new type of civilization, the North. This would be founded on a fourth ethical principle, namely "Others should not behave toward me as I do not behave toward others," impostures of which are "No one should do what I don't do" and "No one should have what I don't have."²² In theory, once Russia had separated itself from the West in this way, conflict between the two could then be avoided by adopting a policy of isolationism, but this would work only if the West agreed to let Russia live in isolation. If, instead, the West adopted the distorted version of its fundamental ethical principle and insisted on the rule that "Others should behave as I behave," then isolationism would become impossible in the face of Western demands that Russia change its behavior. At that point, conflict between Russia and the West would become inevitable.²³

Whereas Krylov defined civilizations in terms of ethics and behavior, another post-Soviet civilizational theorist, Vadim Tsymbursky (1957–2009), defined them in terms of geopolitics. For Tsymbursky, a civilization was a state with sufficient gravitational attraction that other states orbited around it. The United States was the largest such civilization, but Russia also had its satellites and thus also constituted a civilization, albeit a less powerful one. Russia's interests would be best served not by challenging the United States but by coming to an agreement with it to recognize each other's distinct spheres of influence, thereby creating a "one and a half polar world," in which the US constituted the largest civilization but there were also several other smaller ones, such as Russia.²⁴

Like many other civilizational thinkers, Tsymbursky began his intellectual career with liberal and pro-Western inclinations but abandoned these in the aftermath of the collapse of the Soviet Union.²⁵ What brought him to prominence was the publication in 1993 of his article "Island Russia," after which he became probably the leading proponent of isolationism in the post-Soviet era.

Tsymbursky rejected Eurasianist definitions of Russian identity and instead argued that Russia was defined by three main features. The first was that it was the "geopolitical niche of the Russian ethnos, lying to the east of the Romano-German ethno-civilizational platform . . . forming its own special platform between Europe and China." The second was the vastness of its eastern territories, which rendered it safe from attack from that direction. And the third was its "separation in the west from Romano-German Europe, the homeland of liberal civilization, by a belt of peoples and territories bordering the core of Europe but not being part of it." These peoples and territories, which included the Baltic states, the Czech Republic, and Hungary, Tsymbursky called "strait-territories," which he regarded as a buffer zone protecting Russia from Western Europe. Put together, these three features made Russia in effect "a giant island within a continent."²⁶

Russian Westernizers, claimed Tsymbursky, had always wanted Russia to be part of Europe but failed to understand that Russia's immense size meant that Europeans could never accept it and would always regard it as a threat. Whenever Russia sought to come out of its island and involve itself in European affairs, it provoked a negative reaction from Europeans.[27] Europe and Russia, he said, were "two Schopenhaueresque porcupines who are capable of warming each other up with mutual understanding, economic cooperation, and so on, only if they remain a needle's length apart."[28] The obvious conclusion was that Russia should keep its distance from Europe and stay within the safety of its island. The peace that would follow would enable the country to focus on rebuilding itself. Tsymbursky suggested that Russia should embark on a new process of internal colonization, shifting its attention to the development of Siberia and perhaps even moving its capital to the city of Novosibirsk. He concluded, "Central Asia will keep us safe in the south, and the eastern bank [of the island] resting on Siberia will keep Russia out of the natural habitat of the clash between Islam and liberalism, enabling us to stay out of the strife between the 'haves' and 'have-nots' of the world."[29]

One of Tsymbursky's disciples, conservative philosopher Boris Mezhuev (b. 1970), notes that the concept of Island Russia rested on the assumption that the West would not absorb the "strait-territories" of Eastern Europe, thereby destroying Russia's western buffer zone.[30] By the early 2000s, NATO expansion in Eastern Europe, along with the prospect of further expansion in Georgia and Ukraine, had made it clear that this assumption was wrong. This forced Tsymbursky to reconsider parts of his thesis, particularly those that concerned what he called "the shelf of Island Russia . . . the territories connected to the current Russian core through geographical, geostrategy and cultural bonds." He wrote that "there is no doubt that Eastern Ukraine . . . Crimea . . . [and] certain territories in the Caucasus and Central Asia belong to the Russian shelf."[31] Tsymbursky considered Ukraine to be particularly important and felt that its status as part of Russia's buffer zone constituted a fundamental Russian national interest.[32] Should the West move too close to Russia's borders, Russia might have to respond by absorbing its "shelf"—in other words, Crimea and Eastern Ukraine. With this modification of his theory, Mezhuev writes, "the author of 'Island Russia' was no longer confident that Russia's formers borders should not be revised in favor of expansion."[33]

Among those close to Tsymbursky was the conservative culturology professor Svetlana Lurye (1961–2021). In a 2015 article titled "Rapprochement with the East: Lessons of Intercivilizational Indifference," Lurye argued that although Russia's political relations with Asian states were improving, the

Eurasianists were wrong to imagine that Russia could ever become very close to countries such as China and India. Culturally, they were too far apart. The East could never replace the West as the "other" Russians used to evaluate themselves. "We experience this Western civilization as our own, we love it and hate it, we see its ups and downs, we feel its current perversity with our skin. The East is a stranger with whom we do not need to come into contact," wrote Lurye.[34] That said, she continued, Russia's "intercivilizational indifference" toward countries like China and India provided a lesson that Russians could learn by becoming equally indifferent toward the West. She concluded, "The experience of the Eastern Partnership can teach us to be acutely aware of our otherness, including our otherness in relation to the West. To feel the peculiarity of our Orthodox civilization. And this will adjust our position towards the West. It will make it more accurate and adequate, as well as more detached and less passionate. It will make us more aware of ourselves and own identity. It will be a rewarding experience."[35]

Lurye's concept of intercivilizational indifference appears also in the writings of Boris Mezhuev, whom Tsymbursky introduced to Lurye. Mezhuev was one of a group of youthful Russian philosophers who were inspired by Tsymbursky and acquired the collective title of "Young Conservatives." Particularly notable among them were Yegor Kholmogorov and Mikhail Remizov (b. 1978). Kholmogorov is probably the most outspoken. He states that "Russia is an island" and praises Tsymbursky for "showing the necessity of Russian isolationism," but he adds that what he himself favors is "offensive isolationism."[36] Kholmogorov takes a rather skeptical view of Russia's military intervention in Syria on the grounds that Russia has no vital interests in that country. Ukraine, however, is an entirely different matter. He explains, "The point is that strategically, in terms of culture, as a civilization, as a state, Russia is interested in isolation. That is, as much as possible it should not intervene very much in world affairs. It should not be continually supporting the global balance by means of interventions in far away lands. . . . An example is the geopolitically-founded intervention in Syria. . . . [But] in our current objective circumstances, isolationism is impossible as we are under continual threat. American tanks are in Estonia, 100 kilometers from St. Petersburg. NATO military bases might appear in Ukraine. Thus Russia is currently obliged to attack or counter-attack in some way, because it is objectively threatened."[37]

Remizov is rather less belligerent but also sees the West as acting in a way that makes it difficult for Russia to achieve the isolation it needs. A modern-day proponent of the slogan "Russia for the Russians," he complains that "more than once Russia has staked its interests on the service of this or that global mission. . . . One might say that the country has given its best years to 'humanity' (i.e., the realization of a definite conception of global society) and not to itself. This must never happen again."[38] While Remizov believes that Russia should strongly defend its regional interests, he argues that this should not tempt Russians to engage in any sort of "global mission." "We simply do not have the resources to legitimate an imperial/super-national power," he writes, adding that "we have no need to either dispute or lighten the USA's hegemonic burden, turning it into a sparring partner in the global ring."[39] This conclusion, he claims, fits with Tsymbursky's concept of a "one and a half polar" world order.[40]

Remizov's vision runs into much the same problem as Tsymbursky's—it relies on the West, and in particular the United States, accepting Russia as a separate civilization with its own sphere of influence. Remizov recognizes that this is not likely. He concludes therefore that Russia has "to compel the USA towards realism."[41] Consequently, "in the near future there is no alternative to the logic of confrontation."[42]

More than Kholmogorov or Remizov, it is Mezhuev who has taken responsibility for promoting Tsymbursky's legacy. In the early 2010s, Mezhuev worked as deputy editor of the newspaper *Izvestiia*, where he ran the paper's op-ed page and provided an outlet for Lurye, the Young Conservatives, and other sympathetic thinkers. In 2015, he was fired, apparently for political reasons. It seems that his particular brand of isolationist ideology was unwanted by a Kremlin that was hoping to patch up relations with the West following the signing of the 2015 Minsk Agreement, which was meant to bring an end to the war in Eastern Ukraine. Mezhuev now works as a lecturer in the philosophy department at Moscow State University. Deeply conservative, he wants nothing to do with a West that he thinks has permanently abandoned traditional values. He argues that Russia must change direction onto what he calls the "only possible, only sensible path—developing in maximum isolation from Europe."[43]

According to Mezhuev, "Russia cannot but consider itself a social phenomenon different from the West; in other words a special 'civilization' with its own orbit and power of attraction."[44] He describes his philosophy of "civilizational realism" as "a pragmatic breakdown of Vadim Tsymbursky's geopolitical concept" and as resting on several theoretical premises:

> The world is divided into separate "civilizational blocks" made up of core and periphery. Peripheral states often include regions gravitating towards different civilizational centers. Russia is one such civilization. . . . This claim to leadership is permanent but potentially dangerous for the "status quo"

situation in Europe. . . . This contradiction can be resolved by an agreement with the Euro-Atlantic "civilizational leaders" to create a demilitarized buffer zone made up of limitrophe Eastern European states. . . . Russia needs to give up all efforts to become part of the Euro-Atlantic community and should view it as an "alien" civilizational space, with which integration is impossible.[45]

Following Russia's February 2022 invasion of Ukraine, Mezhuev has had to admit that the hope of creating a buffer zone to separate Russia and the West has been destroyed. However the war ends, Russia and the West will most likely have adjacent borders. Consequently, Mezhuev writes that after the war, "Island Russia in Tsymbursky's terms . . . will cease to exist."[46]

Nevertheless, Mezhuev still urges Russia to keep its distance from the West. He remarks that "it is no coincidence that the West is discarding the last biblical taboos, legalizing not only the right to same-sex cohabitation, but also the change of sex and, in general, radical experiments with one's own body. Since the 18th century, the Western civilization's mainstream trends have proceeded within the secularization project. . . . If Russia is sincerely committed to Christian values, if it is really keen on rejecting the path taken by Europe, it should stay away from it at arm's length—if not literally, then culturally."[47] "The period of rapprochement is closing up," claims Mezhuev: "[Russia] has chosen its civilizational path, diverging from that of Europe."[48]

In any case, Mezhuev does not believe that political rapprochement with the West will benefit either side. Any such rapprochement would lead to Russia becoming involved in European affairs, which would in turn inevitably generate fear in the West and lead it once again to unite against Russia. Russia needs to recognize that the West will never accept it and that attempts to make it do so will only backfire. By contrast, "the farther away from us the West is in socio-cultural terms, the easier (potentially) it will be to do business with it."[49] Consequently, like Lurye, Mezhuev argues that Russia should develop the same attitude to the West as it has toward other civilizations such as India and China—namely, "civilizational indifference." Mezhuev concludes, "The 'collective West' will never agree to grant us an entry pass, because should we get it in the end, the 'collective West' would have to be renamed. . . . Currently, the most promising scenario is to maintain a certain degree of 'isolation' from the West. . . . This 'non-rapprochement' will enable us to solve our geo-political, geo-cultural and geo-economic tasks, while distancing ourselves as much as possible from other civilizational centers."[50]

Mezhuev's writings appear from time to time in the prestigious journal *Russia in Global Affairs*, a favored outlet for high-ranking officials when they wish to publish lengthy musings on foreign policy and international affairs. In early 2018, for instance, the journal published an article by Russian diplomat Nikolai Spassky (b. 1961) titled "The Island of Russia," a title that seemed to indicate that Tsymbursky's teachings had reached at least some people in high places.[51] Later that year, *Russia in Global Affairs* published a piece by an even more prominent personality, Vladislav Surkov (b. 1964), formerly first deputy chief of the Presidential Administration (from 1999 to 2011), deputy prime minister (from 2011 to 2013), and personal adviser to President Putin on matters relating to Ukraine and Georgia (from 2014 to 2020).

Often described as "the grey cardinal of the Kremlin," Surkov was long a popular bogeyman in Western Kremlinology and was widely regarded as the ideological mastermind behind the Russian government. Once considered a relative Westernizer, in his 2018 article, titled "The Loneliness of the Half-Breed," he declared that Russia was neither of the West nor of the East. Instead, it stood alone. The events of 2014 (the annexation of Crimea and the war in Eastern Ukraine) marked a turning point, Surkov argued, "the end of numerous fruitless attempts to become part of Western civilization. . . . From 2014 onwards, a new long era . . . stretches into a future in which we will experience a hundred (two hundred? three hundred?) years of geopolitical loneliness."[52]

Surkov stated that for the past four hundred years, the Russian elite had tried to Westernize their country, following whatever seemed to be most in fashion in the rest of Europe, be it socialism a hundred years ago or the free market in the 1990s. None of this had led the West to accept Russia as one of its own. The problem, said Surkov, was that "despite the external similarities of the Russian and European cultural models, their softwares are incompatible and their connectors dissimilar. You can't make a common system out of them."[53]

That did not mean that Russia should turn east, said Surkov. Just as Russia was not Western, it was not Eastern either. Rather, "Russia is a western-eastern half-breed country."[54] It was time for Russians to recognize this, Surkov argued, to abandon attempts to join either the West or the East, and instead strike out on its own. He concluded, "Russia moved East for 400 years, and then moved West for another 400 years. Neither the one nor the other took root. We have gone down both paths. Now we need the ideology of a third path, a third type of civilization."[55]

Surkov's article indicates a belief that Russia and the West are fated to go their separate ways, with the former creating a separate civilization of its own. This viewpoint has gained traction following the 2022 invasion of Ukraine, with even fairly moderate foreign policy analysts accepting the idea that Russia's future will no longer be oriented toward the West. An example is Dmitry Trenin (b. 1955), former head of the Carnegie Moscow Center, many of whose books and articles have been translated into English and who has been described as "arguably the principal interpreter of the Kremlin's international conduct for the Western world."[56] In the early 2000s, Trenin was considered moderately liberal and pro-Western, albeit someone who chose to work with the Russian state rather than in opposition to it. In 2002, Trenin wrote that "Russia stands on the boundary between the post-modern and modern and even pre-modern world. It must make its choice. The only rational option is to fully stress Russia's European identity and engineer its gradual integration into a Greater Europe . . . a clear pro-European choice would facilitate the country's modernization, its adjustment to the 21st century world. . . . A failure to integrate would spell Russia's marginalization and possibly its disintegration. There is no longer an option of withdrawing into 'Eurasia.'"[57] Twenty years later, he had entirely changed his tune. His 2020 book *New Balance of Power: Russia in Search of Foreign Policy Equilibrium* has been described as "Tsymburskian through and through."[58] "The old strategy, beginning with Peter the Great, to Europeanize the country and take its place in that world, is not relevant," Trenin declared in 2023, thereby entirely reversing his position compared with that in 2002.[59]

Events over the past twenty years have destroyed the dream of Island Russia, at least in the territorial sense originally envisioned by Tsymbursky. At the same time, however, Western sanctions have significantly severed political, economic, and cultural ties between Russia and the West, creating an Island Russia of a different sort. For Russian isolationists, the key message is that Russians should not seek to reverse this process but should embrace the opportunity to end the obsession with becoming part of the Western world and should work instead toward creating a "Russia for the Russians." Many of them suspect that those in authority do not share this perspective. Surkov probably would not have considered it necessary to publish his article in *Russia in Global Affairs* had he felt that most of his colleagues in the Kremlin already agreed with him. Meanwhile, Mezhuev's writings make it very clear that he believes that those in power in Moscow do not accept his opinions and even now would gladly integrate Russia with the West if only the West would permit it. As Trenin's intellectual trajectory shows, attitudes have clearly changed. The question remains how far this goes.

Chapter 7

The Rise of Russian Civilizationism

In summer 2019, a professor at Moscow State University lectured a group of foreign visitors on the nature of Russian civilization. Her talk, she told them, was derived from a chapter she and a colleague had written for a book on the prospects of an intercivilizational world order, produced by the eminent German academic publisher Springer.[1] In her lecture and the book, she argued that "Russia represents a distinct civilization with its own spiritual values, national mindset, and national political culture."[2] Russian civilization, the professor said, was founded on an inner spirituality, the concept of strong centralized state power, and *sobornost'*. These characteristics were unique to Russia. To make the point, she showed a chart, taken from the book, that indicated the main characteristics of four different world civilizations—Western, Russian, Islamic, and Chinese. Each was different. This was neither good nor bad, merely a fact. Russia had certain civilizational characteristics that could be observed over the longue durée, just as other civilizations did.

In their book chapter, the lecturer and her colleague elaborated further. If humanity was to build a peaceful world in which civilizations cooperated rather than clashed, three steps were necessary:

> *The first step is to accept* the very fact that civilizations unlike our own do exist and are entitled to exist. Suppose that an earth civilization

came into an encounter with an extraterrestrial civilization, would a wise course of action be to impose on "aliens" a Westminster-inspired political system based on the belief that that is the best system for the whole Universe. Similarly, on what grounds can any great earthly civilization pretend to have the right to impose on all other civilizations and cultures of planet Earth its political institutions? . . . *The second step is to abandon stereotypes and preconceived notions and try to understand the core values, ideas, and meaning of "alien civilizations." . . . The third step is to accept other civilizations and cultures as they are, after we have learned the circumstances from where they emerged and their strengths.*[3]

What was striking about the professor's talk was not the description of Russian civilization, which was not particularly original, but rather the certainty with which she expressed her belief that the world consisted of distinct civilizations, each with different characteristics that, if not permanent, at least lasted over hundreds of years. Civilizational theory has dug such deep roots in Russian thinking that many no longer regard it as a theory but as an obviously truthful description of the world. The fact that different civilizations exist is not in dispute; the only question is what distinguishes them.

A number of factors explain how this mode of thought became so prevalent in Russia. The first is the discrediting of the previous unilinear notion of history promoted by Soviet communism, followed by the discrediting of Western liberalism due to the chaos endured by Russia in the 1990s and the subsequent worsening of Russian-Western relations. A second factor is that the Russian population has been to some extent conditioned to accept civilizational theory through the spread of the academic discipline known as "culturology." And a third factor is the active propagation of civilizational concepts over three decades by senior opposition political figures, notably the leader of the Communist Party of the Russian Federation (CPRF), Gennady Zyuganov (b. 1944), and the late leader of the Liberal Democratic Party of Russia (LDPR), Vladimir Zhirinovsky (1946–2022). The rise of civilizational theory was thus the product of numerous social processes, not of a decision made in the Kremlin.

Having finally triumphed in the early 1990s, by the 2020s the view that history marches inexorably toward Western liberalism had vanished almost entirely from Russian political discourse. One reason may be that after seventy years of Soviet dialectical materialism, most Russians have lost their appetite for utopian views of the future that seem to lead only to disappointment. As disappointing as communism was the experience of the 1990s, when once again utopian historical determinism left chaos in its wake. While some Russians grew very rich indeed, most experienced economic collapse, disintegrating social services, a massive decline in life expectancy, widespread crime, alcoholism, and drug use, and many other social problems. For many Russians, their country's "return to civilization" was a personal disaster. Unsurprisingly, Russians' perceptions of the 1990s are overwhelmingly negative.[4] Given the period's association with Westernization, the idea that Russia is destined to become like the West has lost much of its appeal.

The shifting international balance of power has further contributed to this loss of faith in the West. As the center of financial power has shifted to the Global South, most notably China, the idea that Western models constitute the end of history has also become much less credible. Instead, there is a growing belief that Russia must reorient itself toward the rising powers in the world. As one of Russia's leading foreign policy analysts, Fyodor Lukyanov (b. 1967), puts it, "A new era has dawned.... The realignment of forces on the world stage is taking its course, with China and Russia, whether they like it or not, on one side and the United States and its allies on the other."[5] In these circumstances, end-of-history narratives seem a little out of place.

In recent years, another factor has added to the declining appeal of the West: the spread of identity politics, "wokeism," cancel culture, and the like. Even some onetime Russian liberals view these phenomena with distaste. One reason may be that demands for sexual and racial equality and other rights were part of the rhetorical toolbox that the Soviet Union used to attack Western states during the Cold War. Consequently, some Russians now view similar demands coming from Westerners as something akin to communism and complain that cancel culture shows that the West is adopting a totalitarian mindset.[6] An example of this sort of thinking came in a 2021 article by the theater director Konstantin Bogomolov (b. 1975), a respected member of Moscow's liberal artistic community and the husband of the well-known socialite and onetime presidential candidate Ksenia Sobchak (b. 1981). Bogomolov's article was published in Russia's leading liberal newspaper *Novaia Gazeta*. In it, he complained that "the contemporary Western world is turning into a new ethical Reich with its own ideology.... We find ourselves in the tail of mad train, steaming to a Hieronymous Bosch-style hell, where we will be met by multicultural gender-neutral devils. We simply have to unhitch the wagon, cross ourselves and start building our own world. To build anew our old, good Europe, the Europe of which we dreamed, the Europe we have lost, the Europe of the healthy."[7]

Another liberal turned critic of the West is the journalist and political scientist Aleksei Chadaev (b. 1978). In the late 1990s, Chadaev worked as an assistant to then–deputy prime minister Boris Nemtsov (1959–2015), one of the most prominent pro-Western politicians of the post-Soviet era. At the time a member of Nemtsov's party, the Union of Right Forces, Chadaev subsequently switched to the pro-Putin party United Russia. He supports Russia's war in Ukraine (euphemistically referred to as the Special Military Operation [SMO]) and in September 2022 held a special event of drone operators in the town of Nizhny Novgorod to highlight the Russian army's need for military drones. At this event he delivered a lecture in which he declared that "the real Europeans are the ones who support the SMO, because they are the ones who insist on their birthright," whereas those who opposed the war displayed a "colonial logic. This, of course, has nothing to do with this spirit of Europe."[8] Chadaev later delivered another talk titled "The Drone as an Instrument of Practical Philosophy."[9]

In a third lecture, Chadaev discussed theories of progress and the end of history. Ancient people, he claimed, had no conception of past and present and instead oriented their lives around natural cycles, such as those of the sun and the moon. As humanity's connections to nature faded, this ceased to be the case. The arrival of monotheism then brought with it the idea of a higher being directing history, and with that arose "a different type of time, a linear one, with a beginning and at some point an end." In due course people added to this the idea that the future would be better than the past—in other words, the idea of progress. But, said Chadaev, "what happened in the first half of the twentieth century was a terrible blow to progressive optimism." The modernist project of perfecting human society was abandoned. Instead, says Chadaev, the West embarked on an effort to save the planet from ecological doom by cutting the population. The tools for this included urbanization, digitization, "feminization and female emancipation, including the right to abortion . . . in order to reduce births to a minimum one must first of all remove the figure of the father," LGBTQ+ rights, the struggle against climate change, controlling people's bodies via "biopower" including "covid biofascism," "colored revolutions" designed to destroy national sovereignty and transfer states' powers to international institutions, and so on. "Putting this into one general thesis," declares Chadaev, "in order that humanity and the planet can survive, it is necessary that people stop being people in the sense we are used to. The end of history is above all the end of the history of the species Homo Sapiens, with its gradual replacement by something new, what one might call 'post-human.'"[10] In resisting the West, says Chadaev, Russia "is trying to defend the right of people to remain people, men—men, women—women, God the Father—God the Father, the state—the state, and history—history. . . . Their [the West's] project has a global character, and we also must stand at the center of a global response to a question posed not so much by our enemies as by History itself."[11]

The exact details of Chadaev's thesis are less important than the general sentiment—namely, that the West has altered the terms of the end of history into something that Russians thoroughly dislike and must therefore resist. This is a commonly held point of view. Chadaev's talk of a global challenge also directs our attention to yet another reason for the changing Russian perspective—international politics. Civilizational theory is much more concerned with international affairs than domestic ones, and its rising influence owes a great deal to growing Russian discontent with the West. Over the past twenty-five years, a whole series of events have contributed to this—NATO enlargement, the bombings of Yugoslavia and Libya, the invasion of Iraq, Western support for the 2014 Maidan revolution in Ukraine, Western sanctions, and so on. Journalist Dmitry Sokolov-Mitrich (b. 1975) explained how these events undermined many Russians' belief in the West as the center of civilization:

> Our first journalistic articles always mentioned the "civilized world" and we firmly believed that it was really civilized. . . . The first serious blow to our pro-Western orientation in life was Kosovo. It was a shock; our rose-colored glasses were shattered into pieces. . . . Worldviews turned 180 degrees. . . . Second Iraq, Afghanistan, the final separation of Kosovo, "Arab Spring," Libya, Syria—all of this was surprising, but no longer earth-shattering. Illusions were lost; it was more or less clear to us what the West was about. . . . EuroMaidan and the subsequent fierce civil war [in Ukraine from 2014 onward] made it clear. . . . We see the blood and war crimes, the bodies of women and children, an entire country sliding back into the 1940s, and the Western world, which we loved so much, assures us that none of this is happening. . . . It was a shock stronger than Kosovo. For me and many thousands of middle-aged Russians, who came into the world with the American dream in our heads, the myth of the "civilized world" collapsed completely.[12]

With Westernism discredited, Russians needed an alternative ideology with which to make sense of the world. The fact that they settled on civilizational theory rather than anything else perhaps owes something to the discipline of culturology.

The late Soviet Union was a more intellectually diverse place than one might imagine. The limits of acceptable discourse were ill-defined, and occasionally somebody would wander over a red line and get slapped down hard. But as long as people avoided criticizing the Communist Party or party policy, there was some scope for them to push the boundaries of debate a little further outward. Among other things, this allowed the so-called culturologists to begin to ever so slightly challenge the official Soviet dogma of dialectical materialism.

As the name suggests, culturology is the study of cultures. It emerged as a field of study in Soviet academia in the 1960s and 1970s and challenged Marxist ideas that culture was strictly a product of the mode of economic production that by itself had no impact on social development. Culturology embraces all areas of the humanities and social sciences—philosophy, political science, linguistics, history, and so on—and aims to illustrate the impact that culture has on each of them. Beyond that, culturology seeks to unify these other academic disciplines into what has been called a "meta-science." The French scholar Marlene Laruelle remarked that culturology sees itself "as a new philosophy of history, a future 'organic, complete body of knowledge,'" using culture as the lens through which society as a whole is viewed.[13] According to its critics, therefore, culturology involves the replacement of one all-embracing mode of thought—Marxism—with another, simply substituting culture for the mode of production as the primary factor explaining human history.

Inherent in culturology is the idea that there is a multiplicity of different cultures. As Mikhail Epstein, one of the leading experts on late Soviet philosophy, comments, "Culturology, as a meta-discipline within the humanities, investigates the diversity of cultures and their modes of interaction. . . . In culturology, 'culture' is treated as a descriptive rather than a normative concept, the term itself being used both in the singular and in the plural. *Culture* as an integrity of disciplinary spheres presupposes the diversity of *cultures* as national and historical types, each with its own formative principle, irreducible to others."[14]

One of the most important influences on culturology was the literary critic and theorist Mikhail Bakhtin (1895–1975). Bakhtin argued that true understanding could only ever arise by standing in some way outside of oneself and seeing things from the perspective of others. Bakhtin thus stressed the importance of dialogue. Individual cultures could be understood only by means of dialogue with other cultures. He criticized Spengler for regarding civilizations as closed cultural systems, claiming instead that cultures were in constant dialogue with one another. "Such a dialogic encounter of two cultures does not result in merging or mixing. Each retains its own unity and open totality, but they are mutually enriched," he wrote.[15]

The intellectual historian Vladimir Bibler (1918–2000) built on this dialogical principle, saying that culture required "at minimum two cultures." He wrote that "the twentieth century demonstrated the need for communication . . . of unique, irreducible, but mutually dialogic cultures, each of which is universal and infinitely rich with potential meanings."[16] Yet another important culturologist was the medieval historian Sergei Averintsev (1937–2004), who wrote of the problematic nature of evaluating other cultures based on the assumptions of one's own. He also stressed the importance of religion in shaping world cultures, drawing on differences between Catholicism and Orthodoxy to explain cultural differences between the Soviet Union and the West.[17] Averintsev explained late Soviet realities by reference not to economics, as Marxist doctrine would dictate, but rather to ancient Byzantine history. As the poet Viktor Krivulin (1944–2001) noted, in Averintsev's lectures "the issues of medieval theological debates, the enigmas of Byzantine aesthetics . . . revealed, to numerous listeners, new modes of understanding Soviet daily life. To many, medieval Byzantium began to seem closer than contemporary Europe or America."[18]

Culturology has come to play a central role in post-Soviet Russian education. Soviet schools and universities forced students to take courses on dialectical materialism. After the collapse of the Soviet Union, the courses were abolished. In their place, the Russian government introduced courses in culturology, which from the mid-1990s became compulsory in all primary and secondary Russian schools as well as many universities. Universities have also established entire undergraduate and graduate degree programs in culturology.[19]

The Russian state has encouraged the culturological trend in other ways. In 2010, for instance, the Ministry of Education issued national standards for historical education that listed among their essential skills "mastery of . . . [the use] of the cultural approach in the analysis of social events and global processes" and "developing significant cultural and historical perspectives for understanding . . . the historical legacy of Russia and the world."[20] Guidelines for high school history curricula stress "historical knowledge of cultural, religious, and ethno-national traditions, moral values and social structures, [and] ideological doctrines."[21] In the Soviet era, social structures would have been considered most important. Now they come some way down the list. Culture takes priority.

Culturology and civilizational theory are not identical, for while some civilizational theorists conflate civilizations with cultures, not all do so. Nevertheless, given its emphasis on the existence of a multiplicity of diverse national cultures around the world, culturology lends itself well to civilizational thinking. Courses in culturology could be seen as a well-meaning effort to introduce students to other cultures and to create a degree of understanding of other peoples. In practice, the emphasis on cultural differences easily turns into an emphasis on the specific difference of Russia, and with that on Russia's identity as a unique civilization.

In a study of Russian culturology textbooks from the early 2000s, Marlene Laruelle concluded that

> culturology thinks about the world in terms of civilizations. It insists on the relevance of this perspective and repeatedly draws its inspiration from the work of Spengler and Toynbee.... Huntington ... is also granted favorable treatment.... Although the textbooks' authors do not necessarily share Huntington's vision of world development as one of conflict, all of them identify with the idea that the post cold war world can be explained only in terms of the "civilizationist" map: the western or "Atlanticist" cultural region as against the "Slav-Orthodox" space, while the "Muslim world" will have to choose between an alliance with the West or Russia"[22]

Laruelle notes that "in all the textbooks Russia is portrayed as a world apart."[23] "The subject of culturology," she remarks, "does not hide its conservative tendencies, which often run alongside rejection of the West.... This rejection of the West is not seen as a political choice but as an almost biological necessity because the 20th century is thought to have proved that 'transplanting, mechanically borrowing cultural elements cannot have positive results.'"[24]

For the past thirty years, therefore, culturology has arguably been creating a new generation of Russians that is receptive to civilizational theory, by teaching Russian youth that the world is divided into distinct cultures, that Russian culture is different from that of the West, and that the introduction of Western values and institutions into Russia can only have negative results. Various politicians have been spreading the same message since at least the early 1990s. The most important of these is the Communist Party leader Gennady Zyuganov.

In 1996, Zyuganov won over 40 percent of the vote in the Russian presidential election, losing to Boris Yeltsin (1931–2007). Since then, the CPRF's share of the vote has declined significantly. Nevertheless, it remains the largest opposition party in the Russian Federation. Western commentators have tended not to regard the CPRF or Zyuganov very seriously and since the mid-1990s have paid them little attention. The general feeling is that they are a fake opposition, tolerated by the Kremlin because they do not seriously challenge the existing system. This neglect of Zyuganov and the Communists is a mistake. In some respects, Zyuganov can be seen as an ideological trailblazer, who from the early 1990s onward was propagating political ideas that were at the time considered somewhat outrageous but that nowadays have become part of the mainstream and have even been adopted by President Putin. While Zyuganov has been in permanent opposition, he has helped set the agenda of Russian political ideology. In a way, he is the Nigel Farage of Russian politics—a man who has never won power, but whose dogged persistence has gradually shifted social attitudes in his direction until eventually his ideas have triumphed even while he remains on the political sidelines.

Zyuganov's father was a village teacher who lost a leg in the battle for Sevastopol during the Second World War. Zyuganov initially followed his father's path by becoming a village teacher, but in the late 1960s he joined the Communist Party and became a full-time party worker. In this capacity, he devoted himself to issues of ideology and propaganda, in due course acquiring a doctorate in philosophy and becoming one of the heads of the Communist Party Central Committee's propaganda department.[25] In the final months of the Soviet Union, he became a prominent member of the conservative wing of the party that opposed Mikhail Gorbachev's reforms. Following the collapse of the Soviet Union, he then became leader of the CPRF.

As party leader, Zyuganov set about redefining communist ideology, combining a commitment to social justice with a fervent Russian nationalism, arguing that socialism was congruent with the character of Russian civilization in a way that capitalism was not. He wrote that he saw "Russia as a special world, a complete 'social cosmos' with specific historical, geopolitical, philosophical, national, and economic features in which the general laws of social development are refracted in a unique way.... The main reason for our sociopolitical ailment is the attempt at capitalist restoration, which has undermined the material and spiritual foundations of our society and state and is making the vast differences between Western civilization and Russian civilization ever more apparent. Capitalism is inconsistent with the flesh and blood, with the being, with the habits, and with the psychological makeup of our society."[26]

Zyuganov defines a civilization as "a stable supragovernmental entity, characterized by a very high degree of political, economic, and social integration, that is embodied in a type of mode of production that is progressive at the given historical period, and in the character of social-political relations, in its organically integral cultural milieu."[27] He writes that "when analyzing our theory of civilizations, we should remember the earlier studies of Nikolai Danilevsky and Konstantin Leontyev," while also urging readers to examine foreign authors, most notably Spengler and Toynbee.[28] "We should give attentive consideration to the key postulates of Arnold Toynbee's theory of the historical development of humankind," he writes.²⁹ The Eurasianists provide another source of influence. According to Zyuganov, "Gumilyov's theory of 'passionarity' is a seminal contribution to the theory of ethnogenesis, the genesis of civilizations on the territories of Russia."³⁰ "Since ancient times," he claims, "civilizations have been developed, preserved, and moved along by ethnoses—nations and peoples, as well as their broader groupings. The interactions of these powerful influences determine world politics and culture at any given historical moment. It is clear that history moves in a cyclical, spiral manner. Great minds from Ecclesiastes and Heraclitus, Vico and Leibniz, Hegel and Marx to Lenin, Toynbee, and Kondratyev have identified many such historical cycles."³¹

According to Zyuganov, the collapse of the Soviet Union represented a turning point in the cycle of Russian history—namely, the end of Soviet civilization. Soviet civilization, claims Zyuganov, "differed from those researched by Spengler and Toynbee," because it was the first to embody the principle "He who does not work, does not eat," and the first to give power to the working majority and to enshrine social, sexual, and national equality. The collapse of Soviet civilization led in the 1990s to "anti-civilization," as a result of which "the question of a civilizational alternative to the current era of decay and collapse is more important than ever."³²

To Zyuganov, Soviet civilization and Russian civilization are strongly related, both embodying similar principles. The post-Soviet attempt to rebuild Russia on the basis of Western models was bound to fail, because Western and Russian civilizations are fundamentally different. Citing cosmist and Eurasianist thinkers such as Vernadsky, Savitsky, Trubetskoi, and Gumilyov, Zyuganov argued in the mid-1990s that "modern Western civilization is based on an atomist-mechanical picture of the world. . . . In Russia, such a complete atomization has not taken place. . . . The individual continues to feel part of a collective structure of one type or another. . . . The most important spiritual category for Eurasians is the people [the nation], which is rejected by our Westernizers."³³ He concluded, "Experience, common sense, scientific analysis, and cultural tradition confirm that: from a historical point of view, Russia is a unique civilization . . . geopolitically, Russia is the core and mainstay of the Eurasian continental bloc, whose interests oppose the hegemonic tendencies of the 'oceanic power' of the United States . . . [and] in ideology and worldview, Russia represents the cultural-historical and moral traditions and fundamental values of communality, collectivism, great-power sovereignty (state self-sufficiency), and the aspirations to embody the highest ideas of good and justice."³⁴ Addressing Americans, he wrote, "During centuries of their existence, the peoples of Russia have created their special world—the world of Russian civilization. . . . You [Americans] have gone your own way, relying on your own religions and your own national ideas and values. . . . Let Russia be Russia and let America be America. Ours is a big and diverse world. We should not try to destroy and level this diversity; rather, we should ensure, through tolerance and compromise, that diverse and unique civilizations coexist peacefully with each other."[35]

After the CPRF, the next largest opposition party in the Russian Federation is the LDPR, which until his recent death was led by the firebrand nationalist politician Vladimir Zhirinovsky. Due to his habit of making provocative statements, Zhirinovsky has often been viewed as a clown rather than as a serious politician, but his high-profile role as leader of the LDPR for thirty years means that his pronouncements require detailed analysis. Among other things, Zhirinovsky was a civilizational theorist in his own right, writing several books about different global civilizations. In addition, in 1999 he founded the Institute of Global Civilizations, which nowadays offers a number of undergraduate and graduate degree programs and which in 2022 was renamed the V. V. Zhirinovsky University of Global Civilizations.

In a 2017 book titled *Zhirinovsky as Philosopher*, the rector of the Institute of Global Civilizations, Oleg Slobotchikov, described Zhirinovsky as "a contemporary representative of Russian Cosmism," whose thinking rested on the writings of the likes of Solovyov, Fyodorov, Vernadsky, Tsiolkovsky, and Chizhevsky. Apart from cosmism, the other guiding principle of Zhirinovsky's thought, according to Slobotchikov, was his "civilizational approach to history."[36] Zhirinovsky wrote that "civilization is a living reality. Various civilizations exist and have been developing for more than a thousand years. They have a complex dynamic nature that resists simple definition. Each civilization has its own force field, which either attracts or repels specific ethnic and other communities. It [civilization] is a kind of 'oil paint' that allows one more realistically and accurately to represent the ethno-geopolitical map of the world."[37] In an article for the journal of the Institute of Global Civilizations, the LDPR leader acknowledged the difficulty of defining civilizations but, referring to Toynbee, argued that if one defined them in terms of religion, the modern world contained six civilizations: the "Western-Christian," "Eastern-Christian," "Eastern-Islamic," "Eastern-Buddhist," "pagan," and "hidden," the last of which consisted of civilizations existing within the confines of other civilizations (Jewish people being the main example, according to Zhirinovsky).[38]

According to Zhirinovsky, "The strategic task of Western-Christian civilization is the introduction of the 'new world order.'" By contrast, "For Eastern-Christian Orthodox civilization it is self-preservation of the ethnos, potential aggressiveness arises only as an instinct of self-preservation."[39] The difference, therefore, was that the West was "actively aggressive," whereas Russia was normally passive but reacted aggressively when it felt under threat. Zhirinovsky suggested three scenarios for future intercivilizational relations. The first involved "the dissolution of local civilizations into a unified global supersociety based on the Western model." The second was a Huntingtonian "clash of civilizations," something that Zhirinovsky argued had already been underway for several decades. And the third involved the "transformation of civilizations"—for instance, the breakup of Western civilization into separate North American, South American, and European civilizations.[40] Zhirinovsky considered the third scenario the most probable. China's power was rising, Eastern-Islamic civilization was experiencing a "burst of passionarity," and Eastern-Christian civilization was in a period of decay, with parts of it possibly transforming into a Eurasian civilization under Russian leadership. Although this was uncertain, the likely outcome was "the construction of a multipolar geopolitical world, in which each civilization becomes a reasonably independent and powerful center of geopolitical power."[41] To avoid conflict during a period of change, a "continual and active dialogue" of civilizations was necessary. Zhirinovsky concluded, "The West itself sees that the twenty year experience of a unipolar model of world order has been unsuccessful. But a pluralistic model of a multipolar order has not yet been created. While striving for such a model, we must look for different variants of intercivilizational interaction, of transforming civilizations for the support and development of the contemporary world order."[42]

A 2017 study of Russian political rhetoric revealed an interesting fact. Putin's rhetoric, as well as that of the ruling, pro-Putin United Russia party, trailed behind that of the CPRF and LDPR. Putin and United Russia moved in the direction of the CPRF and LDPR, and not vice versa. In short, things that Zyuganov and Zhirinovsky said in due course found their way into Putin's speeches also.[43]

This finding is somewhat counterintuitive for those used to imagining Russia as an entirely top-down political system in which all ideas emanate outward from the Kremlin into Russian society rather than from Russian society into the Kremlin. There are a couple of explanations, neither of which is exclusive of the other. The first is that changes in the international situation forced Russia's rulers to change their positions in such a way as to bring them closer to their political rivals. The second is that Russian political leaders are quite responsive to public opinion and are adept at reading the political tea leaves and shifting their rhetoric to respond to popular attitudes.

Putin's success as a politician may be seen as being in part a product of his ability to defang his opponents by co-opting their positions as his own. In this sense, he is a follower rather than an initiator of ideological change.

This becomes clear when one examines civilizational discourse. Zyuganov and Zhirinovsky engaged in this discourse long before Putin, who initially adopted a very different position, but who over time has come to sound increasingly like them. We shall now examine how this change came about.

CHAPTER 8

The Triumph of Russian Civilizationism

The history of the past twenty years shows a decisive shift in official Russian rhetoric. In the early 2000s, the Russian government imagined its future as being part of a broader Europe stretching "from Lisbon to Vladivostok." In line with this, Putin emphasized Russia's nature as part of European civilization. As time went on, as it became clear that European integration was impossible, and as Russian-Western relations became increasingly conflictual, the tone of government statements changed. References to Russia's European character disappeared and were replaced with statements emphasizing that Russia was a unique civilization of its own. In addition, Putin and other officials increasingly complained that the West was seeking to impose its civilizational model on others and argued that the world was, and ought to be, multicivilizational in character.

The change in rhetoric was a gradual one, but by 2022 it was almost complete. Civilizational theory had in effect conquered the Kremlin. Faced by Western attempts to isolate Russia, Putin turned to civilizational discourse in an effort to shore up domestic support, to justify his resistance of the West, and to woo the developing world and persuade it not to join the West's anti-Russian campaign. In this way, ideology became an important battleground in the political struggle between Russia and the West.

Far from claiming that Russia was a distinct civilization, in the years of his first two presidencies (2000–2008) Putin consistently maintained that Russia was a European country. Speaking at a Russia–European Union summit meeting in May 2001, Putin declared that the basis of Russia's relations with the European Union was "common civilizational roots and ancient trading, economic, and cultural ties, and of course an enormous historical experience of cooperation."[1] In an interview with a Finnish newspaper in September 2001, Putin was even more forthright, declaring that "Russia is a European country, and consequently the European direction of our foreign policy will be a priority. After the Second World War and the emergence of blocs as a result of the Cold War, Russia suffered more than anybody else from the division of Europe. We have learnt this lesson well, and of course all our actions will be directed both now and in the future towards ensuring that there will be no such dividing lines again."[2] Likewise, Putin told an audience in Germany on September 26, 2001, that "from the time of Peter I, Russia has not only felt itself to be but in reality was part of the European continent in the broadest sense of the word. Firm foundations of European economics and culture were laid down in Russia. . . . Today, fundamental European values are an organic part of the Russian way of life."[3]

Such language continued throughout Putin's first two presidencies. Speaking in July 2005 at the unveiling of a plaque in honor of Immanuel Kant, Putin remarked that "we are, and must feel ourselves to be, successors to the great European traditions. We will build our relations with European and other countries of the world precisely on this basis."[4] And in a press release for another Russia-EU summit in October 2007, he declared that "Russia is a country with deep European roots and traditions. Over centuries it has made an invaluable contribution to the development of European spirituality, culture, and simply to the development of civilization. And we quite naturally recognize our responsibility for preserving wellbeing and stability in the common 'European home.'"[5]

What one might call the early Putin was far from being an advocate of civilizational theory. That said, from the very start one can observe some trends of thought that in due course would develop in that direction. As early as December 31, 1999, when he was still only acting president following the resignation of Russia's first post-Soviet leader, Boris Yeltsin, Putin declared that "Moscow will strive to create a multipolar world."[6] It is noticeable that most of Putin's declarations that Russia was a European country came on occasions when he was addressing a European audience. Speaking to representatives of other countries, he tended to focus on a different theme—namely, the necessity of organic national development and consequently the error of trying to impose Western models on others. For instance, at a May 2005 press conference with the Egyptian president, Hosni Mubarak, Putin commented that "the institutions and principles of democracy cannot be effectively instilled in this or that territory without taking into account national traditions and history."[7] And in a February 2007 interview with the Qatari media organization Al-Jazeera, he remarked that "I would like to say that after the fall of the Berlin wall we many times, often and in detail, said that we should create a Europe without dividing lines. . . . I do not understand why several of our partners are returning to a situation in which they consider themselves more intelligent, more civilized, and consider that they have the right to impose their standards on others. . . . If standards are imposed from outside, and not a product of natural development from within society itself, it can only end in tragedy. . . . We will strive to create a multipolar world."[8]

In due course, Putin took this message to Western audiences as well, the most famous example being his speech to the Munich security conference in February 2007. In this he said, "What is a unipolar world? However you color it, in the end in practice it means only one thing: one center of power, one center of strength, all decisions made by one center. This is a world of one master, one sovereign. . . . This, of course, has nothing in common with democracy."[9] And in an interview with *Time* magazine in December 2007, Putin said,

> Why do think that you have the right to interfere in our affairs? As far as I am concerned, this is the basic problem in our relationship. Over the past few years people tell us: we are waiting for you, we want to receive you into our family, into our civilized Western family. But, first, why have you decided that your civilization is the best? There are far older civilizations than the American one. And second, people quietly let us know, whisper in our ears: "We are willing to receive you, but you must bear in mind that we are a patriarchal family, and we are the senior ones, and you must obey us." You can't have relationships like that in the modern world.[10]

It was at this time, at the end of Putin's second presidency, that civilizational language first began to creep into Russian official discourse. An example was an article by Foreign Minister Sergei Lavrov (b. 1950) that appeared in *Russia in Global Affairs* in 2008. In this Lavrov declared, "As regards the content of the new stage in humankind's development, there are two basic approaches to it among countries. The first one holds that the world must gradually become a

Greater West through the adoption of Western values. It is a kind of 'the end of history.' The other approach—advocated by Russia—holds that competition is becoming truly global and acquiring a civilizational dimension; that is, the subject of competition now includes values and development models."[11]

This was the first time that a senior Russian official had endorsed the civilizational vision of the world. This vision then found its way into the Foreign Policy Concept of the Russian Federation that was published by the Russian government later in 2008, by which time Dmitry Medvedev (b. 1965) had taken over from Putin as Russian president. The Foreign Policy Concept declared that "for the first time in contemporary history global competition is acquiring a civilizational dimension which suggests a competition between different value systems and development models within the framework of universal democratic and market economy principles. As the constraints of the bipolar confrontation are being overcome, the cultural and civilizational diversity of the modern world is increasingly in evidence."[12] The concept stated that the Russian Federation would aim to "promote and propagate, in foreign States, the Russian language and Russian people's culture constituting a unique contribution to cultural and civilizational diversity of the contemporary world and to the development of an intercivilizational partnership."[13]

While this document painted a Huntingtonian picture of the world being increasingly divided up into competing civilizations, it did not describe this development as either a positive or negative phenomenon, merely depicting it as a fact of life that needed regulating. Moreover, the addition of the words "within the framework of universal democratic and market economy principles" suggested a belief in such principles and as such constituted a recognition of the universal validity of key Western values. Neither Medvedev nor Lavrov nor the Foreign Policy Concept stated that Russia was a separate civilization from the West. Indeed, Medvedev said quite the opposite, telling the World Policy Conference in October 2008 that "historically, Russia is part of European civilization and for us, as Europeans, it matters a lot what values will shape the future world."[14] The Russian government at this time hoped that a way could be found to revise European institutions in such a way as to include Russia. To this end, Medvedev proposed a European Security Treaty that would create a new institutional order in Europe, including Russia and replacing NATO as the main guarantor of European security. The treaty found no support in the West and nothing came of it, but the proposal indicated that the Russian government still viewed its country's future as lying with Europe and not as a separate civilization.

Putin returned to the Russian presidency in 2012. His return gave a new impetus to civilizational discourse. In an article published in *Izvestiia* in January 2012, Putin wrote that "Russia can and must play a role predicated upon its civilization model, its great history, geography and its cultural 'genome' that organically combines the fundamental principles of European civilization and many centuries of cooperation with the East."[15] And in an article the same month for the newspaper *Nezavisimaia Gazeta*, Putin for the first time referred to Russia as a "unique civilization." This uniqueness derived from Russia's multiethnic, multiconfessional nature, which made Russia "a type of state civilization where there are no ethnicities, but where 'belonging' is determined by a common culture and shared values."[16] This definition of Russia as a "state civilization" has since become a preferred means of discourse. At the 2013 meeting of the Valdai Discussion Club, for instance, Putin stated that "a spontaneously constructed state and society does not work, and neither does mechanically copying other countries' experiences. Such primitive borrowing and attempts to civilize Russia from abroad were not accepted by an absolute majority of our people. . . . Russia—as philosopher Konstantin Leontyev vividly put it—has always evolved in 'flowering complexity' as a state civilization. . . . It is precisely the state civilization model that has shaped our state polity. It has always sought to flexibly accommodate the ethnic and religious specificity of particular territories, ensuring diversity in unity."[17] The use of the term "state civilization" was less radical than it might at first seem, as the stress was much more on the state than on the civilization. Russia, Putin was saying, was not the home of a single national people but a multiethnic country. What united it and made it a civilization was the state. Despite the civilizational language, this was thoroughly in line with the traditional orientation of Russia's rulers, who have generally stressed loyalty to the state rather than loyalty to a given ethnic or religious group.

What was new about Putin's statements was the emphasis on culture, such as his mention of Russia's cultural "genome." This perhaps reflected his own growing cultural conservatism, resting in part on a belief that the Western world had abandoned traditional values and was attempting to make Russia follow suit. As Putin told the Valdai Club in September 2013,

> We can see how many of the Euro-Atlantic countries are actually rejecting their roots, including the Christian values that constitute the basis of Western civilization. They are denying moral principles and all traditional identities: national, cultural, religious and even sexual. They are implementing policies that equate large families with same-sex partnerships, belief in God with the belief in Satan. . . . At the same time, we see attempts to somehow revive a standardized model

of a unipolar world.... Such a unipolar, standardized world does not require sovereign states; it requires vassals. In a historical sense this amounts to a rejection of one's own identity, of the God-given diversity of the world.[18]

These concerns found expression in a document titled "Foundations of State Cultural Policy," published by the Russian Ministry of Culture in 2015. This spoke of the danger of the "devaluation of generally recognized values," called for "affirmation in the social consciousness of traditional family values," and declared Russia to be a "civilizationally self-contained country."[19] Since then, use of the term "self-contained civilization" (*samobytnaia tsivilizatsiia*) has become increasingly common, perhaps in reaction to Russia's increasing isolation from the West and the concomitant need to build a more self-reliant economy. Putin has also combined it with "state civilization" to describe Russia as a "self-contained state civilization." The term "unique civilization" is also sometimes used. In November 2018, for instance, Putin cited Danilevsky for the first time in one of his speeches and told the World Russian Peoples' Council,

> There is one thing I am certain about: the voice of Russia will resound with dignity and confidence in the future world. It is defined by both our tradition and internal spiritual culture, our identity and finally, by the history of our country as an authentic civilization, a unique one, but one which does not assertively and aggressively claim its exceptionalism. Because it is impossible to imagine the history of humanity without such unique civilizations as India, China, Western Europe, America, and many others. It is really a multifaceted complexity where each facet supplements and enriches the others. I would like to remind you of the words said by a prominent Russian thinker of the 19th century, Nikolai Danilevsky: no civilization can call itself supreme, the most developed one. Today the understanding of the complexity of civilizational development is the foundation for the multipolar world and for defending the principles of international law.[20]

Despite all this, Putin and other senior officials remained somewhat ambivalent about Russia's status as a unique, self-contained civilization, occasionally making comments that suggested quite the opposite. At a March 2013 meeting in Moscow with European Commission president Jose Manuel Barroso, for instance, Putin stated that "we have a common civilization and we share so many things in common in terms of our history and culture. When I am here in Moscow I feel like I could be in any other European city. I'm sure that you feel the same when you go to the capitals of the European Union. I think that this common civilizational matrix is indeed a very important driver for progressively building a relationship that is stronger every day."[21] And in April 2014, Putin told Russian television viewers that "Russia's particularities are not distinguishable in a cardinal, deep manner from European values. We are all people of one civilization. Yes, we are all different, we have our own particularities, but our deep values are identical."[22]

The ambivalence on this issue can be seen in an article by Sergei Lavrov published in *Russia in Global Affairs* in 2016. In this, Lavrov declared that "problems in the modern world can be solved effectively only through serious and fair cooperation between leading states. . . . Such cooperation should take into account the multivariate nature of the modern world, its cultural and civilizational diversity. . . . Long-term success can only be achieved if we move towards a partnership of civilizations based on respectful cooperation between different cultures and religions."[23] But in the same article, Lavrov described Russia as being "essentially one of the branches of European civilization."[24] For the most part, the article consisted of assertions that Russia was a European country that needed to be included within European security institutions, along with complaints that the West had refused to allow this. "All attempts to unite Europe without Russia and against it always led to big tragedies," Lavrov wrote, adding that "we continue to believe that the best way to ensure the interests of Europe is to form a common economic and humanitarian space from the Atlantic to the Pacific."[25] Despite the use of civilizational language, the article thus asserted a belief that Russia's future rightfully belonged in Europe.

Indeed, it is worth noting that even after the 2014 annexation of Crimea and the outbreak of war in Eastern Ukraine, the Russian state continued to hope that a way could be found to patch up relations with the West. In this atmosphere, anti-Western civilizational rhetoric was somewhat unwelcome, as shown by the fact that in 2014 Aleksandr Dugin was fired from his job teaching at Moscow State University and subsequently disappeared off mainstream TV screens. Boris Mezhuev's dismissal from *Izvestiia* in 2015 showed that Tsymbursky-style isolationism was equally out of sync with government policy.

Russian official rhetoric in the 2010s was often contradictory, sometimes asserting Russia's nature as a unique civilization and sometimes denying it. The Kremlin varied its language according to its audience. The contradictions in government discourse were also possibly a product of the need to satisfy different groups within the ruling system. Putin is often seen as a balancer, who has succeeded in maintaining his power by occupying a central position between different ideological factions. A need to satisfy both pro- and anti-Western elements within the state and wider Russian society may have helped cause the variations in civilizational discourse. Another reason for these variations may have been that the decade from 2012 onward was a transitional period in which the idea of Russia as a European civilization was gradually replaced by the idea of Russia as an independent one. Pro-European references were a residual leftover of a dying philosophy that faded with each passing year.[26] These explanations are not entirely exclusive. But at least until 2021, the idea of Russia as a unique civilization had not entirely supplanted the idea of Russia as European. Nevertheless, the concept that the world is made up of a multiplicity of civilizations had become well established. So had the idea that international security depended on recognition of civilizational diversity and on the rejection of the forcible imposition of Western models on other civilizations.

Following Russia's invasion of Ukraine in February 2022, civilizational discourse has achieved victory over the pro-European alternative, as evidenced by Putin's speech to the Valdai Club in October 2022. As mentioned in the introduction, in this speech Putin used the words "civilization" and "civilizational" fifteen times. He began by remarking, "The loss of biodiversity is one of the most dangerous consequences of disrupting the environmental balance. This brings me to the key point all of us have gathered here for. Is it not equally important to maintain cultural, social, political and civilizational diversity? At the same time, the smoothing out and erasure of all any differences is essentially what the modern West is all about. What stands behind this? First of all, it is the decaying creative potential of the West and a desire to restrain and block the free development of other civilizations."[27] He continued,

> I am convinced that real democracy in a multipolar world is primarily about the ability of any nation—I emphasize—any society or civilization to follow its own path and organize its own socio-political system.... I would like to cite the words of the great Russian philosopher Nikolai Danilevsky. He believed that progress did not consist of everyone going in the same direction, as some of our opponents seem to want. This would only result in progress coming to a halt, Danilevsky said. Progress lies in "walking the field that represents humanity's historical activity, walking in all directions," he said, adding that no civilization can take pride in being the height of development. I am convinced that dictatorship can only be countered through free development of countries and peoples; the degradation of the individual can be set

off by the love of a person as a creator; primitive simplification and prohibition can be replaced with a flowering complexity of culture and tradition.²⁸

With its repetition of the word "civilization," its citation of Danilevsky, and its nod in the direction of Leontyev ("primitive simplification" and "flourishing complexity"), Putin's speech represented a full-blown acceptance of the essential tenets of civilizational theory. Shortly after, these found official expression in the form of the latest version of the Foreign Policy Concept of the Russian Federation, published in early 2023.

According to the Russian academic Mikhail Suslov, the government official responsible for the ideological framing of the 2023 Foreign Policy Concept was Aleksei Dobrynin (b. 1974), director of the department of external political planning in the Russian Ministry of Foreign Affairs.²⁹ Little is known about Dobrynin, but he made his views known in an article in *Russia in Global Affairs* in spring 2023, shortly after the publication of the Foreign Policy Concept. The article was probably the most forthright exposition of civilizational theory ever produced by a Russian official. In his article, Dobrynin cited Danilevsky and Tsymbursky, using vocabulary (such as "civilizational platforms") that was clearly derived from the latter. He wrote,

> Strictly speaking, the civilizational approach is just one of the possible ways of describing the world. However, in the current critical phase, it provides the most reliable "point of view" for an adequate interpretation of the processes transforming the world order. . . . The crystallization of civilizations [we call them civilizational platforms] each with its own unique structure, as well as the development of links between them, is laying the path for the formation of an entirely new system. This is replacing the old paradigm, characterized by the domination of one civilization and its expansion under the slogans of globalization, Westernization, Americanization, universalization, liberalization, and the eradication of national borders. . . . And thus, the world is moving from globalization towards the formation of a multiplicity of civilizational platforms [one may also call them centers of strength or "poles"].³⁰

Dobrynin noted that, "before our eyes, the West is losing its five-hundred year old dominance. . . . The rules of the game are changing."³¹ The West, or rather the "Anglo-Saxons," were, however, resisting this process. According to Dobrynin, "The Anglo-Saxons, or more precisely their ruling elites, are banking on the forcible restoration of the 'unipolar moment' of the early 1990s. To this end, they are seeking to dismember civilizational communities into easily swallowed segments, according to the principle of divide and rule."[32] There was thus a growing ideological conflict between supporters of a unipolar world and supporters of civilizational diversity.

These ideas found their reflection in the 2023 Foreign Policy Concept, which singled out the "Anglo-Saxon states" for their "unfriendly course toward Russia." The concept declared that "more than a thousand years of independent statehood . . . determines Russia's special position as a unique country-civilization." Russia, said the concept, "is striving towards a system of international relations that would guarantee reliable security, preservation of its cultural and civilizational identity, and equal opportunities for the development of all states. . . . In order to meet these criteria, the system of international relations should be multipolar and based on the following principles: sovereign equality of states, respect for their right to choose models of development . . . diversity of cultures, civilizations and models of social organization, non-imposition on other countries by all states of their models of development, ideology and values."[33]

Putin commented on the Foreign Policy Concept in his Valdai speech of October 2023. He noted that

> in Russia's Foreign Policy Concept, approved this year, our country is characterized as a self-contained state civilization. This formulation precisely and fully reflects our understanding not only of our own development but also of the basic principles of the international order. . . . The essential qualities of a state-civilization are diversity and self-sufficiency. . . . Every state and society wants to independently work out its own path of development on the basis of its own culture and traditions. . . . I am convinced that humanity is moving . . . not towards the soulless universalism of the new globalization but, on the contrary, towards a synergy of state-civilizations, big spaces, and communities that recognize themselves as such.[34]

Unfortunately, he concluded, the West refused to recognize this dynamic and instead was determined "to push through its own interests here and now at any price."[35] This was the root of the world's problems.

Almost simultaneous with the Foreign Policy Concept, civilizationism also became a formal part of state educational policy. In September 2023, the Russian Ministry of Education issued guidelines for a new university course titled "Foundations of Russian Statehood." A kind of civics course for undergraduates, the course seeks to instill in students "an awareness of belonging to Russian society, the development of a sense of patriotism and citizenship, the creation of a spiritual, moral and cultural foundation of a developed and integral personality, awareness of the features of the historical path of the Russian state, the identity of its political organization and the pairing of individual dignity and personal success with social progress and political stability." To this end, the course is divided into five sections, including "Russia as a State-Civilization" and "Russian Worldview and Values of Russian Civilization." Learning objectives include "to present the history of Russia in its continuous civilizational dimension," "to consider fundamental achievements, inventions, discoveries and achievements related to . . . Russian civilization," "to investigate the most probable external and internal challenges facing the Russian civilization," and "to identify the fundamental value principles (constants) of Russian civilization . . . as well as related value orientations of Russian civilization."[36]

All this indicates how civilizational language has thoroughly infiltrated official discourse and become the lens through which Russians are encouraged to view the world. One should be careful about what this means. The Russian state has not endorsed Eurasianism, Island Russia, or any other specific variant of civilizational theory. Rather, what one observes is a vision that is reduced to its fundamental core, minus all the detailed ideological trappings that go along with the specific variants. This has the political advantage of being easily comprehensible while also not committing Moscow to policies that it might later find inconvenient.

It is impossible to determine whether Putin and other state officials believe their civilizational rhetoric or have resorted to it solely because it is politically convenient. Certainly, it is not something that Putin appeared to believe in twenty years ago. That said, much has changed in the past twenty years, and it is not unreasonable to imagine that Putin's thinking has evolved in the process. Civilizationism has deep roots in Russian society, and it is perhaps to be expected that at least some of those who work in the Russian government believe it, if not in full then at least in part. Arguably, though, it is not very important whether they believe what they are saying. What matters is that this is the ideological terrain on which they have chosen to plant their flag. Domestically, civilizationism helps promote the idea of Russian distinctiveness and through that helps boost patriotism and support for the state. It also justifies Russia's political battle against the West and on the international scene provides the Russian state with a powerful tool for persuading countries in the developing world not to join with the West against it.

One can observe this last point in a decree issued by Putin approving the new Foreign Policy Concept. In this, Putin declared that Russia was "a self-contained state civilization" and then pointed to Russia's status as the "legal successor of the Soviet Union," and as such a state with a "long role in the creation of the contemporary system of international relations and in the liquidation of the global system of colonialism."[37] Putin continued, "Humanity is passing through a period of revolutionary change. . . . It is impossible to return to the past, unequal model of global development, which for centuries guaranteed the rapid economic growth of the colonial powers by exploiting the resources of dependent territories in Asia, Africa, and the Western hemisphere." Power was shifting, said Putin, but "some states . . . refuse to recognize the reality of a multipolar world . . . and try to hold back the natural march of history."[38]

The desire to appeal to the developing world helps explain the heavy use Putin made of civilizational language in his 2022 and 2023 Valdai Club speeches. Until 2021, representatives of Western countries made up a large part of those invited to the club's annual meeting. In 2022 and 2023, the Westerners for the most part stayed away, meaning that Putin was speaking to an audience consisting largely of citizens of countries of other parts of the world. His calculation may well have been that a denunciation of Western hegemony couched in civilizational language and the right of different peoples to develop according to their own paths would go down well with people whose own countries had experience of Western colonialism. Indeed, in his 2023 speech, Putin made the connection between civilizationism and anticolonialism quite explicit. He said, "As we understand it, the concept of civilization is a multifaceted phenomenon. It can be interpreted in many ways. There was an openly colonial interpretation according to which there is a 'civilized world' which serves as a model for everyone else, and everyone must conform to its standards, and anyone who disagrees is forced into 'civilization' by means of the master's cudgel. These times, as I have already said, are past, and our understanding of civilization is completely different."[39]

Since the start of the war in Ukraine, Putin has repeatedly played the anticolonial card to paint Russia as the ally of the developing world against the former colonial powers. In March 2023, for instance, representatives of forty African parliaments attended a conference in Moscow titled "Russia-Africa in a Multipolar World." Putin told the African delegates that it was "common knowledge that the Soviet Union provided significant support to the peoples of Africa in their fight against colonialism, racism, and apartheid, how it helped many African countries to gain and protect their sovereignty, and consistently supported them in building their statehood, strengthening defence, laying the foundations of their national economies and workforce training."[40] On hearing these words, the delegates applauded.

Since the start of 2023, denunciations of neocolonialism have increasingly gone hand in hand with mentions of civilizations and a multipolar order.

In May 2023, for instance, Putin told an audience of international security officials that "we highly appreciate the fact that Russia has many partners in different regions and on different continents and [appreciate] the historically strong, friendly and trust-based ties with the countries of Asia, Africa and Latin America . . . I am sure that acting together we will build a more just multipolar world, and the exceptionalism-driven ideology as well as the neo-colonial system that made it possible to exploit the resources of the whole world will inevitably become a thing of the past."[41] And in June 2023, he told the St. Petersburg International Economic Forum that "the ugly and de-facto neo-colonial international system no longer works, while the multipolar world order is, on the contrary, becoming stronger. This is an inevitable process."[42]

The current conflict between Russia and the West is not ideological in origin. The Russian government's shift toward civilizational theory took place alongside growing tensions with the West and to a large degree in response to them. It did not precede those tensions, let alone cause them. Having said that, the conflict has taken on an ideological tinge, due to the different manner in which the two sides have chosen to frame it. Western leaders portray it as a struggle between autocracy and democracy. Russian leaders describe it as a struggle between those who believe in a world made up of diverse civilizations and those who believe that there is but one civilization, represented by the West, and as a struggle between those who believe that history marches in many directions and those who believe that it marches only in one.

Each of these framings appeals to a different constituency. The talk of autocracy versus democracy plays an important role in rallying support for the struggle against Russia in the West. It also helps bind Western states together, creating a common identity against the autocratic "other." It is therefore a framing that is primarily directed inward. The weakness of this framing is that it seems to have little appeal outside the West. By contrast, Russia is looking outward, seeking to generate support, or at least neutrality, among non-Western countries. So far, both framings seem to be successful in their chosen goals. The West has succeeded in solidifying domestic support for the actions it has taken against Russia and in support of Ukraine. Russia's message, meanwhile, seems to have been received reasonably well in large parts of the world. Outside of Europe, North America, Australasia, Japan, and South Korea, few states are declaring themselves Russia's supporters, but none are declaring themselves its enemy. Not even Mexico has levied sanctions against Russia.

Putin's talk of the "natural march of history" and an "inevitable process" points to confidence that the move toward a multipolar, multicivilizational world is unstoppable. Civilizational theory poses a genuine challenge to Western liberalism's claims to universalism, and with that to the West's desire to spread its values and institutions around the globe. At the end of the Cold War, some in the West imagined that great ideological battles were a thing of the past and that history had come to an end. Instead, a new ideological struggle is emerging, between civilizationism on the one hand and liberal universalism on the other. Russia's critics sometimes say that it exports nothing but oil and gas. But it also exports ideas, and with this it is able to win the hearts and minds of other nations. Since the end of the Cold War, the West has grown accustomed to thinking that it has a monopoly on soft power. That way of thinking may have to change.

Conclusion

Russian civilizationism draws on a wide variety of sources. These include both Russian thinkers, such as the Slavophiles, cosmists, and Eurasianists, and Western authors, such as Spengler, Toynbee, and Sorokin. Its policy proposals vary widely too, from the confrontational politics of Dugin at one extreme to the isolationism of Tsymbursky at the other. All of the varieties described in this book do, however, have some things in common. All take the view that Russia and the West are distinct entities, Western models are not universally valid, and consequently Russia, like other civilizations, has a right to develop in its own way. Over the past twenty years, these core precepts have become increasingly prevalent in Russian state discourse, to the extent that civilizationism now functions as an unofficial ideology. This ideology both cements loyalty to the Russian state and justifies Russia's geopolitical struggle against the West to non-Russian audiences.

It could be argued that this ideological turn is a temporary phenomenon and that Russian history has seen a succession of pro- and anti-Western waves of sentiment, none of which lasted very long before being replaced by their opposite. For instance, the universal hostility of Western Europe toward Russia during the Crimean War caused an intense anti-Western backlash among some Russians, as shown by Danilevsky's *Russia and Europe*. All the same, the reign of Alexander II following the Crimean War was an era of relative

Westernization. This then went into reverse under Alexander III, who in 1870, while still heir to the throne, had written with pleasure of Russia's intention to rebuild its Black Sea fleet (disbanded after the Crimean War), declaring, "The first step is taken, and all that remains is to beseech God to help us in this matter and save Russia from the Western yoke that eternally weighs down on us."[1] Yet under Alexander's son, Nicholas II, the anti-Western rhetoric again diminished. Similar swings of the pendulum back and forth can be observed during the Soviet era. One could view the current popularity of civilizational theory as just one more phase in Russia's on-again, off-again relationship with the West that will sooner or later be superseded by a new era of relative friendship.

This may be the case, but there are also grounds for thinking that we may be at a historical turning point at which Russia and the West go their separate ways, if not forever then at least for a very long time. The situation today is somewhat different from that in the past. First, despite occasional anti-Western rhetoric, the Russian state has never before quite so specifically identified Russia as a distinct civilization. Second, at the time of writing, it is somewhat difficult to imagine how the war in Ukraine could end in a manner that would mend Russian-Western relations. There seems to be a higher likelihood that an eventual ceasefire in Ukraine will be followed by many years, if not decades, of mutual suspicion, during which the West will continue to try to isolate Russia and contacts between the two parties will remain few. By the time the freeze in relations ends, the world may well be a very different place. The ongoing shift in economic power to the East may mean that the West will no longer be as powerful as it once was and may no longer be able to claim with quite so much assurance that it represents the end of history. Once the window to the West opens up again, Russians may not be as interested as before in what lies on the other side.

In any event, civilizationism is likely to remain an important part of the discourse of international politics for the simple reason that Russia is not alone in promoting it. Civilizational rhetoric has been spreading for some time. In 1998, for instance, the then–Iranian president Seyyed Mohammad Khatami called on the United Nations (UN) to lead a "dialogue among civilizations." In due course, this led to the UN declaring 2001 to be "the year of dialogue among civilizations" as well as to the creation of the UN Alliance of Civilizations in 2005. The initiative failed to make significant headway, however, due to the indifference of Western states.[2] Meanwhile, in recent years Chinese international relations theorists have been promoting their own version of civilizational theory, known as *Tianxia* (everything under the heaven). Leading *Tianxia* scholar Zhao Tinyang states that Kant's concept of perpetual peace cannot succeed because "Kantian peace requires all countries to have homogeneous systems and common values," and such systems and values do not currently exist.³ "In contrast," writes Zhao, "a concept of perpetual peace based on non-exclusion, rooted in the Chinese tradition of polytheism with an almost equal respect to every god, which tianxia embraced, is better suited to today's globalized world."⁴ Zhao adds that "if a new tianxia is to be possible, it quite obviously cannot mean the universalization of Chinese values. On the contrary, it should take in and take on any value that proves universally good, no matter where it originated, just as the concept of 'all under heaven' transcendentally implies."⁵

The Chinese government has lent its support to the concept of *Tianxia* as well as to civilizational theory more broadly. In 2023, Chinese president Xi Jinping declared the establishment of a "Global Civilization Initiative." According to a statement by the State Council Information Office of the People's Republic of China,

> The Global Civilization Initiative, proposed by Chinese President Xi Jinping, will inject fresh and strong energy into the common development and progress of human society.... In the history of humanity, over thousands of years, various civilizations have come into being, developed, and have in return promoted the overall development of human society. Diversity has been a prominent feature of civilizations.... People need to keep an open mind in appreciating how different civilizations perceive values, and refrain from imposing their own values or models on others, and from stoking ideological confrontation.... The diversity of civilizations is in nature a source of vitality and momentum in human development.... A single flower does not make spring, while one hundred flowers in full blossom bring spring to the garden. Together, we can make the garden of world civilizations full of colors and life.⁶

The last sentence reminds one of Konstantin Leontyev's phrase "flowering complexity." It fits also with the statement of Russian philosopher Ivan Ilyin (who has been much quoted by Putin) that "each people has its own, special mental makeup.... And this is good. This is beautiful. The grasses and the flowers in the field are diverse. The trees and the clouds are diverse. God's garden is rich and beautiful; it has abundant forms and glitters with colors and views."⁷ Modern Western states stress the need for diversity within societies. Civilizational theory challenges them to accept diversity between societies as well. However strange some of the ideas expressed in this book may seem to many readers, they are helping shape the world and thereby determine its future.

Notes

Introduction

1. Vladimir Putin, "Zasedanie mezhdunarodnogo diskussionogo kluba 'Valdai,'" Kremlin.ru, October 27, 2022, http://kremlin.ru/events/president/news/69695.
2. Vladimir Putin, "Zasedanie diskussionnogo kluba 'Valdai,'" Kremlin.ru, October 5, 2023, http://kremlin.ru/events/president/news/72444.
3. Constitution of the Russian Federation, art. XIII, http://archive.government.ru/eng/gov/base/54.html.
4. Kåre Johan Mjør, "Civilizationism in Russia from the Slavophiles to Vladimir Putin," in *Civilization: Global Histories of a Political Idea*, ed. Patricia Chiantera-Stutte and Giovanni Borgognone (Lanham: Lexington, 2022), 179–80.
5. For a detailed exposition of these points, see Nicholas Ross Smith, *A New Cold War? Assessing the Current US-Russia Relationship* (Cham: Springer International, 2020).
6. Robert A. Manning, "Does Biden's 'Democracy v. Autocracy' Framework Make Sense?," *Hill*, June 13, 2022, https://thehill.com/opinion/national-security/3521187-does-bidens-democracy-v-autocracy-framework-make-sense/.
7. German Lopez, "Putin vs. Democracy," *New York Times*, February 27, 2022, https://www.nytimes.com/2022/02/27/briefing/putin-democracy-ukraine.html.
8. Joe Biden, "Remarks by President Biden at the Summit for Democracy Opening Session," December 9, 2021, White House, https://www.whitehouse.gov/briefing-room/speeches-remarks/2021/12/09/remarks-by-president-biden-at-the-summit-for-democracy-opening-session/.
9. David A. Graham, "The Wrong Side of the 'Right Side of History,'" *Atlantic*, December 21, 2015, https://www.theatlantic.com/politics/archive/2015/12/obama-right-side-of-history/420462/.
10. "Russia's Pockets of Support Are Growing in the Developing World," Economist Intelligence Unit, March 7, 2023, https://www.eiu.com/n/russias-pockets-of-support-are-growing-in-the-developing-world/.
11. Oksana Drozdova and Paul Robinson, "In Others' Words: Quotations and Recontextualization in Putin's Speeches," *Russian Politics* 2, no. 2 (2017): 227–53.
12. Andrei Tsygankov, "In the Shadow of Nikolai Danilevskii: Universalism, Particularism, and Russian Geopolitical Theory," *Europe-Asia Studies* 69, no. 4 (2017): 585.

1. Two Concepts of History

1. Brett Bowden, *The Empire of Civilization: The Evolution of an Imperial Idea* (Chicago: Chicago University Press, 2009), 27, 31.
2. Bowden, *Empire of Civilization*, 32.

3. Giovanni Borgognone and Patricia Chiantera-Stutte, "Introduction: Assembling the Civilizational Jigsaw," in *Civilization: Global Histories of a Political Idea*, ed. Patricia Chiantera-Stutte and Giovanni Borgognone (Lanham: Lexington, 2022), 5.

4. Krishan Kumar, "The Return of Civilization—and of Arnold Toynbee," *Comparative Studies in Society and History* 56, no. 4 (2014): 821 (emphasis in the original).

5. Borgognone and Chiantera-Stutte, "Introduction," 6.

6. John Gray, *Black Mass: Apocalyptic Religion and the Death of Utopia* (Toronto: Doubleday Canada, 2007), 6.

7. Gray, *Black Mass*, 4.

8. Nicolas Berdyaev, *The Meaning of History* (London: Geoffrey Bles, 1945), 33.

9. Gray, *Black Mass*, 5.

10. W. Warren Wagar, "Definitions and Origins," in *The Idea of Progress since the Renaissance*, ed. W. Warren Wagar (New York: John Wiley, 1969), 19, 31.

11. Herbert Spencer, *Social Statics; or, The Conditions Essential to Human Happiness Specified, and the First of Them Developed* (New York: D. Appleton, 1883), 456–57.

12. Bowden, *Empire of Civilization*, 48.

13. Marquis de Condorcet, "Outline of an Historical Picture of the Human Mind," in Wagar, *Idea of Progress*, 77.

14. Bowden, *Empire of Civilization*, 55.

15. Immanuel Kant, "Idea for a Universal History with a Cosmopolitan Aim," in *Kant's Idea for a Universal History with a Cosmopolitan Aim: A Critical Guide*, ed. Amélie Rorty and James Schmidt (Cambridge: Cambridge University Press, 2009). 10 (emphasis in the original).

16. Kant, "Idea for a Universal History," 14.

17. Kant, "Idea for a Universal History," 20 (emphasis in the original).

18. Kant, "Idea for a Universal History," 21.

19. Immanuel Kant, *Kant's Perpetual Peace: A Philosophical Proposal* (London: Sweet and Maxwell, 1927), 26.

20. Kant, *Kant's Perpetual Peace*, 31.

21. Condorcet, "Outline," 77.

22. Condorcet, "Outline," 84.

23. Condorcet, "Outline," 84–86.

24. Auguste Comte, "The First System," in *Auguste Comte and Positivism: The Essential Writings*, ed. Gertrud Lenzer (London: Routledge, 2017), 71.

25. Comte, "First System," 72.

26. Comte, "First System," 73 (emphasis in the original).

27. Comte, "First System," 77.

28. Georg Wilhelm Friedrich Hegel, *Lectures on the Philosophy of World History* (Cambridge: Cambridge University Press, 1975), 93.

29. Jack Fox-Williams, "Hegel's Understanding of History," *Philosophy Now*, no. 140 (2020), https://philosophynow.org/issues/140/Hegels_Understanding_of_History.

30. Georg Wilhelm Friedrich Hegel, *The Philosophy of History* (New York: Cosimo, 2007), 40.

31. Adam Smith, *The Theory of Moral Sentiments* (Cambridge: Cambridge University Press, 2002), 373. Adam Smith, *Essays on Philosophical Subjects* (London: T. Cadell Jun. and W. Davies, 1795), 107.

32. Lukasz Hardt, *Economics without Laws: Towards a New Philosophy of Economics* (Cham: Palgrave Macmillan, 2017), 23.

33. Oscar Valdes Viera, "The Neoclassicals' Conundrum: If Adam Smith Is the Father of Economics, It Is a Bastard Child" (Levy Economics Institute Working Paper, no. 893, 2017).

34. Karl Marx, "A Contribution to the Critique of Political Economy," in Wagar, *Idea of Progress*, 100.

35. Marx, "Contribution," 100.

36. Marx, "Contribution," 101.

37. David Ekbladh, *The Great American Mission: Modernization and the Construction of an American World Order* (Princeton, NJ: Princeton University Press, 2015), 67.

38. Ekbladh, *Great American Mission*, 103, 112.

39. R. N. Gwynne, "Modernization Theory," in *International Encyclopedia of Human Geography*, ed. N. J. Thrift and Rob Kitchen (Amsterdam: Elsevier, 2009), 164–65; Nils Gilman, "Modernization Theory Never Dies," *History of Political Economy* 50 (2018): 141–42.

40. W. W. Rostow, *The United States in the World Arena: An Essay in Recent History* (New York: Harper & Brothers, 1960), xxi, 6.

41. Francis Fukuyama, "The End of History?," *National Interest* 16 (1989): 3.

42. Fukuyama, "End of History?," 4.

43. Fukuyama, "End of History?," 5.

44. Fukuyama, "End of History?," 8.

45. Fukuyama, "End of History?," 9.

46. Francis Fukuyama, *The End of History and the Last Man* (New York: Free Press, 1992), xiv.

47. Fukuyama, *End of History*, 48.

48. Niall Ferguson, *Civilization: The West and the Rest* (New York: Penguin, 2011), 5.

49. Ferguson, *Civilization*, 12.

50. Jeevan Vasagar, "Niall Ferguson: Admirable Historian or Imperial Mischief Maker?," *Guardian*, June 18, 2012, https://www.theguardian.com/books/2012/jun/18/niall-ferguson-bbc-reith-lecturer-radio4.

51. Ferguson, *Civilization*, 323.

52. Johann Gottfried Herder, *Another Philosophy of History and Selected Political Writings* (Indianapolis: Hackett, 2004), 46.

53. Herder, *Another Philosophy*, 26 (emphasis in the original).

54. Herder, *Another Philosophy*, 7 (emphasis in the original).

55. Herder, *Another Philosophy*, 30 (emphasis in the original).

56. Herder, *Another Philosophy*, 58–59, 62–64, 68 (emphasis in the original).

57. Johann Gottfried Herder, *On World History: An Anthology* (London: Routledge, 1997), 37.

58. Herder, *Another Philosophy*, 90–91 (emphasis in the original).

59. David Engels, "Oswald Spengler and the Decline of the West," in *Key Thinkers of the Radical Right: Behind the New Threat to Liberal Democracy*, ed. Mark Sedgwick (New York: Oxford University Press, 2019), 5

60. Oswald Spengler, *The Decline of the West* (New York: Alfred A. Knopf, 1939), 16–17.

61. Spengler, *Decline of the West*, 21 (emphasis in the original).
62. Spengler, *Decline of the West*, 24, 39.
63. Spengler, *Decline of the West*, 104, 107.
64. Spengler, *Decline of the West*, 106.
65. Spengler, *Decline of the West*, 167.
66. Marvin Perry, *Arnold Toynbee and the Western Tradition* (New York: Peter Lang, 1996), 16–19.
67. Patricia Chiantera-Stutte, "Challenges to the West: Civilizational Theory, Imperialism, and Liberal Internationalism," in Chiantera-Stutte and Borgognone, *Civilization*, 26.
68. Perry, *Arnold Toynbee*, 63.
69. Chiantera-Stutte, "Challenges to the West," 26–27.
70. Chiantera-Stutte, "Challenges to the West," 27.
71. Arnold J. Toynbee, *Civilization on Trial* (New York: Oxford University Press, 1948), 10.
72. Luca Castellin, "A Historian's Approach to Civilization: Arnold J. Toynbee and the Study of International Affairs in the Twentieth Century," in Chiantera-Stutte and Borgognone, *Civilization*, 61.
73. Arnold J. Toynbee and G. R. Urban, *Toynbee on Toynbee: A Conversation between Arnold J. Toynbee and G. R. Urban* (New York: Oxford University Press, 1974), 34–35.
74. Toynbee, *Civilization on Trial*, 222.
75. Toynbee, *Civilization on Trial*, 222–23.
76. Toynbee and Urban, *Toynbee on Toynbee*, 35.
77. Chiantera-Stutte, "Challenges to the West," 35.
78. Castellin, "Historian's Approach," 61.
79. Perry, *Arnold Toynbee*, 27.
80. Perry, *Arnold Toynbee*, 30. See also Kumar, "Return of Civilization," 831.
81. Toynbee, *Civilization on Trial*, 13.
82. Toynbee, *Civilization on Trial*, 90.
83. Pitirim Sorokin, *Social and Cultural Dynamics. Volume One. Fluctuations of Form and Art* (New York: Bedminster Press, 1962), ix.
84. Vladimir Alalykin-Izvekov, "Phenomenon of Civilization: Pitirim A. Sorokin's Integralist Approach and Its Limitations," *Biocosmology – Neo-Aristotelism* 4, no. 3 (2014): 323, 325–26.
85. Pitirim Sorokin, *Society, Culture, Personality: Their Structure and Dynamics* (New York: Harper, 1947), 639.
86. Sorokin, *Society, Culture, Personality*, 644.
87. Sorokin, *Society, Culture, Personality*, 702–3.
88. Sorokin, *Society, Culture, Personality*, 320.
89. Alalykin-Izvekov, "Phenomenon of Civilization," 319.
90. Pitirim Sorokin, *Modern Historical and Social Philosophies* (New York: Dover, 1963), 7.
91. Sorokin, *Modern Historical and Social Philosophies*, 8.
92. Sorokin, *Modern Historical and Social Philosophies*, 275. See also Pitirim Sorokin, *Sociological Theories of Today* (New York: Harper and Row, 1966), 378–83.
93. Alalykin-Izvekov, "Phenomenon of Civilization," 331.

94. Carroll Quigley, "General Crises in Civilizations" (paper presented at the 139th meeting of the American Association for the Advancement of Science, Washington, DC, December 29, 1972), http://www.carrollquigley.net/Lectures/General_Crises_in_Civilizations.htm. See also Carroll Quigley, *The Evolution of Civilizations* (New York: Macmillan, 1961), 27.

95. Quigley, "General Crises."

96. Quigley, *Evolution of Civilizations*, 70.

97. Quigley, "General Crises."

98. Quigley, "General Crises."

99. Daniel Rueda, "Alain de Benoist: Ethnopluralism and the Cultural Turn in Racism," *Patterns of Prejudice* 55, no. 3 (2021): 223.

100. Rueda, "Alain de Benoist," 223–24.

101. Rueda, "Alain de Benoist," 226.

102. Alain de Benoist, "Une Europe unifiée est nécessaire," Les Amis d'Alain de Benoist, August 20, 2020, https://www.alaindebenoist.com/2020/08/05/une-europe-unifiee-est-necessaire.

103. Alain de Benoist, *Europe: Tiers monde, même combat* (Paris: Robert Laffont, 1986), 17.

104. Giovanni Borgognone, "Governable Masses and Manageable Democracy: Samuel Huntington and the Origins of the Clash of Civilizations Theory," in Chiantera-Stutte and Borgognone, *Civilization*, 88.

105. Samuel P. Huntington, "The Clash of Civilizations?," *Foreign Affairs* 72, no. 3 (1993): 23.

106. Huntington, "Clash of Civilizations?," 23.

107. Huntington, "Clash of Civilizations?," 24.

108. Huntington, "Clash of Civilizations?," 29.

109. Huntington, "Clash of Civilizations?," 22.

110. Samuel Huntington, *The Clash of Civilizations and the Remaking of World Order* (New York: Touchstone, 1996), 20, 28.

111. Huntington, *Clash of Civilizations*, 53.

112. Huntington, *Clash of Civilizations*, 20–21.

113. Huntington, *Clash of Civilizations*, 310.

114. David Graeber and David Wengrow, *The Dawn of Everything: A New History of Humanity* (London: Allen Lane, 2022).

115. Gregorio Bettiza, "Empty Signifier in Practice: Interrogating the 'Civilizations' of the United Nations Alliance of Civilizations" (Robert Schuman Centre for Advanced Studies Research Paper No. RSCAS 2014/95, September 25, 2014), 18, https://papers.ssrn.com/sol3/papers.cfm?abstract_id=2501363.

116. Perry, *Arnold Toynbee*, 106. For a detailed description of the criticisms of Toynbee's work, see Ronald N. Stromberg, *Arnold J. Toynbee: Historian for an Age of Crisis* (Carbondale: Southern Illinois University Press, 1972), 39–76.

117. Alalykin-Izvekov, "Phenomenon of Civilization," 332.

118. Ferguson, *Civilization*, 198.

119. Vladimir Alalykin-Izvekov, "Civilizational Theory in Russia—Past, Present, and Future," *Biocosmology—Neo-Aristotelism* 4, no. 4 (2014): 454; Sergei V. Lavrov, "Russia's Foreign Policy in a Historical Perspective," *Russia in Global Affairs*, no. 2 (2016), https://eng.globalaffairs.ru/articles/russias-foreign-policy-in-a-historical-perspective/.

2. Russian Historical Determinism

1. N. Tourgueneff, *La Russie et les russes. Tome III. De l'avenir de la Russie* (Brussels: Meline, Cans et Compagnie, 1847), 3.

2. Nikolai Ivanovich Turgenev, "Ideas on the Organization of a Society," in *The Decembrist Movement*, by Marc Raeff (Englewood Cliffs, NJ: Prentice-Hall, 1966), 67.

3. "Sledstevennoe delo polkovnika Mit'kova," in *Vosstanie dekabristov*, vol III, ed. N. M. Chentsov (Moscow-Leningrad: Tsentrarkhiv, 1927), 192.

4. "Murav'ev-Apostol (Matvei). Otstavnoi podpolkovnik," in *Vosstanie dekabristov*, vol IX, ed. N. M. Chentsov (Moscow-Leningrad: Tsentrarkhiv, 1950), 216.

5. Paul Robinson, *Russian Conservatism* (DeKalb: Northern Illinois University Press, 2019), 43.

6. Lesley Chamberlain, *Ministry of Darkness: How Sergei Uvarov Created Conservative Modern Russia* (London: Bloomsbury, 2020).

7. Cynthia H. Whittaker, "The Ideology of Sergei Uvarov: An Interpretative Essay," *Russian Review* 37, no. 2 (1978): 159.

8. S. S. Uvarov, *Rech' prezidenta Imperatorskoi Akademii Nauk, popechitelia Sankt-Peterburgskogo uchebnogo okruga, v torzhestvennom sobranii Glavnogo pedagogicheskogo instituta, 22 marta 1818* (St Petersburg: Tipografiia departamenta narodnogo prosveshcheniia, 1818), 49.

9. Uvarov, *Rech'*, 51–53.

10. Whittaker, "Ideology of Sergei Uvarov," 163.

11. Robinson, *Russian Conservatism*, 49.

12. Vanessa Rampton, *Liberal Ideas in Tsarist Russia: From Catherine the Great to the Russian Revolution* (Cambridge: Cambridge University Press, 2020), 48.

13. Quoted in Andrzej Walicki, *The Flow of Ideas: Russian Thought from the Enlightenment to the Religious-Philosophical Renaissance* (Frankfurt: Peter Lang, 2015), 235.

14. Alexander Polunov, *Russia in the Nineteenth Century: Autocracy, Reform, and Social Change, 1814–1914* (Armonk: M. E. Sharpe, 2005), 59.

15. Randall A. Poole, "Religious Toleration, Freedom of Conscience, and Russian Liberalism," *Kritika: Explorations in Russian and Eurasian History* 13, no. 3 (2012): 621. See also A. V. Gorlov, "Dva 'vzgliada' russkogo liberala XIX veka: K.D. Kavelin o razvitii instituta sobstvennosti v Rossii," *Vestnik gosudarstvennogo i munitsipal'nogo upravleniia* 3 (2012): 39–49; R. A. Arslanov, "Istoriia rossiiskogo gosudarstva v kontseptsii K.D. Kavelina," Vestnik RUDN 1 (2007): 37–47.

16. K. D. Kavelin, "Vzgliad na iuridicheskii byt drevnei Rossii," in *Nash umstvennyi stroi: Stat'i po filosofii russkoi istorii i kul'tury* (Moscow: Pravda, 1989), 13.

17. Kavelin, "Vzgliad," 23.

18. Kavelin, "Vzgliad," 19 (emphasis in the original).

19. Kavelin, "Vzgliad," 22.

20. Kavelin, "Vzgliad," 48.

21. Kavelin, "Vzgliad," 65–66.

22. Kavelin, "Vzgliad," 66.

23. Kavelin, "Vzgliad," 66.

24. "Pis'mo K. D. Kavelina k T. N. Granovskomu," September 5, 1848, quoted in W. Bruce Lincoln, *In the Vanguard of Reform: Russia's Enlightened Bureaucrats, 1825–1861* (DeKalb: Northern Illinois University Press, 1982), 85.

25. Paul Milyukov, "The Influence of English Political Thought in Russia," *The Slavonic Review*, 5, no. 14 (1926): 270.
26. P. N. Miliukov, *Ocherki po istorii russkoi kul'tury*, 5th ed., vol. 1 (St Petersburg: Mir Bozhii, 1904), 272, quoted in Thomas Riha, *A Russian European: Paul Miliukov in Russian Politics* (Notre Dame, IN: University of Notre Dame Press, 1969), 32–33.
27. Paul Milyoukov, *Russia and Its Crisis* (London: Collier, 1962), 29.
28. Milyoukov, *Russia and Its Crisis*, 30, 34.
29. "Ot russkikh konstitutsionalistov," *Osvobozhdenie* no. 1 (1902): 12.
30. P. Miliukov, *God bor'by* (St Petersburg: Biblioteka Obshchestvennoi pol'zy, 1907), 22.
31. G. Plekhanov, *The Development of the Monist View of History* (Moscow: Foreign Languages Publishing House, 1956), 255–56.
32. Plekhanov, *Development of the Monist View*, 222.
33. Plekhanov, *Development of the Monist View*, 302.
34. Plekhanov, *Development of the Monist View*, 273–75.
35. Geoffrey Roberts, *Stalin's Library: A Dictator and His Books* (New Haven, CT: Yale University Press, 2022), 85–87.
36. Joseph Stalin, *Dialectical and Historical Materialism* (New York: International Publishers, 1940), 17, 19.
37. Stalin, *Dialectical and Historical Materialism*, 27, 30.
38. Stalin, *Dialectical and Historical Materialism*, 34.
39. Stalin, *Dialectical and Historical Materialism*, 37.
40. Stalin, *Dialectical and Historical Materialism*, 38.
41. Roger Kanet, "The Recent Soviet Assessment of Developments in the Third World," *Russian Review* 27, no. 1 (1968): 27–41.
42. James P. Scanlan, *Marxism in the USSR: A Critical Survey of Current Soviet Thought* (Ithaca, NY: Cornell University Press, 1985), 193.
43. Scanlan, *Marxism in the USSR*, 194–203.
44. Robert D. English, *Russia and the Idea of the West: Gorbachev, Intellectuals, and the End of the Cold War* (New York: Columbia University Press, 2000), 3–5.
45. Julia Sushytska and Alisa Slaughter, "Introduction," in *A Spy for an Unknown Country: Essays and Lectures by Merab Mamardashvili*, by Merab Mamardashvili (Stuttgart: Ibidem, 2020), 17.
46. Merab Mamardashvili, "The 'Third' State," in Mamardashvili, *Spy for an Unknown Country*, 165, 176.
47. Leonid Batkin, "Turn to Be Europe," *XX Century and Peace* 8 (1988): 31.
48. Batkin, "Turn to Be Europe," 32, 33.
49. "Nuzhna li zheleznaia ruka?," *Vremia i my* 107 (1989): 127.
50. "Nuzhna li zheleznaia ruka?," 125.
51. "Nuzhna li zheleznaia ruka?," 126.
52. Guillaume Sauvé, *Subir la victoire: Essor et chute de l'intelligentsia libérale en Russie (1987–1993)* (Montreal: Les Presses de l'Université de Montréal, 2019), 160.
53. Igor' Kliamkin, "Kakaia ulitsa vedet k khramu?" *Novyi mir* no. 11 (1987): 186.
54. Peter Reddaway and Dmitri Glinski, *The Tragedy of Russia's Reforms: Market Bolshevism against Democracy* (Washington, DC: United States Institute of Peace, 2000).
55. Joachim Zweynert, "Economic Ideas and Institutional Change: Evidence from the Soviet Economic Debates 1987–1991," *Europe-Asia Studies* 58, no. 2 (2006): 191–92.

56. Olga Malinova, "Encounters with Liberalism in Post-Soviet Russia," in *In Search of European Liberalisms: Concepts, Languages, Ideologies*, ed. Michael Freeden, Javier Fernandez-Sebastian, and Jörn Leonhard (New York: Berghahn, 2019), 284.

57. Yegor Gaidar, *Days of Defeat and Victory* (Seattle: University of Washington Press, 1996), 191.

58. Yegor Gaidar, *Russia: A Long View* (Cambridge, MA: MIT Press, 2012), xiv.

59. Egor Gaidar, "Novyi kurs," *Izvestiia*, February 10, 1994, quoted in Lynn D. Nelson and Irina Y. Kuzes, *Radical Reform in Yeltsin's Russia: Political, Economic, and Social Dimensions* (Armonk: M. E. Sharpe, 1995), 66.

60. Quoted in Hilary Appel, *A New Capitalist Order: Privatization and Ideology in Russia and Eastern Europe* (Pittsburgh: University of Pittsburgh Press, 2004), 167.

3. The Origins of Russian Civilizationism

1. Leonid Heretz, *Russia on the Eve of Modernity: Popular Religion and Traditional Culture under the Last Tsars* (Cambridge: Cambridge University Press, 2008), 105.

2. Heretz, *Russia on the Eve of Modernity*, 103.

3. Heretz, *Russia on the Eve of Modernity*, 53–54, 62.

4. Victor Shnirelman, "Russia as Katechon: 'Civilizationism' and Eschatological Discourse in Putin's Russia," *Russia Post*, July 1, 2022, https://www.russiapost.info/society/katechon.

5. Egor Kholmogorov, *Russkii proekt. Restavratsiia budushchego* (Moscow: Algoritm, 2005), 18–19, quoted in Maria Engström, "Contemporary Russian Messianism and the New Russian Foreign Policy," *Contemporary Security Policy* 35, no. 3 (2014): 367.

6. Petr Chaadaev, *Filosofskie pis'ma* (Kazan: Tipografiia D. M. Gran, 1906), 11.

7. Michael Hughes, "Independent Gentlemen: The Social Position of the Moscow Slavophiles and Its Impact on Their Political Thought," *Slavonic and East European Review* 71, no. 1 (1993): 72–73.

8. K. Aksakov, "Stat'i K. Aksakova iz 'Mol'vy,'" in *Rannye slavianofily: A. S. Khomiakov, I. V. Kireevskii, K. S. i A. S. Aksakovy*, ed. N. L. Brodskii (Moscow: Tipografiia T-va I. D. Sytina, 1910), 111–12.

9. Susanna Rabow-Edling, *Slavophile Thought and the Politics of Cultural Nationalism* (Albany: State University of New York Press, 2006), 65–67, 104–7; Nicholas V. Riasanovsky, *Russia and the West in the Teaching of the Slavophiles: A Study of Romantic Ideology* (Gloucester, MA: Peter Smith, 1965), 15–18.

10. Andrzej Walicki, *A History of Russian Thought from the Enlightenment to Marxism* (Stanford: Stanford University Press, 1979), 106.

11. For instance, Henry Lanz, "The Philosophy of Ivan Kireevsky," *Slavonic Review* 4, no. 12 (1926): 594–604.

12. Aksakov, "Stat'i," 115–16. See also Peter K. Christoff, *An Introduction to Nineteenth Century Slavophilism: I. V. Kireevskii* (The Hague: Mouton, 1972), 145.

13. A. I. Koshelev, "Poezdka Russkogo zemledel'tsa v Angliiu i na vsemirnuiu vystavku," *Moskovskii sbornik* (1852): 242–43.

14. I. V. Kireevskii, "V otvete A. S. Khomiakovu," in *Polnoe sobranie sochinenii I. V. Kireevskogo*, vol. 1, by I. V. Kireevskii (Moscow: Tipografiia Imperatorskogo Moskovskogo Universiteta. 1911), 112.

15. A. S. Khomiakov, "To the Serbians: A Message from Moscow," in *An Introduction to Nineteenth Century Slavophilism: A. S. Xomjakov*, by Peter K. Christoff (The Hague: Mouton, 1961), 250.

16. A. S. Khomiakov, "Mechta," in Brodskii, *Rannye slavianofily*, 146.

17. Christoff, *I. V. Kireevskii*, 181, 321.

18. Ivan Kireevsky, "On the Nature of European Culture and on Its Relationship to Russian Culture," in *On Spiritual Unity: A Slavophile Reader*, by Aleksei Khomiakov and Ivan Kireevsky (Hudson, NY: Lindisfarne, 1998), 190–91, 228.

19. Christoff, *A. S. Xomjakov*, 142.

20. K. S. Aksakov, "Kratkii istoricheskii ocherk zemskikh soborov," in *Polnoe sobranie sochinenii Konstantina Sergeevicha Aksakova*, vol. 1, by K. S. Aksakov (Moscow: Tipografiia M. Bakhmeteva, 1861), 292.

21. K. S. Aksakov, "O sovremennom cheloveke," in *Bratskaia pomoshch' postradavshim semeistvam Bosnii*, ed. A. S. Aksakov (St Petersburg: Peterburskii otdel Slavianskogo komiteta, 1876), quoted in Christoff, *K. S. Aksakov*, 257–58.

22. A. S. Khomiakov, "Po povodu Gumbol'dta," in *Polnoe sobranie sochinenii Alekseia Stepanovicha Khomiakova*, 3rd ed., vol. 1, by A. S. Khomiakov (Moscow: Universitetskaia tipografiia, 1900), 174.

23. Aleksei Khomiakov, "Some Remarks by an Orthodox Christian Concerning the Western Communions, on the Occasion of a Letter Published by the Archbishop of Paris," in Khomiakov and Kireevsky, *On Spiritual Unity*, 114–15.

24. Wayne Dowler, *Dostoevsky, Grigor'ev, and Native Soil Conservatism* (Toronto: University of Toronto Press, 1982), 91.

25. Fyodor Dostoevsky, *Winter Notes on Summer Impressions* (Richmond: Alma, 2016), 13.

26. Dostoevsky, *Winter Notes*, 29.

27. F. M. Dostoevskii, *Dnevnik pisatelia*, in *Polnoe sobranie sochinenii v tridsati tomakh* (Leningrad: Nauka, 1981), 21:38, 22:114.

28. F. M. Dostoevskii, "Pushkin," in *Polnoe sobranie sochinenii*, 26:148.

29. F. M. Dostoevskii, "A. A. Romanovu (nasledniku)," in *Polnoe sobranie sochinenii*, 29:1:260.

30. Vladimir Solov'ev, "Tri svidaniia," in Vladimir Solov'ev, *Stikhotvoreniia i shutochnye p'esy* (Leningrad: Sovetskii pisatel', 1974), 130.

31. Paul Valliere, *Modern Russian Theology: Bukharev, Soloviev, Bulgakov—Orthodox Theology in a New Key* (Grand Rapids, MI: William B. Eerdmans, 2000), 124–25.

32. Valliere, *Modern Russian Theology*, 114.

33. Vladimir Solov'ev, *Sobranie sochinenii Vladimira Sergeevicha Solov'eva*, supplementary Vol. 11 (Brussels: Izdatel'stvo Zhizn' s Bogom, 1969), 21–22, quoted in Valliere, *Modern Russian Theology*, 186.

34. Vladimir Solovyov, *The Justification of the Good: An Essay on Moral Philosophy* (New York: Cosimo, 2010), 170, 193.

35. Solovyov, *Justification of the Good*, 1.

36. Vladimir Soloviev, *Politics, Law and Morality: Essays by V. S. Soloviev* (New Haven, CT: Yale University Press, 2000), 12.

37. Soloviev, *Politics*, 20.

38. Soloviev, *Politics*, 19.

39. Vladimir Solovyov, *War, Progress, and the End of History: Three Conversations, Including a Short Story of the Anti-Christ* (Hudson, NY: Lindisfarne, 1990), 20.

40. Solovyov, *War*, 58.

41. Solovyov, *War*, 20.

42. Solovyov, *War*, 106.

43. Solovyov, *War*, 20.

44. Solovyov, *War*, 148.

45. Solovyov, *War*, 149, 155.

46. Solovyov, *War*, 165.

47. Solovyov, *War*, 185.

48. Solovyov, *War*, 193.

49. Vladmir Sergeevich Solov'ev, *Pis'ma Vladimira Sergeevicha Solov'eva*, vol. 2 (St Petersburg: n.p., 1910), 345, quoted in George M. Young, *The Russian Cosmists: The Esoteric Futurism of Nikolai Fedorov and His Followers* (Oxford: Oxford University Press, 2012), 98.

50. Young, *Russian Cosmists*, 69.

51. L. N. Tolstoy writing to V. I. Alexeev, 1881, quoted in Nikolai Nikolaevich Fedorov, *What Was Man Created For? The Philosophy of the Common Task* (Bath: Honeyglen/L'Age de Homme, 1990), 7.

52. Fedorov, *What Was Man Created For?*, 113.

53. Fedorov, *What Was Man Created For?*, 120.

54. Fedorov, *What Was Man Created For?*, 53-54.

55. Fedorov, *What Was Man Created For?*, 55-56.

56. Fedorov, *What Was Man Created For?*, 70.

57. Fedorov, *What Was Man Created For?*, 97.

58. Fedorov, *What Was Man Created For?*, 108.

59. Fedorov, *What Was Man Created For?*, 139.

60. Fedorov, *What Was Man Created For?*, 96.

61. Fedorov, *What Was Man Created For?*, 96.

62. Fedorov, *What Was Man Created For?*, 127.

63. Fedorov, *What Was Man Created For?*, 134.

64. Young, *Russian Cosmists*, 146.

65. Young, *Russian Cosmists*, 149.

66. George M. Young, "Navigating Spaceship Earth: Four Russian Cosmists," *Quest* 101, no. 3 (2013): 105-8, 120, https://www.theosophical.org/publications/quest-magazine/navigating-spaceship-earth-four-russian-cosmists.

67. Young, "Navigating Spaceship Earth."

68. Alexander Chizhevsky, "'The World-Historical Cycles,' from *The Earth in the Sun's Embrace*," in *Russian Cosmism*, ed. Boris Groys (New York: e-flux, 2018), 31.

69. Konstantin Tsiolkovsky, "Panpsychism, or Everything Feels," in Groys, *Russian Cosmism*, 134.

70. Tsiolkovsky, "Panpsychism," 136.

71. Tsiolkovsky, "Panpsychism," 148.

72. Tsiolkovsky, "Panpsychism," 148.

73. Tsiolkovsky, "Panpsychism," 154.

74. Tsiolkovsky, "Panpsychism," 154.

75. Tsiolkovsky, "Panpsychism," 144.

4. The Emergence of Russian Civilizationism

1. Robert E. MacMaster, *Danilevsky: A Russian Totalitarian Philosopher* (Cambridge, MA: Harvard University Press, 1967), 16.
2. Nikolai N. Strakhov, "The Life and Works of N. Ia. Danilevskii," in *Russia and Europe: The Slavic World's Political and Cultural Relations with the Germanic-Roman West*, by Nikolai Iavkovlevich Danilevskii (Bloomington, IN: Slavica, 2013), xl.
3. MacMaster, *Danilevsky*, 49.
4. MacMaster, *Danilevsky*, 56.
5. MacMaster, *Danilevsky*, 66.
6. Quoted in S. J. Holmes, "K. E. von Baer's Perplexities over Evolution," *Isis* 37, no. 1/2 (1947): 10.
7. Holmes, "K. E. von Baer's Perplexities," 11.
8. Holmes, "K. E. von Baer's Perplexities," 12.
9. MacMaster, *Danilevsky*, 148.
10. Nikolai Danilevskii, "Kosmos. Opyt fizicheskogo miroopisaniia Aleksandra von Gumbol'dta," *Otechestvennye zapiski* (1848), http://az.lib.ru/d/danilewskij_n_j/text_1848_kosmos.shtml.
11. Danilevskii, "Kosmos."
12. Nikolai Danilevskii, *Rossiia i Evropa: Vzgliad na kul'turnye i politicheskye otnosheniia slavianskogo mira k germano-romanskomu* (St Petersburg: Glagol', 1995), 39–40, 42.
13. Danilevskii, *Rossiia i Evropa*, 48–49.
14. Danilevskii, *Rossiia i Evropa*, 59.
15. Danilevskii, *Rossiia i Evropa*, 62.
16. Danilevskii, *Rossiia i Evropa*, 77–78.
17. Danilevskii, *Rossiia i Evropa*, 92.
18. Danilevskii, *Rossiia i Evropa*, 101.
19. Danilevskii, *Rossiia i Evropa*, 104–5.
20. Danilevskii, *Rossiia i Evropa*, 137–38.
21. Danilevskii, *Rossiia i Evropa*, 143.
22. Danilevskii, *Rossiia i Evropa*, 337.
23. Danilevskii, *Rossiia i Evropa*, 308.
24. Danilevskii, *Rossiia i Evropa*, 255.
25. Danilevskii, *Rossiia i Evropa*, 277.
26. Danilevskii, *Rossiia i Evropa*, 277.
27. Danilevskii, *Rossiia i Evropa*, 360–62.
28. K. Benois, "About the Author," in *Byzantinism and Slavdom*, by Konstantin Leontyev (Zloven: Taxiarch, 2020), xviii.
29. Glenn Cronin, *Disenchanted Wanderer: The Apocalyptic Vision of Konstantin Leontyev* (DeKalb: Northern Illinois University Press, 2021), 19.
30. Cronin, *Disenchanted Wanderer*, 55.
31. Cronin, *Disenchanted Wanderer*, 75.
32. Cronin, *Disenchanted Wanderer*, 76.
33. Quoted in Benois, "About the Author," viii.
34. Constantine Leontyev, "The Average European as an Ideal and Instrument of Universal Destruction," in *Russian Philosophy*, vol. 2, ed. James Edie, James P. Scanlan, and Mary-Barbara Zeldin (Chicago: Quadrangle, 1965), 279.

35. Leontyev, "Average European," 275–76.
36. K. N. Leont'ev, *Polnoe sobranie sochinenii i pisem v dvenadsati tomakh*, vol. 2 (St Petersburg: Vladimir Dal', 2000), 158, quoted in Cronin, *Disenchanted Wanderer*, 77.
37. Leont'ev, *Polnoe sobranie*, vol. 2, 45–46, quoted in Cronin, *Disenchanted Wanderer*, 31.
38. Leont'ev, *Polnoe sobranie*, vol. 2, 152, quoted in Cronin, *Disenchanted Wanderer*, 40.
39. Leont'ev, *Polnoe sobranie*, vol. 6.1, 130–31, quoted in Cronin, *Disenchanted Wanderer*, 79.
40. Leontyev, "Average European," 280.
41. K. N. Leont'ev, *Vizantizm i Slavianstvo* (Moscow: Izdanie Obshchestva Istorii i Drevnostei Rossiiskikh pri Moskovskom Universitete, 1876), 2.
42. Leont'ev, *Vizantizm i Slavianstvo*, 24.
43. Leont'ev, *Vizantizm i Slavianstvo*, 22.
44. Leont'ev, *Vizantizm i Slavianstvo*, 29.
45. Leont'ev, *Vizantizm i Slavianstvo*, 30–31.
46. Leont'ev, *Vizantizm i Slavianstvo*, 29.
47. Leont'ev, *Vizantizm i Slavianstvo*, 70.
48. Leont'ev, *Vizantizm i Slavianstvo*, 72–73.
49. Leont'ev, *Vizantizm i Slavianstvo*, 77.
50. Leont'ev, *Vizantizm i Slavianstvo*, 87.
51. Leont'ev, *Vizantizm i Slavianstvo*, 100–101.
52. Leont'ev, *Vizantizm i Slavianstvo*, 103, 112.
53. Leont'ev, *Vizantizm i Slavianstvo*, 123.
54. Leont'ev, *Vizantizm i Slavianstvo*, 125.

5. The Eurasianist Strand of Russian Civilizationism

1. Petr Savitskii, P. Suvchinskii, Prince N. S. Trubetskoi, and George Florovskii, introduction to *Exodus to the East: Forebodings and Events—an Affirmation of the Eurasians* (Idyllwild, CA: Charles Schlacks Jr., 1996), 1–3.
2. Paul Robinson, *Russian Conservatism* (DeKalb: Northern Illinois University Press, 2019), 136.
3. N. S. Trubetskoi, *Evropa i chelovechestvo* (Moscow: Direkt-Media, 2015), 113.
4. Trubetskoi, *Evropa i chelovechestvo*, 5.
5. Trubetskoi, *Evropa i chelovechestvo*, 14.
6. Trubetskoi, *Evropa i chelovechestvo*, 18.
7. Trubetskoi, *Evropa i chelovechestvo*, 39, 61.
8. Trubetskoi, *Evropa i chelovechestvo*, 62.
9. Trubetskoi, *Evropa i chelovechestvo*, 88.
10. Trubetskoi, *Evropa i chelovechestvo*, 91–92.
11. Trubetskoi, *Evropa i chelovechestvo*, 97.
12. Trubetskoi, *Evropa i chelovechestvo*, 108.
13. Nicholas Riasanovsky, "Prince N. S. Trubetskoi's 'Europe and Mankind,'" *Jahrbücher für Geschichte Osteuropas* 12, no. 2 (1964): 212.
14. Riasanovsky, "Prince N. S. Trubetskoi's 'Europe and Mankind,'" 214.
15. Nikolai S. Trubetskoi, "The Upper and Lower Stones of Russian Culture (The Ethnic Basis of Russian Culture)," in Savitskii et al., *Exodus to the East*, 83, 89–91.

16. Trubetskoi, "Upper and Lower Stones," 91.

17. Petr N. Savitskii, "A Turn to the East," in Savitskii et al., *Exodus to the East*, 6.

18. George Florovskii, "The Cunning of Reason," in Savitskii et al., *Exodus to the East*, 39.

19. Nikolai S. Trubetskoi, "On True and False Nationalism," in Savitskii et al., *Exodus to the East*, 70.

20. Trubetskoi, "On True and False Nationalism," 74–75.

21. Anna Akhmatova, "Requiem," Best Poems, accessed June 27, 2024, https://www.best-poems.net/anna_akhmatova/requiem.html.

22. Charles Clover, *Black Wind, White Snow: The Rise of Russia's New Nationalism* (New Haven, CT: Yale University Press, 2016), 94–100.

23. Mark Bassin, *The Gumilev Mystique: Biopolitics, Eurasianism, and the Construction of Community in Modern Russia* (Ithaca, NY: Cornell University Press, 2016), 195.

24. Alexander Titov, "Lev Gumilyov, Ethnogenesis and Eurasianism" (PhD diss., University College London, 2005), 151; Mark Bassin, "Narrating Kulikovo: Lev Gumilyov, Russian Nationalists, and the Troubled Emergence of New Eurasianism," in *Between Europe and Asia: The Origins, Theories, and Legacies of Russian Eurasianism*, ed. Mark Bassin, Sergey Glebov, and Marlene Laruelle (Pittsburg: University of Pittsburgh Press, 2015), 171.

25. Clover, *Black Wind, White Snow*, 138.

26. Lev Gumilev, "Seek Out What Is True," *Soviet Literature* 1 (1990): 72–76, quoted in Glenn Cronin, *Disenchanted Wanderer: The Apocalyptic Vision of Konstantin Leontyev* (DeKalb: Northern Illinois University Press, 2021), 8.

27. Clover, *Black Wind, White Snow*, 138. For a detailed comparison of Gumilyov and Toynbee, see Titov, "Lev Gumilyov."

28. Lev Gumilyov, *Ethnogenesis and the Biosphere* (Moscow: Progress, 1990), 9, 29, 56.

29. Gumilyov, *Ethnogenesis*, 173.

30. Gumilyov, *Ethnogenesis*, 105.

31. Gumilyov, *Ethnogenesis*, 204.

32. Gumilyov, *Ethnogenesis*, 223, 231.

33. Gumilyov, *Ethnogenesis*, 264.

34. Gumilyov, *Ethnogenesis*, 278, 282.

35. Gumilev, L. N., and K. P. Ivanov, "Etnicheskie protsessy: dva pokhoda k izucheniiu," *Sotsiologicheskie issledovaniia* 1 (1992): 52, quoted in Mark Bassin, "Lev Gumilev and the European New Right," *Nationalities Papers* 43, no. 6 (2015): 844.

36. Gumilev, L. N., and V. Iu. Ermolaev, "Gore ot illiuzii," in Lev Gumilev, *Ritmy Evrazii: Epokky i tsivilizatsiia* (Moscow: Ekopros, 1993), 174, quoted in Bassin, *Gumilev Mystique*, 213–14.

37. Dmitry E. Muza, "Mnogovektornost' razvitiia sovremennogo mira," *Problemy tsivilizatsionnogo razvitiia* 3, no. 2 (2021): 6–7.

38. A. S. Panarin, *Rossiia v tsivilizatsionnom protsesse* (Moscow: Rossiiskaia Akademiia Nauk, 1995), 4.

39. Andrei P. Tsygankov, *The "Russian Idea" in International Relations: Civilization and National Distinctiveness* (London: Routledge, 2023), 77–84.

40. For instance, Marina Peunova, "An Eastern Incarnation of the European New Right: Aleksandr Panarin and the New Eurasianist Discourse in Contemporary Russia," *Journal of Contemporary European Studies* 16, no. 3 (2008): 407–19.

41. A. S. Panarin, *Russkaia al'ternativa* (Lewiston, NY: Edwin Mellen, 1999), 3.
42. Panarin, *Russkaia al'ternativa*, 51.
43. Panarin, *Russkaia al'ternativa*, 386.
44. Panarin, *Rossiia v tsivilizatsionnom protsesse*, 48.
45. A. S. Panarin, *Pravoslavnaia tsivilizatsiia* (Moscow: Institut Russkoi Tsivilizatsii, 2014), 447.
46. Panarin, *Russkaia al'ternativa*, 389, 435.
47. Panarin, *Russkaia al'ternativa*, 56.
48. Panarin, *Russkaia al'ternativa*, 245.
49. Panarin, *Russkaia al'ternativa*, 247–48, 250.
50. Panarin, *Rossiia v tsivilizatsionnom protsesse*, 243.
51. Panarin, *Russkaia al'ternativa*, 496–97.
52. Panarin, *Russkaia al'ternativa*, 499.
53. Panarin, *Russkaia al'ternativa*, 340.
54. Panarin, *Russkaia al'ternativa*, 340–42.
55. Panarin, *Rossiia v tsivilizatsionnom protsesse*, 246, 252.
56. Panarin, *Russkaia al'ternativa*, 294.
57. Panarin, *Rossiia v tsivilizatsionnom protsesse*, 215.
58. Panarin, *Russkaia al'ternativa*, 301.
59. Panarin, *Russkaia al'ternativa*, 499.
60. I. V. Il'in and O. G. Leonova, "Global'nye universal'nye tsennosti i gumanitarnye tekhnologii v mezhdunarodnoi politike," *Vestnik Moskovskogo Universiteta: Globalistika i geopolitika* 27, no. 1 (2018): 4.
61. Il'in and Leonova, "Global'nye universal'nye tsennosti," 10.
62. "About Us," Katehon, accessed June 27, 2024, https://katehon.com/en/about-us.
63. Alexander Dugin, "Apocalyptic Realism," Katehon, April 20, 2022, https://katehon.com/en/article/apocalyptic-realism.
64. Dugin, "Apocalyptic Realism."
65. Aleksandr Dugin, *Absoliutnaia Rossiia* (Moscow: Arktogeia, 1999), 670.
66. Paul Robinson, "Interview with Alexander Dugin," *Irrussianality*, September 13, 2017, https://irrussianality.wordpress.com/2017/09/13/interview-with-alexander-dugin/.
67. Aleksandr Dugin, *Ukraina: Moia voina* (Moscow: Tsentrpoligraf, 2015), 40.
68. Marlene Laruelle, "Two Faces of Contemporary Eurasianism: An Imperial Version of Russian Nationalism," *Nationalities Papers* 32, no. 1 (2004): 128.
69. Dugin, *Ukraina*, 439.
70. Michael Millerman, *Inside "Putin's Brain": The Political Philosophy of Alexander Dugin* (n.p.: Millerman School, 2022), 62.
71. Millerman, *Inside "Putin's Brain,"* 37.
72. Millerman, *Inside "Putin's Brain,"* 39.
73. Robinson, "Interview with Alexander Dugin."
74. Anton Barbashin and Hannah Thoburn, "Putin's Brain: Alexander Dugin and the Philosophy behind Putin's Invasion of Crimea," *Foreign Affairs*, March 31, 2014, https://www.foreignaffairs.com/articles/russia-fsu/2014-03-31/putins-brain.
75. Robinson, "Interview with Alexander Dugin."

76. Dugin, *Ukraina*, 441.
77. Dugin, *Absoliutnaia Rossiia*, 659.
78. Alexander Dugin, *The Fourth Political Theory* (London: Arktos, 2012), 155.
79. Dugin, *Absoliutnaia Rossiia*, 601.
80. Dugin, *Fourth Political Theory*, 45–46.
81. Dugin, *Fourth Political Theory*, 64.
82. Dugin, *Fourth Political Theory*, 116–17.
83. Dugin, *Fourth Political Theory*, 120.
84. Dugin, *Fourth Political Theory*, 165, 192.

6. The Isolationist Strand of Russian Civilizationism

1. Dina Khapaeva, "Putin Is Just Following the Manual," *Atlantic*, March 26, 2022, https://www.theatlantic.com/ideas/archive/2022/03/putin-kremlin-foreign-policy-strategy/629388/.
2. Khapaeva, "Putin."
3. Mikhail Iur'ev, "Krepost' Rossiia," in *Krepost' Rossiia*, ed. Mikhail Leont'ev, Mikhail Iur'ev, Mikhail Khazin, and Anatoloii Utkin (Moscow: Iauza Eksmo, 2008), https://litresp.ru.
4. Iur'ev, "Krepost' Rossiia."
5. Iur'ev, "Krepost' Rossiia."
6. A. A. Ivanov, "Lozung 'Rossiia dlia russkikh' v konservativnoi mysli vtoroi poloviny XIX veka," *Tetradi po konservatizmu* 4 (2015): 34 (emphasis in the original).
7. Ivanov, "Lozung," 36.
8. Alexander Solzhenitsyn, "A World Split Apart," Alexander Solzhenitsyn Center, June 8, 1978, https://www.solzhenitsyncenter.org/a-world-split-apart.
9. Aleksandr Solzhenitsyn, "Three Key Moments in Modern Japanese History," *National Review* 35, no. 24 (1983): 1536.
10. Eric E. Ericson Jr., *Solzhenitsyn and the Modern World* (Washington, DC: Regnery Gateway, 1993), 232.
11. Alexander Solzhenitsyn, *Letter to Soviet Leaders* (London: Collins/Harvill, 1974), 21–22, 31–32, 41.
12. Aleksandr Solzhenitsyn, "Raskaianie i samoogranichenie kak kategorii natsional'noi zhizni," in *Publitsistika v trekh tomakh* (Yaroslavl: Verkhe-Volzhskoe Knizhnoe Izdatel'stvo, 1995), 1:64–65, 84.
13. Aleksandr Solzhenitsyn, "Kak nam obustroit' Rossiiu?," in *Publitsistika v trekh tomakh*, 1:542.
14. Egor Kholmogorov, "Konstantin Krylov: Povedenie," *Voprosy natsionalizma* 33, no. 1 (2021): 21.
15. Konstantin Krylov, "Russkaia ideia," Krylov.ru, July 31, 2004, https://krylov.ru/tpost/fojsirdfy1-russkaya-ideya.
16. Kholmogorov, "Konstantin Krylov," 23.
17. Konstantin Krylov, "O natsional'nom dukhe," Krylov.ru, November 22, 1999, https://krylov.ru/nation.
18. Konstantin Krylov, *Povedenie* (Moscow: Al'kor, 2021), 105.
19. Krylov, *Povedenie*, 105.

20. Krylov, *Povedenie*, 80-84, 114–17.
21. Krylov, *Povedenie*, 122–23.
22. Krylov, *Povedenie*, 133–37.
23. Paul Grenier, "Konstantin Krylov's Ethical Theory and What It Reveals about the Propensity for Conflict between Russia and the West," *Telos* 201 (2022): 118.
24. Boris Mezhuev, "'Island Russia' and Russia's Identity Politics," *Russia in Global Affairs*, no. 2 (2017), https://eng.globalaffairs.ru/articles/island-russia-and-russias-identity-politics/.
25. S. V. Khatuntsev, "Vspominaia Vadima Tsymburskogo," *Polis: Politicheskie issledovaniia* 3 (2013): 157.
26. Vadim Tsymburskii, "Ostrov Rossiia," *Russkii Arkhipelag*, 1993, https://archipelag.ru/ru_mir/ostrov-rus/cymbur/island_russia/.
27. Tsymburskii, "Ostrov Rossiia."
28. Vadim Tsymburskii, "Osnovaniia rossiiskogo geopoliticheskogo konservatizma," *Tetradi po konservatizmu* 1 (2015): 42.
29. Tsymburskii, "Ostrov Rossiia."
30. Mezhuev, "Island Russia."
31. Quoted in Igor Torbakov, "Towards 'Island Russia,'" *Eurozine*, May 14, 2021, https://www.eurozine.com/towards-island-russia/.
32. A. P. Tsygankov, "'Ostrovnaia' geopolitika Vadima Tsymburkogo," *Tetradi po konservatizmu* 1 (2015): 18.
33. Mezhuev, "Island Russia."
34. Svetlana Lurye, "Sblizhenie s Vostokom—urok mezhtsivilizatsionnogo ravnodushiia," *Russkaia istina*, June 3, 2015, https://politconservatism.ru/experiences/sblizhenie-s-vostokom-urok-mezhtsivilizatsionnogo-ravnodushiya.
35. Lurye, "Sblizhenie s Vostokom."
36. Egor Kholmogorov, *Revansh russkoi istorii* (Moscow: Knizhnyi mir, 2016), 7–8.
37. Paul Robinson, "Interview with Egor Kholmogorov," *Irrussianality*, November 18, 2017, https://irrussianality.wordpress.com/2017/11/18/interview-with-egor-kholmogorov/.
38. Mikhail Remizov, *Russkie i gosudarstvo* (Moscow: Eksmo, 2006), 95–96.
39. Remizov, *Russkie i gosudarstvo*, 366.
40. Remizov, *Russkie i gosudarstvo*, 367.
41. Remizov, *Russkie i gosudarstvo*, 368–69.
42. Remizov, *Russkie i gosudarstvo*, 20.
43. Boris Mezhuev, "Ostorozhno: 'Drugaia Evrope'!," *Russkaia istina*, February 4, 2023, https://politconservatism.ru/blogs/ostorozhno-drugaya-evropa.
44. Boris Mezhuev, "Civilizational Realism," *Russia in Global Affairs*, no. 4 (2018), https://eng.globalaffairs.ru/articles/civilizational-realism/.
45. Mezhuev, "Civilizational Realism."
46. Boris Mezhuev, "Civilizational Indifference: Can Russia Keep Up Cultural Distancing in Relations with Europe?," *Russia in Global Affairs*, no. 4 (2022), https://eng.globalaffairs.ru/articles/civilizational-indifference/.
47. Mezhuev, "Civilizational Indifference."
48. Mezhuev, "Civilizational Indifference."
49. Mezhuev, "Civilizational Indifference."
50. Mezhuev, "Civilizational Indifference."

51. Nikolai Spasskiy, "The Island of Russia," *Russia in Global Affairs*, no. 1 (2018), https://eng.globalaffairs.ru/articles/the-island-of-russia-2/.

52. Vladislav Surkov, "The Loneliness of the Half-Breed," *Russia in Global Affairs*, May 28, 2018, https://eng.globalaffairs.ru/articles/the-loneliness-of-the-half-breed/.

53. Surkov, "Loneliness."

54. Surkov, "Loneliness."

55. Surkov, "Loneliness."

56. Torbakov, "Towards 'Island Russia.'"

57. Dmitrii Trenin, *The End of Eurasia: Russia on the Border between Geopolitics and Globalization* (Washington: Carnegie Endowment for International Peace, 2002), 311–12.

58. Torbakov, "Towards 'Island Russia.'"

59. Dmitry Trenin, "Why Building a New World Order Is Now an Existential Issue for Russia," *RT*, February 3, 2023, https://www.rt.com/russia/570912-building-new-world-order/.

7. The Rise of Russian Civilizationism

1. Ilya Ilyin and Olga Leonova, "Russian Civilization and Global Culture: Alternative or Coexistence?," in *Challenges of Globalization and the Prospects for an Intercivilizational World Order*, ed. I. Rossi (Cham: Springer, 2020), 983–96 (emphasis in the original).

2. Ilyin and Leonova, "Russian Civilization," 989.

3. Ilyin and Leonova, "Russian Civilization," 995 (emphasis in the original).

4. Gulnaz Sharafutdinova, *The Red Mirror: Putin's Leadership and Russia's Insecure Identity* (Oxford: Oxford University Press, 2020), 127.

5. Fyodor Lyukanov, "China Is Finally Stepping Up to Its Role as a Superpower. This Will Change the World," *RT*, March 4, 2023, https://www.rt.com/news/572465-china-is-finally-superpower/.

6. For an example of such thinking, see Konstantin Eggert, "Letter to Dr Niblett," X, November 10, 2021, https://twitter.com/kvoneggert/status/1458379001593008128. For a discussion of this general subject, see Jan Surman and Ella Rossman, "New Dissidence in Contemporary Russia: Students, Feminism and New Ethics," *New Perspectives* 30, no. 1 (2022): 27–46.

7. Konstantin Bogomolov, "Pokhishchenie Evropy 2.0," *Novaia gazeta*, February 10, 2021, https://novayagazeta.ru/articles/2021/02/10/89120-pohischenie-evropy-2-0.

8. Aleksei Chadaev, "Novgorodskaia lektsiia. Filosofiia oruzhiia. Sovremennoe i vnevremennoe," *Aleksei Chadaev: Nabliudeniia, zamechaniia i predlozheniia*, September 12, 2022, https://chadayev.ru/blog/2022/09/12/novgorodskaya-lektsiya-filosofiya-oruzhiya-sovremennoe-i-vnevremennoe/.

9. Aleksei Chadaev, "Dron kak instrument prakticheskoi filosofii," *Aleksei Chadaev: Nabliudeniia, zamechaniia i predlozheniia*, December 20, 2022, https://chadayev.ru/blog/2022/12/21/dron-kak-instrument-prakticheskoj-filosofii/.

10. Aleksei Chadaev, "Chto takoe sovremennost', pochemu tuda bilety, pochemu nas ottuda vygnali i mozhno li ee importozamestit'," *Aleksei Chadaev: Nabliudeniia, zamechaniia i predlozheniia*, July 12, 2022, https://chadayev.ru/publications/2022/07/12/chto-takoe-sovremennost-pochyom-tuda-bilety-pochemu-nas-ottuda-vygnali-i-mozhno-li-eyo-importozamestit/.

11. Chadaev, "Chto takoe sovremennost'."

12. Dmitry Sokolov-Mitrich, "The Russia They Lost," Slavyangrad, September 24, 2014, https://slavyangrad.org/2014/09/24/the-russia-they-lost/.

13. Marlene Laruelle, "The Discipline of Culturology: A New 'Ready Made Thought' for Russia," *Diogenes* 51, no. 4 (2004): 22.

14. Mikhail Epstein, *The Phoenix of Philosophy: Russian Thought of the Late Soviet Period (1953–1991)* (New York: Bloomsbury, 2019), 175, 177 (emphasis in the original).

15. M. M. Bakhtin, "Response to a Question from *Novy Mir*," in *Speech Genres and Other Late Essays*, by M. M. Bakhtin (Austin: University of Texas Press, 1986), 7.

16. V. S. Bibler, "Iz 'zametok vprok'," *Voprosy filosofii*, no. 6 (1991): 37.

17. Epstein, *Phoenix of Philosophy*, 215–16.

18. Viktor Krivulin, "Konets epokhi Ryb," *Novoe russkoe slovo*, February 17, 1995, 36, quoted in Epstein, *The Phoenix of Philosophy*, 217.

19. Laruelle, "Discipline of Culturology," 22.

20. Liudmila Aleksashkina and Joseph Zajda, "National History Curriculum and Standards for Secondary Schools in the Russian Federation," in *Nation Building and History Education in a Global Culture*, ed. Joseph Zajda (Dordrecht: Spring, 2017), 172.

21. Aleksashkina and Zajda, "National History Curriculum," 172–73.

22. Laruelle, "Discipline of Culturology," 25–26.

23. Laruelle, "Discipline of Culturology," 30.

24. Laruelle, "Discipline of Culturology," 32.

25. Veljko Vujacic, "Gennadiy Zyuganov and the 'Third Road,'" *Post-Soviet Affairs* 12, no. 2 (1996): 129–30.

26. Gennady Zyuganov, *My Russia: The Political Autobiography of Gennady Zyuganov* (London: Routledge, 2015), 137.

27. Gennadii Ziuganov, "Sovetskaia tsivilizatsiia—vospominanie o budushchem," *Kommunisticheskaia Partiia Rossiiskoi Federatsii—Sankt Peterburgskoe Gorodskoe Otdelenie*, accessed June 28, 2024, http://www.old.cprfspb.ru/9446.html.

28. Zyuganov, *My Russia*, 99–100.

29. Zyuganov, *My Russia*, 100.

30. Zyuganov, *My Russia*, 100.

31. Zyuganov, *My Russia*, 100, 124.

32. Ziuganov, "Sovetskaia tsivilizatsiia."

33. Zyuganov, *My Russia*, 74.

34. Zyuganov, *My Russia*, 101.

35. Zyuganov, *My Russia*, xiii.

36. Oleg Slobotchikov, *Zhirinovskii kak filosof* (Moscow: Institute mirovykh tsivilizatsii, 2017).

37. Vladimir Zhirinovskii, *Sotsiologiia mirovykh tsivilizatsii: Vostochno-khristianskaia pravoslavnaia tsivilizatsiia* (Moscow: LitRes Samizdat, 2013), 5.

38. Vladimir Zhirinovskii, "Sud'by mirovykh tsivilizatsii v xxi veke," Institut Mirovykh Tsivilizatsii, *Vestnik* 3 (2011): 4–5.

39. Zhirinovskii, "Sud'by," 6.

40. Zhirinovskii, "Sud'by," 7–8.

41. Zhirinovskii, "Sud'by," 9.

42. Zhirinovskii, "Sud'by," 9.

43. Irakli Gelukashvili, "Le processus du raisonnement géopolitique et la construction identitaire chez l'élite russe: Les narratives géopolitiques russes à l'égard de la Géorgie et de l'Ukraine (1999–2014)" (PhD diss., Université du Quebec à Montréal, 2017).

8. The Triumph of Russian Civilizationism

1. Vladimir Putin, "Vstupitel'noe slovo na plenarnom zasedanii vstrechi na vysshem urovne Rossia-Evropeiskii soiuz," Kremlin.ru, May 17, 2001, http://kremlin.ru/events/president/transcripts/21237.

2. Vladimir Putin, "Interv'iu finskoi gazete 'Khel'singen sanomat,'" Kremlin.ru, September 1, 2001, http://kremlin.ru/events/president/transcripts/21315.

3. Vladimir Putin, "Vystuplenie na vstreche s predstaviteliami delovykh i obshchestvennykh krugov FRG," Kremlin.ru, September 26, 2001, http://kremlin.ru/events/president/transcripts/21342.

4. Vladimir Putin, "Vystuplenie na otkrytii memorial'noi doski Immanuilu Kantu na zdanii Rossiiskogo gosudarstvennogo universiteta," Kremlin.ru, July 3, 2005, http://kremlin.ru/events/president/transcripts/23076.

5. Vladimir Putin, "Zaiavlenie dlia pressy i otvety na voprosy po itogam xx sammita Rossiia-Evrosoiuz," Kremlin.ru, October 26, 2007, http://kremlin.ru/events/president/transcripts/24624.

6. Vladimir Putin, "Ispolniaiushchii obiazannosti Presidenta Rossii, prem'er-ministr Vladimir Putin provel rasshirennoe zasedanie Soveta Bezopasnosti Rossii," Kremlin.ru, December 31, 1999, http://kremlin.ru/events/president/news/37390.

7. Vladimir Putin, "Sovmestnaia press-konferentsiia s Presidentom Egipta Khosni Mubarakom," Kremlin.ru, May 27, 2005, http://kremlin.ru/events/president/transcripts/22933.

8. Vladimir Putin, "Interv'iu mezarabskomu sputnikovomu telekanalu 'Al'-Dzhazira,'" Kremlin.ru, February 10, 2007, http://kremlin.ru/events/president/transcripts/24035.

9. Vladimir Putin, "Vystuplenie i diskussiia na Miunkhenskoi konferentsii po voprosam politiki bezopastnosti," Kremlin.ru, February 10, 2007, http://kremlin.ru/events/president/transcripts/24034.

10. Vladimir Putin, "Interv'iu zhurnalu 'Taim,'" Kremlin.ru, December 19, 2007, http://kremlin.ru/events/president/transcripts/24735.

11. Sergei Lavrov, "Russia and the World in the 21st Century," *Russia in Global Affairs*, no. 3 (2008), https://eng.globalaffairs.ru/articles/russia-and-the-world-in-the-21st-century/.

12. "The Foreign Policy Concept of the Russian Federation," Permanent Mission of the Russian Federation to the European Union, July 12, 2008, https://russiaeu.ru/userfiles/file/foreign_policy_concept_english.pdf.

13. "Foreign Policy Concept," 2008.

14. Dmitrii Medvedev, "Speech at World Policy Conference," Kremlin.ru, October 8, 2008, http://kremlin.ru/events/president/transcripts/48308.

15. Vladimir Putin, "Russia Muscles Up—the Challenges We Must Rise to Face," *Izvestiia*, January 16, 2012, https://russialist.org/archives/russia-putin-article-izvestia-russia-muscles-up-214.php.

16. Vladimir Putin, "Russia—the Ethnicity Issue," *Nezavisimaia Gazeta*, January 23, 2012, http://archive.premier.gov.ru/eng/events/news/17831/.

17. Vladimir Putin, "Zasedanie mezhdunarodnogo diskussionogo kluba 'Valdai,'" Kremlin.ru, September 19, 2013, http://kremlin.ru/events/president/news/19243.

18. Putin, "Zasedanie mezhdunarodnogo diskussionogo kluba 'Valdai,'" 2013.

19. Ministerstvo Kul'tury Rossiiskoi Federatsii, *Osnovy gosudarstvennoi kul'turnoi politiki*, 2015, 3–4, 16, http://www.folkcentr.ru.

20. Vladimir Putin, "Zasedanie vsemirnogo russkogo narodnogo sobora," Kremlin.ru, November 1, 2018, http://kremlin.ru/events/president/news/59013.

21. Vladimir Putin, "Vstrecha s presidentom Evropeiskoi komissii Zhoze Manuelom Barrozu," Kremlin.ru, March 21, 2013, http://kremlin.ru/events/president/news/17720.

22. Ministerstvo Kul'tury, *Osnovy*, 54.

23. Sergei Lavrov, "Russia's Foreign Policy in a Historical Perspective," *Russia in Global Affairs*, no. 2 (2016), https://eng.globalaffairs.ru/articles/russias-foreign-policy-in-a-historical-perspective/.

24. Lavrov, "Russia's Foreign Policy."

25. Lavrov, "Russia's Foreign Policy."

26. Fabian Linde, "The Civilizational Turn in Russian Political Discourse: From Pan-Europeanism to Civilizational Distinctiveness," *Russian Review* 75, no. 4 (2016): 604–25.

27. Vladimir Putin, "Zasedanie mezhdunarodnogo diskussionogo kluba 'Valdai,'" Kremlin.ru, October 27, 2022, http://kremlin.ru/events/president/news/69695.

28. Putin, "Zasedanie mezhdunarodnogo diskussionogo kluba 'Valdai,'" 2022.

29. Mikhail Suslov, "Isolationism, a Broad Eurasian Partnership, and a Left Tinge," *Russia Post*, April 20, 2023, https://russiapost.info/politics/isolationism.

30. Aleksei Dobrynin, "Obraz mnogopoliarnogo mira," *Russia in Global Affairs*, no. 2 (2023), https://globalaffairs.ru/articles/obraz-mnogopolyarnogo-mira/ (bracketed text in the original).

31. Dobrynin, "Obraz mnogopoliarnogo mira."

32. Dobrynin, "Obraz mnogopoliarnogo mira."

33. "The Concept of the Foreign Policy of the Russian Federation," Ministry of Foreign Affairs of the Russian Federation, March 31, 2023, https://mid.ru/en/foreign_policy/fundamental_documents/1860586/.

34. Vladimir Putin, "Zasedanie diskussionnogo kluba 'Valdai,'" Kremlin.ru, October 5, 2023, http://kremlin.ru/events/president/news/72444.

35. Putin, "Zasedanie diskussionnogo kluba 'Valdai.'"

36. "Foundations of Russian Statehood," Higher School of Economics, School of History, 2023–24, https://hist.hse.ru/en/courses/844166102.html.

37. Vladimir Putin, "Ukaz ob utdverzhdenii Kontseptsii vneshnei politiki Rossiiskoi Federatsii," Kremlin.ru, March 31, 2023, http://kremlin.ru/events/president/news/70811.

38. Putin, "Ukaz."

39. Putin, "Zasedanie diskussionnogo kluba 'Valdai.'"

40. Vladimir Putin, "Mezhdunarodnaia parlamentskaia konferentsiia 'Rossiia—Afrika v mnogopoliarnom mire,'" Kremlin.ru, March 20, 2023, http://kremlin.ru/events/president/news/70745.

41. Vladimir Putin, "Videoobrashchenie k uchastnikam 11-i Mezhdunarodnoi vstrechi vysokikh predstavitelei, kuriruiushchikh voprosy bezopasnosti," Kremlin.ru, May 24, 2023, http://kremlin.ru/events/president/news/71189.

42. Vladimir Putin, "Plenarnoe zasedanie Peterburgskogo mezhdunarodnogo ekonomicheskogo foruma," Kremlin.ru, June 16, 2023, http://kremlin.ru/events/president/news/71445.

Conclusion

1. I. E. Dronov, *Imperator Aleksandr III i ego epokha* (Moscow: Akademicheskii proekt, 2016), 183.

2. Jeffrey Haynes, *From Huntington to Trump: Thirty Years of Civilizations* (Lanham, MD: Lexington, 2019), 107–30.

3. Tingyang Zhao, *Redefining a Philosophy for World Governance* (Beijing: Palgrave Macmillan, 2019), 47.

4. Zhao Tingyang, "Tianxia: All under Heaven," *Noéma*, June 19, 2020, https://www.noemamag.com/tianxia-all-under-heaven/.

5. Zhao, "Tianxia."

6. "Global Civilization Initiative Injects Fresh Energy into Human Development," State Council Information Office of the People's Republic of China, March 19, 2023, http://english.scio.gov.cn/topnews/2023-03/19/content_85177312.htm.

7. I. A. Il'in, *O sushchnosti pravosoznaniia* (Moscow: Rarog, 1993), 101–2.

Index

Akhmatova, Anna, 79
Aksakov, Ivan, 50
Aksakov, Konstantin, 50–51, 53
Alexander I, Emperor, 35
Alexander II, Emperor, 35, 38, 63, 132
Alexander III, Emperor, 38, 55, 133
Antichrist, 48–49, 57, 86
anticolonialism, 77
apocalypse, 12, 48–49, 86
Arbatov, Georgy, 44
Averintsev, Sergei, 111

Baer, Karl Ernst von, 65
Bakhtin, Mikhail, 110
barbarism, 10–11, 13, 15, 28, 45
Batkin, Leonid, 45
Benoist, Alain de, 29–30, 82, 87
Berdiaev, Nikolai, 9, 11
Bibler, Vladimir, 110
Biden, Joe, 6–7
Bogomolov, Konstantin, 107
Bulgakov, Sergei, 70

capitalism, 4, 20, 40–46, 88, 94, 113
Chaadaev, Pyotr, 50
Chadaev, Aleksei, 107–109
Chizhevsky, Aleksandr, 60–61, 81–82, 115
Christianity, 11–12, 26, 38, 48, 55, 122
civilization: benefits of, 20; contrasted with civilizations, 10; definitions of, 10, 28–30, 113; differences, Russian and Western, 113; Eurasian, 78, 90; European, 34, 56, 73, 76, 121, 124; homogenizing effect of, 39; mentioned by Putin, 2–3, 8, 119–20, 122–25; modern, 45; as opposed to barbarism, 10–11, 13, 15, 28; Orthodox, 100; Pan-Slav, 75; return to, 107; Russian, 87, 92, 95, 106, 113–15; saving of, 44; social evolution, 13; Sorokin's view of, 27; Soviet, 114; technical, 81; universal, 4–5, 67–69, 78. *See also* Western civilization
civilizational indifference, 92, 102

civilizational realism, 101
civilizational theory, 3–8, 27–29, 31–34, 82, 133; challenge to Western liberalism, 131; Chinese, 133–34; culturology, 111; deep roots of, 106, 128; international focus of, 109; isolationist branch of, 91; Putin and, 119; receptivity to, 112; Russian, 47, 50, 63, 92, 128, 130; themes of, 22; triumph of, 118, 126
civilizationism: and anticolonialism, 129; enduring importance of, 133; as political tool, 3, 7; Russian, 4, 82, 127–28; sources of, 132
civilizations: clash of, 30–31, 85, 105, 116; as closed systems, 110; contrasted with civilization, 10; definitions of, 27, 111, 115; diversity of, 7; equality of, 3; extraterrestrial, 106; higher and lower, 77; liberal, 98; life cycles of, 24–29, 67, 70, 73; origins of, 61, 80, 114; partnership of, 124; plurality of, 87; rights of, 7; types of, 97–98, 115. *See also* dialogue of civilizations
Cold War, 6, 18–19, 44, 93, 107, 119, 131
colonialism, 7–8, 20, 22, 30, 51, 77, 129
common task, the, 8, 59, 62
communism, 3, 23, 30, 94, 106–107; collapse of, 18–19, 45, 63; as end of history, 5, 17, 40, 43
Comte, Auguste, 15–16, 20, 23, 28, 32
Condorcet, Marquis de, 13, 15, 23, 28
cosmism, 58, 62, 80, 84, 115, 132
culturology, 43, 99, 106, 109–12

Danilevsky, Nikolai, 2, 62–69, 82, 113, 132; cited by Putin 2, 9, 123, 125–26; Pan-Slavist views of, 74–75, 94
Darwin, Charles, 12, 65
Decembrist revolt, 35
democracy, 27, 30, 130; liberal, 4, 19–20, 39–40, 46; Russian attitudes to, 6–7, 47, 88, 94–95, 97
democratic peace theory, 14

157

development, theories of, 18, 35
dialectical materialism, 17, 40–44, 60, 106, 110–11
dialogue of civilizations, 4, 25, 85, 116, 133
Dialogue of Civilizations Research Institute, 85
diversity, 29, 70, 73; civilizational, 3, 69, 74, 82, 124–25, 127, 134; cultural, 3, 84, 110; ethnic, 81; national, 51; need for, 83, 86, 115; West as threat to, 123
Dobrynin, Aleksei, 126
Dostoevsky, Fyodor, 54–55, 58, 64, 82
Dugin, Aleksandr, 4, 86–89, 92, 124, 132

end of history, the, 20, 22, 48, 89; apocalypse, 49; Chadaev on, 108; Christianity and, 11; communism as, 42; consumer society as, 18; cosmist conception of, 62; democracy as, 4, 40; denial of, 66, 95; desire to accelerate, 34; Europe as, 13; Fukuyama on, 19; Solovyov on, 56–57; the West as, 83, 95, 107, 109, 121, 133
ethnogenesis, 79–81, 114
ethnopluralism, 29–30
Eurasianism, 75–76, 78–79, 87, 128
Eurasianists, 74, 78, 91, 95–96; characteristics of, 90; influence of, 80, 114, 132; rejection of, 98, 100
Eurocentrism, 20, 81

Ferguson, Niall, 20, 32
First World War, 23–24, 26–27, 39, 47, 75, 76
Florovsky, Georgy, 76
flowering complexity, 2–3, 63, 73–74, 122, 126, 134
Fukuyama, Francis, 19, 52
Fyodorov, Nikolai, 57–60, 115

Gaidar, Yegor, 46–47
Global Civilization Initiative, 134
Gorbachev, Mikhail, 44–45, 81–82, 113
Granovsky, Timofei, 37
Gumilyov, Lev, 9, 61, 79–82, 114
Gumilyov, Nikolai, 79

Hegel, George, 16–17, 19–20, 28, 32, 37–38, 52, 114
Heidegger, Martin, 87
Herder, Johann, 21–23, 32, 51
Herzen, Aleksandr, 9
historical determinism, 12, 33–35, 41, 43, 66, 107

historical materialism, 20, 43, 45
historicism, 21
history: apocalyptic view of, 49; civilizational approach to, 115; cyclical, 114; direction of, 5–6, 9, 25, 35–38, 44–46, 55–56, 64–65; driving forces of, 17, 43; goal of, 14, 37, 45, 56, 76; judgment of, 21; laws of, 37–38, 41, 46, 65; natural march of, 129, 131; Norman Theory of, 36; process of, 61; progressive course of, 68; revenge of, 84–85; stages of, 16, 42; unilinear theory of, 10, 13, 23, 32–33, 76, 82, 94, 106; universal, 52, 62, 84. *See also* end of history
Huntington, Samuel, 30–31, 85, 121

Ilyin, Ivan, 134
Institute of Global Civilizations, 115
intercivilizational indifference, 99–100
Island Russia, 84, 90–91, 98–99, 104, 128
isolationism, 91, 93–95, 98, 100–102, 124, 132

Kant, Immanuel, 13, 15, 21, 56, 119
katechon, 8, 49, 86
Katehon think tank, 86
Kavelin, Konstantin, 37–38
Khatami, Seyyed Mohammad, 133
Kholmogorov, Yegor, 49, 96–97, 100
Khomiakov, Aleksei, 50, 52
Kireevsky, Ivan, 50, 53, 55
Kliamkin, Igor, 46
Koshelev, Aleksandr, 50
Krylov, Konstantin, 96–97

Lavrov, Sergei, 120–21, 124
laws: economic, 17, 47; general, 15; of history, 37–38, 41, 46, 65; of nature, 14, 16, 24, 42; of political biology, 40; of social evolution, 20; universal, 14, 16–17, 47, 89
Lenin, Vladimir, 41
Leontyev, Konstantin, 2, 70–75, 126, 134; influence of, 9, 80, 82, 113
liberal internationalism, 4, 14, 24
liberalism, 11, 23, 30, 73, 87–89; conservative, 33; radical, 34; Western, 19, 29, 71, 82–83, 106, 131
Limonov, Eduard, 87, 96
Lukyanov, Fyodor, 107
Lurye, Svetlana, 99–101

Mackinder, Halford, 87
Mamardashvili, Merab, 44–45

Marx, Karl, 17–18, 20, 32, 40–44, 114
Medvedev, Dmitry, 121
Mezhuev, Boris, 99–101, 104, 124
Mezhuev, Vadim, 4
Migranian, Andranik, 46
Mikhailovsky, Nikolai, 40
Miliukov, Pavel, 39–40
modernization, 20, 49, 84
modernization theory, 18–20, 81
Morgan, Lewis Henry, 13
multipolar world, 5, 7, 30, 89, 116, 119; inevitability of, 131; Putin on, 2, 125, 129–30
Muravyov–Apostol, Matvei, 35

Nemtsov, Boris, 108
neo–Eurasianists, 82, 86
New Cold War, 5
Newton, Isaac, 12
Nicholas I, Emperor, 35, 64–66
Nicholas II, Emperor, 38, 133
Nouvelle droite, 29, 82

Obama, Barack, 6
Old Believers, 49

Panarin, Aleksandr, 9, 82–86
Pan–Slavism, 74–75, 94
passionarity, 8, 80–82, 114
perestroika, 45, 82
perpetual peace, 14, 56
Peter I, Emperor, 49, 92, 104
Petrashevsky Circle, 64–65
Plekhanov, Georgy, 40–41, 43
pluriversalism, 89
Pogodin, Mikhail, 36–37
polycultural world, 75
polylogue, 85–86
positivism, 15–16, 27
progress, 11–12, 14–18, 20–21, 39, 67, 69, 125; belief in, 6, 23, 27, 35; desirable pace of, 36; historical, 37, 40–41, 45; loss of faith in, 24, 75; multicivilizational, 83; negative views of, 49, 56–58, 89, 95; resurrection as goal of, 57, 59; technological, 22; theories of, 28, 108; universal, 51, 54
Putin, Vladimir, 1, 5–9, 69, 88, 92, 103, 113; anticolonialism, 129–30; as balancer, 124; civilizational rhetoric, 2–3, 122–23, 125, 127–31; conservatism, 122; criticisms of West, 120, 127, 129; evolution of thinking, 128; as follower of ideological change, 116–17; pro–European statements, 118–19, 122–24; protests against, 97; return to presidency, 121

Quigley, Carroll, 28–29

Remizov, Mikhail, 100–101
Romanticism, 51
Rostow, Walt, 18
Russia: as different from the West, 50, 94, 97–98, 101, 113, 121, 132; as distinct civilization, 72, 74–75, 105, 119; Eurasian identity, 85; as European country, 118–19, 121, 123–25; mission of, 53–54, 75–77, 95, 101; as self–contained civilization, 91, 123, 127; as state civilization, 122–23, 127–28; as unique civilization, 5, 67, 103, 112, 114, 122–25, 127
Russian Orthodoxy, 48–49, 51, 53, 59, 64, 92, 111
Russian revolution, 23, 26, 34, 75–76

Samarin, Iury, 50
Savitsky, Pyotr, 9, 76, 78, 80
Schelling, Friedrich, 51
Second World War, 24, 79, 113, 119
Slavophiles, 50–52, 75, 90, 96, 132
Slavophilism, 8, 51
Smith, Adam, 16–17
sobornost', 8, 53, 84, 105
social Darwinism, 12, 20, 40
social evolution, 13, 20, 22
socialism, 11, 27, 30, 42–43, 66, 87, 103; congruence with Russian character, 113; peasant, 40; with a human face, 44
Solovyov, Vladimir, 9, 55–58, 60, 82, 115
Solzhenitsyn, Aleksandr, 94–96
Sorokin, Pitirim, 9, 26–28, 31–32, 47, 76, 132
Spassky, Nikolai, 103
Spencer, Herbert, 12–13
Spengler, Oswald, 28, 32, 47, 64, 75, 113–14, 132; criticism of, 110; *The Decline of the West*, 23–24
Staley, Eugene, 18
Stalin, Joseph, 41–43
Surkov, Vladislav, 103–104
Suvchinsky, Pyotr, 76

Tianxia, 133–34
Tolstoy, Lev, 58
Toynbee, Arnold, 24–26, 28–32, 47, 75; influence on Russian authors, 61, 80–82, 84, 113–15, 132

Trenin, Dmitry, 104
Trubetskoi, Nikolai, 9, 76–78
Tsiolkovsky, Konstantin, 60–62, 115
Tsymbursky, Vadim, 98–101, 103–104, 124, 126, 132
Turgenev, Nikolai, 34–35

Ukraine, invasion of, 2, 67, 85–86, 92, 102–103, 125
UN Alliance of Civilizations, 133
unipolar world, 2, 7, 85, 89, 116, 123, 126–27
Uvarov, Sergei, 35–36

Valdai Discussion Club, 1, 2, 7, 122, 125
values: Christian, 102; European, 119; traditional, 123; universal, 3–5, 20, 93; Western, 6–7, 24, 45, 83, 112, 131
Vernadsky, Vladimir, 9, 60, 80–82, 115
vseedinstvo (all-unity), 55, 60, 62, 84

West, the, 2–4, 6–9, 12–13, 17, 20–22, 24, 72; alleged superiority of, 20; Anglo-Saxon element of, 87, 126–27; arrogance of, 22; ascendancy of, 25; decline of, 52, 68, 78, 90, 126; fading appeal of, 133; inevitability of conflict with, 82; loss of faith in, 107, 109; as model of civilization, 2, 7, 13, 20, 44–45, 47, 81; need to resist, 108–109; negative portrayals of, 49, 52–55, 62, 116, 118, 124; praise of, 51; relations with Russia, 4–6, 92, 98, 100–104, 106, 118, 130–33; Russian copying of, 36–39; triumph of, 19; unilinear conception of history, 94; universalist pretensions of, 31, 84, 131
Western civilization, 67–68, 74, 78, 100, 102–103; definition of, 11; errors of, 50; inevitable march of, 12; as only valid civilization, 2, 93; Putin on, 120, 122; supremacy of, 20; Toynbee on, 25–26; Zhirinovsky on, 115–16
Westernism, 3, 37, 83, 109
Westernization, 5, 74, 107, 126, 133; destructive nature of, 84; need to avoid, 53, 81, 93
Westernizers, 34, 36–37, 44, 51, 99, 103, 114
World Wars. *See* First World War; Second World War

Yakunin, Vladimir, 85
Yeltsin, Boris, 46–47, 112, 119
Young Conservatives, 100–101
Yuriev, Mikhail, 92–93

Zhirinovsky, Vladimir, 106, 115–17
Zyuganov, Gennady, 106, 112–14, 116–17